insects & spiders

**An EXPLORE
YOUR WORLD™
Handbook**

D0711232

DISCOVERY COMMUNICATIONS, INC., produces high-quality television programming, interactive media, books, films, and consumer products. DISCOVERY NETWORKS, a division of Discovery Communications, Inc., operates and manages the Discovery Channel, TLC, Animal Planet, Travel Channel and the Discovery Health Channel.

Insects & Spiders, An Explore Your World ™ Handbook, was created and produced by ST. REMY MEDIA INC.

Library of Congress Cataloging-in-Publication Data
Insects & spiders: an explore your world handbook.
    p. cm.
  Includes bibliographical references (p.).
  ISBN 1-56331-841-5 (pbk.)
      1. Insects. 2. Spiders. I. Title: Discovery channel insects and spiders. II. Title: Insects & spiders. III. Discovery Channel (Firm)
  QL463.D57 2000
  595.7--dc21   99-087177

Random House website address:
http://www.atrandom.com
Discovery Channel Online website address:
http://www.discovery.com
Printed in the United States of America on acid-free paper
First Edition   10 9 8 7 6 5 4 3 2

CONSULTANTS

Dr. Robert Anderson is a research scientist in entomology at the Canadian Museum of Nature in Ottawa, Canada, specializing in the study of beetles. Obsessed with insects as a child, he has pursued this interest into adulthood. He graduated from the University of Toronto and continued with additional studies at Carleton University and the University of Alberta. He is the author of more than fifty technical publications on insects, and has traveled extensively in Central and South America in the course of his research.

Paula E. Cushing, Ph.D. is the curator of Entomology and Arachnology at the Denver Museum of Natural History in Denver, Colorado. She has been doing research and publishing both scientific and popular articles on spiders for the past sixteen years. Recently she began the Colorado Spider Survey research project to document the biodiversity of spiders in the state.

Dr. David J. Lewis is a graduate of Memorial University in Newfoundland and has been a professor of entomology at McGill University in Montreal since 1978. His main research interests include the ecology and distribution of aquatic insects and the biology and control of the biting flies. He teaches courses in entomology, environmental science, limnology, and zoology.

James R. Nechols is a professor of entomology at Kansas State University in Manhattan, Kansas. He specializes in biological control of insect pests and weeds. He also has a particular interest in the ecology and behavior of parasitic wasps as well as insect dormancy. A graduate of Cornell University, he has served as an editor for the journal *Crop Protection* and has co-edited two books on biological control. His current research concerns evaluating the impact of natural enemies on target and non-target species.

insects & spiders

An EXPLORE YOUR WORLD™ Handbook

DISCOVERY BOOKS
NEW YORK

CONTENTS

SECTION ONE
6 INSECTS

8 Form & Function
- Wings
- Limbs & Feet
- Eyes
- Antennae

24 From Egg to Adult
- Mating Methods
- *Insect Clues*

32 Staying Alive
- Camouflage
  & Mimicry
- Versatile
  Communicators
- Truly Social
- *Insect Architects*

46 Allies & Enemies
- *D. Melanogaster*

SECTION TWO
54 SPIDERS

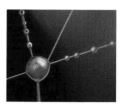

56 **Spiders Up Close**
- Top Notch Predators
- Spider Silk
- Spider Courtship

SECTION THREE
66 BACKYARD & BEYOND

68 **Backyard Bug Primer**
- *Identifying Insects by Order*
- Taking a Closer Look

86 **Insects & Spiders:**
An International Biome Guide

174 **Resource Guide**
- International Directory • Taxonomy of Insects
- Taxonomy of Spiders • Endangered Species
- Glossary

184 **Index**

192 **Acknowledgments**
& Picture Credits

INSECTS

FORM & FUNCTION

Even the tiniest insects possess the working parts of more complex animals, including digestive organs and a nervous system linked to muscles, all well protected by an exterior armor: the exoskeleton.

If this planet were to belong to the most diverse group of creatures living on it, insects would reign. They have adapted and multiplied until they represent 80 percent of animal species on Earth. About 900,000 have been described so far; six thousand to ten thousand more are discovered each year. Recent estimates suggest that the final tally may be tens of millions of species.

Each time a new insect is discovered, scientists establish where it fits in the overall animal classification system. All insects fall into the class Hexapoda in the phylum Arthropoda, along with other classes that include Arachnida (spiders), *(page 54)*, Chilopoda (centipedes), and Diplopoda (millipedes). In keeping

> *"Otherness is what
> I have always liked
> about bugs."*
>
> — Sue Hubbell

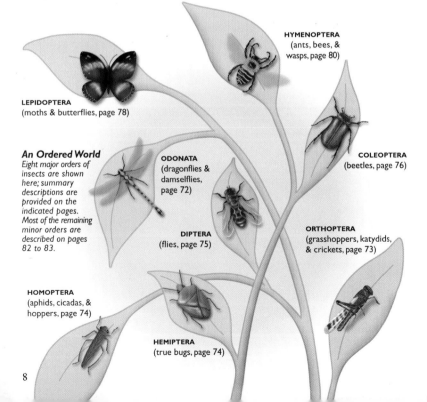

HYMENOPTERA
(ants, bees, & wasps, page 80)

LEPIDOPTERA
(moths & butterflies, page 78)

An Ordered World
Eight major orders of insects are shown here; summary descriptions are provided on the indicated pages. Most of the remaining minor orders are described on pages 82 to 83.

ODONATA
(dragonflies & damselflies, page 72)

COLEOPTERA
(beetles, page 76)

DIPTERA
(flies, page 75)

ORTHOPTERA
(grasshoppers, katydids, & crickets, page 73)

HOMOPTERA
(aphids, cicadas, & hoppers, page 74)

HEMIPTERA
(true bugs, page 74)

with taxonomic rules *(page 176)*, insects are further classified into groups called orders, each of which possesses its own set of distinguishing characteristics that reflect a pattern of common ancestry. The orders, in turn, are composed of families, genera, and species.

As with all animal and plant species, the scientific naming of different kinds of insects uses a two-word Latin system that was introduced in 1753 by the Swedish botanist and taxonomist Carolus Linnaeus *(page 176)*. Among entomologists, the honeybee, for example, is known by its scientific name *Apis mellifera*.

SUCCESSFUL INVADERS

Species proliferation and adaptability go hand in hand. Insects have invaded almost every possible terrestrial habitat; there are even glacier midges that thrive on the ice and snow of the Himalayas, larvae of the brine fly *Ephydra buresi* that flourish in the hotsprings of Yellowstone Park, and larvae of the shore fly *Helaeopmyia petrolia* that survive in crude petroleum. Only in marine habitats do the number of insect species fail to exceed those of all other creatures. Their extraordinary success everywhere else is due in part to their small size. Most insects range between 0.04 and 0.4 inch (1 to 10 mm) and are therefore much smaller than the leaves they may munch on. The smallest known insect, the fairyfly wasp *(Alaptus magnanimus)*, measures about 0.0067 inch

All in the Same Class
Despite their obvious dissimilarities, the three insects shown here all share the same basic body design.

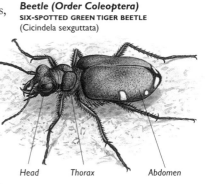

Beetle (Order Coleoptera)
SIX-SPOTTED GREEN TIGER BEETLE
(Cicindela sexguttata)

Head   Thorax   Abdomen

Butterfly (Order Lepidoptera)
OLD WORLD SWALLOWTAIL
(Papilio machaon)

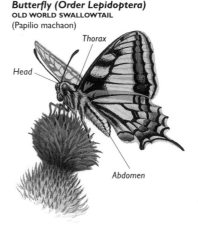

Thorax

Head

Abdomen

Locust (Order Orthoptera)
RED-LEGGED LOCUST
(Melanoplus femurrubrum)

Head

Thorax   Abdomen

(0.2 mm). It is so tiny that it lays its eggs inside the eggs of other insects. Even the very largest butterflies and moths have wingspans of no more than a foot (300 mm).

While the first insects to evolve about 400 million years ago were not as diminutive as the fairyfly wasp, they were extremely small. Some of these Apterygota, or "wingless" insects, were similar to modern silverfish. Diverse in the early days of their evolution, they started to decline as soon as winged insects began to appear fifty million years later.

With the greater mobility provided by wings, the Pterygota, or "wing bearers," eventually displaced apterygotes from most habitats. By about 225 million years ago, most major lineages of today's winged insects were in existence. They did not, however, become abundant until flowering plants

The first entomologists were amateurs like the celebrated Jean Henri Fabre, a nineteenth-century school teacher who devoted himself to the study of, in particular, wasps, bees, beetles, grasshoppers, and crickets. Although he did not believe in evolution, his writing earned him high praise from Charles Darwin, who described him as "an incomparable observer."

began to appear in great numbers some millions of years later.

FROM HEAD TO TERMINALIA

Although insects come in countless shapes and sizes, most adult insects follow the same basic body design: three pairs of jointed legs and three distinct regions—the head, the thorax, and the abdomen. On the head, most bear a pair of compound eyes *(page 20)*, a pair of antennae *(page 22)*, and mouthparts that derive from ancestral appendages *(page 13)*.

Each of these structures can vary a great deal, depending on the demands of habitat and lifestyle. The eyes, for instance, can be small, like those of an ant, which uses its sense of smell, not its eyes, to navigate. Or they can be large, like those of dragonflies, which hunt prey primarily by sight. Some insects also have simple eyes, or ocelli, that aid in the detecting of light.

The design of an insect's body gives it great strength. Beetles can carry loads eighty times their weight, ants ten times their weight.

An insect's thorax is divided into three segments, each having its own pair of legs *(page 18)*. If the insect possesses wings *(page 14)*, they are present on the second and/or the third thoracic segment. Unlike the thorax and the head, the abdomen does not usually bear appendages on its segments, except for the terminalia, which is located at the hind tip of the abdomen. These appendages are associated with egg-laying, mating, or defense functions. The stings of wasps and bees are examples of such structures.

The entire body of an insect is covered in cuticle, a protective material that makes up the exoskeleton. The relative weight of the exoskeleton explains in part why terrestrial insects remain so small. It can be rigid, as with most adult beetles, or flexible, as is the case with many immature insects. The cuticle shields an insect's soft internal tissues against injury, provides support for the muscles, and, because it is water resistant, reduces water loss through evaporation.

Cuticle is made of various combinations of proteins and polysaccharide molecules, called chitin, that are linked together in flexible bundles to provide great tensile strength. A lifeless material, chitin does not grow, so insects must molt; the number of times that they shed their exoskeleton in the course of their life depends on the species. Each time the exoskeleten is shed is followed by a brief period during which the soft inner body has a chance to expand a bit before the new cuticle hardens.

Cuticle also makes up, in whole or in part, the insect's locomotory, sensory, and digestive organs. It even lines the system of tracheal tubes and air sacs that allows insects to breath air, carrying oxygen from sphincterlike openings, or spiracles, on the thorax and abdomen to the inner tissues. This network of successively smaller branches is also used by

Giant Forebears

The small size of today's insects is partly due to the limitations of their tracheal system in assisting the diffusion of oxygen to cells throughout the body. Insects grew much larger 300 million years ago—some had wingspans of about two feet (0.6 m) or more—because, one view has it, the concentration of atmospheric oxygen was almost twice as high then as today. The more oxygen available in the atmosphere, the more was available for metabolism.

gaseous wastes and water as they exit the body through spiracles on the posterior abdomen.

For insects living in arid habitats, water loss through the spiracles can be substantial, so they open only when necessary. Water loss naturally poses no problem for aquatic insects, which instead need to find ways to maximize their oxygen intake since the concentration of oxygen in water is so much less than in air. To compensate, these insects acquire small amounts of oxygen by diffusion through the cuticle and may also use additional respiratory structures, such as the rectal

pump of dragonfly nymphs, which allows them to breathe through their rear end.

Although insects do not breathe with their mouth, they do ingest food with it. Enzymes produced by the salivary glands start to break down food almost immediately. The food travels along the esophagus, through the crop, and into the proventriculus, which, for insects that eat solid food, acts like a bird's gizzard to break it up. Termites feast on wood thanks to a proventriculus armed with folds and spines for shredding.

Once food has passed through the proventriculus, it enters the midgut, where enzymes are produced and nutrients are absorbed. In the hindgut, the last section of

Inside an Insect
An insect has an open circulatory system, which means that blood, or hemolymph, circulates freely around the internal organs as it transports nutrients, hormones, and wastes to different regions of the body. Oxygen is carried by the tracheal system of tubules and air sacs.

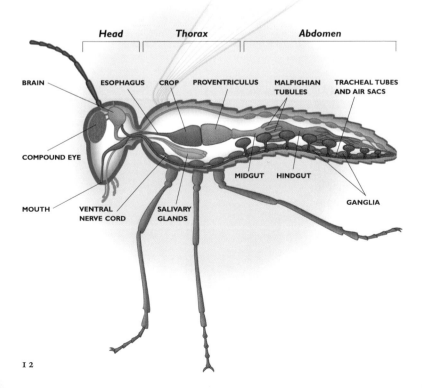

| Head | Thorax | Abdomen |

BRAIN — ESOPHAGUS — CROP — PROVENTRICULUS — MALPIGHIAN TUBULES — TRACHEAL TUBES AND AIR SACS

COMPOUND EYE

MIDGUT — HINDGUT

GANGLIA

MOUTH — VENTRAL NERVE CORD — SALIVARY GLANDS

Variations on a Theme

The appendages surrounding the mouth of insects are designed to chew, to suck, or to do both. Chewing insects have mandibles (cutting jaws), maxillae (secondary jaws), a labium (lower lip), and a labrum (upper lip). The mouthparts of sucking insects developed from the basic chewing structures and are extremely varied.

Leaf Chewer

Palps on the maxillae of the leaf-chewing grasshopper are used to get food to the mouth; palps on the labium help in tasting.

the digestive tract, water absorption, ion balance, and elimination of nitrogenous wastes (analogous to urine) are regulated by outgrowths. Called Malpighian tubules, they were named after the seventeenth-century Italian microscopist Marcello Malpighi, who first discovered them while examining the anatomy of the silkworm. The tubules and the midgut are the only parts of the digestive tract that are not protected by a layer of cuticle.

Nectar Feeder

Butterflies and moths suck on liquid nectar with a hollow proboscis. When not in use, the proboscis rolls up like a coiled spring.

NOT JUST A PRETTY FACE

The insect brain is a nerve center in their head that is linked to other, smaller nerve centers, called ganglia, by nerves that usually span the entire length of the body. The brain, which is larger in more sophisticated insects such as social bees and ants, makes sense of much of the information obtained by the sense organs, especially the eyes and the antennae. The ganglia are paired and each pair is responsible only for certain specific functions, so other functions can still occur if one pair happens to be damaged or missing. For example, a male praying mantis is programmed to release sperm (and thus complete mating) even after its head has been severed from its body by its partner.

Blood Sucker

Female mosquitoes stab human and animal skin with their needle-like proboscis, which they then use to suck blood. Male mosquitoes feed only on nectar.

Predator

Carnivorous insects, such as tiger beetles, bite and chew their food with jagged mandibles.

Sponger

Many flies, including the house fly, lap up liquid with paired lobes at the tip of the proboscis.

Wings

Insects became the first animals—and the only invertebrates—to fly when they took to the sky about 350 million years ago, some 200 million years before birds. The evolution of wings contributed enormously to their success. Wings allowed them to find mates and escape their enemies more easily, exploit more food sources, and colonize new territory—even migrate thousands of miles, as is the case of some butterflies and moths *(box below)*.

Although early insects lacked wings, their absence is not necessarily a sign of primitiveness. Every

Long-distance Fliers

The evolution of wings has allowed insects to expand their range tremendously. Most species stay within a few miles of their emergence site, but some have specialized in long-distance travel:
• Monarch butterfly (*Danaus plexippus*): In autumn, these butterflies migrate from northern United States and Canada to hibernate in California or Mexico. They fly back north in the spring.
• Silver-Y moth (*Plusia gamma*): Every year this grayish moth travels from North Africa and southern Europe to Britain.
• Migratory locust (family Acrididae): In 1985 these insects swarmed from Ethiopia and the Sudan to the west coast of Africa. From there, a fraction of the swarm continued to fly across the Atlantic to Barbados, nearly three thousand miles (4,800 km) away.

---

insect order has a few species with only vestigial wings—sometimes appearing as simple bumps on the exoskeleton—having found an even better way to survive. Fleas and lice, for instance, have abandoned their wings for strong legs, which are much more convenient for clinging to the hair and feathers of their particular host. Other insects have wings for a short time in their life cycle—for courtship and mating, for example—and then lose them. Winglessness can be linked to sexual dimorphism, where male and female are markedly dissimilar in appearance. Typically in such cases, the male sports wings and the female doesn't; she waits for the male to come to her.

THE ORIGIN OF WINGS
Unlike birds, which bear wings that evolved from their forelegs, insects

Beetles, such as this ladybird, have hardened, veinless forewings called elytra, which cover and protect the membranous hindwings at rest and are usually held out of the way during flight.

forms in wing evolution, so it is still unclear what function the small outgrowths, or proto-wings, may have had before evolving into structures capable of sustained, powered flight. The most commonly accepted hypothesis at the moment is that the proto-wings were gill-like structures that once helped insects breathe underwater. Another possibility is that they originally functioned as stabilizers during long jumps or drops from trees.

did not sacrifice a complete limb in order to grow a wing. Although researchers once believed that wings developed from the thorax wall, today it is generally believed that insect wings evolved from outgrowths on the upper segment of their articulated legs. The fossil record has not yet produced any specimens that display intermediate

WING STRUCTURE

Most insect wings are made of two very thin layers of chitin, the main component of the exoskeleton. Typically the two chitin layers are interlaced with a complex network of wing veins that help provide strength and support to the whole frame. The veins usually contain tracheal tubes, nerve fibers, and blood, which flows in the space around the tubes *(page 11)*. When insects emerge from cocoons, their wings are crumpled until the air pumps

Up Beat

VERTICAL
MUSCLE

HORIZONTAL
MUSCLE

Down Beat

The Basic Wing Stroke
The powered flight of more advanced insects requires the use of indirect muscles that are attached not to the wing itself, but to the wing-bearing thoracic walls. The wings, which fit between the upper and lower thoracic sections, move like levers on a fulcrum. For the up beat, the vertical muscles contract, pulling down the thorax and levering the wings upward. For the down beat, horizontal muscles contract, raising the thorax and causing the wings to lower.

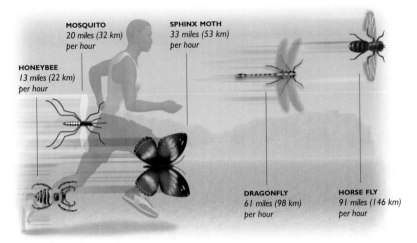

MOSQUITO
20 miles (32 km)
per hour

SPHINX MOTH
33 miles (53 km)
per hour

HONEYBEE
13 miles (22 km)
per hour

DRAGONFLY
61 miles (98 km)
per hour

HORSE FLY
91 miles (146 km)
per hour

Flight Speeds
The flight of an insect is usually faster than a running person—although not necessarily when the runner is Maurice Greene, who in 1999 ran 22.9 miles (36.7 km) per hour to cover 100 meters in 9.79 seconds. Shown here are some of the maximum flight speeds that have been recorded for certain types of insects.

through the tubes, causing them to unfurl. The pattern of the veins, or venation, varies from species to species and is therefore used as an identification tool, particularly for butterflies and moths.

All flying insects, with the exception of the true flies, possess two pairs of wings, but they exhibit a wide assortment of wing shapes and sizes. Although most insects, particularly dragonflies and locusts, can glide considerable distances on their wings, flight is usually carried out by beating the wings. The most primitive groups, such as dragonflies, mantids, and grasshoppers, flap each pair of wings independently. Although this system still allows for effective flight, it consumes a great deal of energy and will generally restrain beating frequency to less than fifty beats per second, although the wing speed of

some dragonflies has been recorded at a hundred beats per second.

The most advanced groups, which include butterflies and bees, have a much more efficient flying apparatus, one involving hooks and grapples that lock both pairs of wings together in a single propulsion unit. This system, which relies on the internal attachment of muscles to the thorax to indirectly move the wings *(page 15)*, allows insects, such as some midges, to achieve a thousand beats per second. In comparison, the fastest hummingbird will never exceed two hundred wing beats per second.

True flies have taken flight one step further by modifying their hind wings into a pair of clubbed structures called halteres. Halteres act as balancing organs, helping to steer and stabilize during flight. If the halteres are removed, flies spin around

Some insects, such as fleas (Siphonaptera), are wingless. Crawling and jumping are their only modes of locomotion.

until they hit the ground. Halteres vibrate along with the forewings and are packed with a variety of sense organs that help the flies monitor flight conditions and react swiftly to any changes.

MULTIPURPOSE ASSETS

While the main purpose of wings is aerial propulsion, wings can also serve other functions. Some butterflies and moths use their wings for camouflage and mimicry *(page 36)*. The hind wings of the Io moth *(Automeris io)*, for example, bear intimidating eyespots that are covered by the forewings in the resting position. When disturbed, the moth flashes its wings, revealing the false eyes. Other lepidopterans, such as dark-winged arctic butterflies, use their wings as solar panels to increase body temperature. Darker wings absorb more of the incoming solar radiation, allowing them to reach the warmer temperatures needed for flight. Wings are also used in courtship. Midges from the family Chironomidae, for example, beat their wings at certain frequencies to locate another midge of the right gender and species, even from within swarms containing thousands of individuals of various species.

Iridescent Beauty

The wings of butterflies and moths are covered with millions of tiny overlapping scales, which are responsible for the wing patterns. Each scale is individually pegged into the wing membrane, and from the moment the insect starts to fly the scales begin to fall off. Scales can be pigmented or transparent and covered with thin parallel plates that successively reflect light to create shimmering, iridescent colors, such as the blue of the South American morpho *(Morpho amathonte)* shown here. There are some 35,000 scales per square inch (5,400 scales per square centimeter) on the wings of a morpho and each scale is lined with tiny grooves that contribute to the iridescent effect.

Limbs & Feet

Adult insects typically have one pair of legs attached to each thoracic segment. From the thorax outward, each leg is made up of the coxa, trochanter, femur, tibia, and tarsus—articulated segments that connect with each other on a ball-and-socket basis. Muscles run

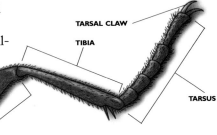

Anatomy of an Insect Leg
The principal parts of an insect's leg are named after the corresponding parts on a vertebrate's limb.

TARSAL CLAW

TIBIA

TROCHANTER

COXA

TARSUS

FEMUR

the length of the leg, the most powerful ones residing in the femur, the segment that is analogous to the human thigh. The tarsus, or foot, has up to five subsegments and usually bears a pair of claws, sometimes separated by membranous sacs or pads at the end. On flies, these pads are shaped like suction cups. Covered with fine hairs kept sticky by the oily secretions of oil glands, the pads enable the insect to adhere to sheer surfaces and walk upside down on ceilings.

The legs of most terrestrial insects are slender and of even length. Because the insects are six-legged, they walk and run by assuming a highly stable tripod position, raising the foreleg and hindleg on one side and the midleg on the other side. The resulting zigzag gait is remarkably efficient.

Other types of locomotion—jumping, swimming, crawling, burrowing, and even skating on water—are reflected in a variety of leg modifications. Jumpers, such as fleas and grasshoppers, have developed very strong femoral muscles in their hindlegs, which are armored in an extra-tough, elastic cuticle. The hindlegs of fleas are also equipped with a pad of rubberlike protein called resilin that they compress and release when they jump. The added boost can propel them up to 150 times their own height. To perform an equivalent feat, a person would

Leg Modifications

DIVING BEETLE
Swimming leg feathered with hair

HONEYBEE
Hindleg with pollen basket

Water striders navigating a pond in New Mexico take advantage of the surface tension of water, which creates a thin, elastic film to walk on. The striders have water-repellent hairs on their feet that help keep them afloat.

have to leap about one thousand feet (305 m) in the air.

Insects that spend their lives on or under the surface of lakes, ponds, and streams have legs adapted to swimming. Predacious diving beetles, for example, have flattened hindlegs fringed with hair. To swim, the beetle moves its legs simultaneously in broad strokes, just like oars. Another aquatic insect, the whirligig beetle, has flattened hindlegs and midlegs, but these are moved alternately as though the beetle were jogging through water.

Legs serve many other purposes besides locomotion. The praying mantises have forelegs armed with spines to grasp their prey. Mole crickets have forelegs modified for digging rather than hunting. Their enlarged, flat forelegs allow them to excavate burrows reaching as much as eight inches (20 cm) below the surface. Worker honey bees' hindlegs are equipped with pollen-collecting baskets consisting of depressions fringed with hair.

SENSORY ADAPTATIONS

Sensory structures are often present on the legs of insects. For example, the fine hairs on the tip of the house fly's legs "taste" liquids so the fly can evaluate the sugar content. In katydids, sounds are perceived by an auditory organ located on the tibia of the foreleg. But possibly the most unusual leg modification is that of the beetle genus *Melanophila*. Their midlegs are equipped with a sensory organ that can detect infrared wavelengths emitted by forest fires. Once they sense a fire, the beetles fly toward it, avoiding the flames, to lay their eggs on the charred wood of the newly burnt trees.

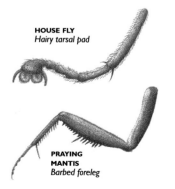

HOUSE FLY
Hairy tarsal pad

PRAYING MANTIS
Barbed foreleg

19

Eyes

The compound eyes of the harlequin beetle (Acrocinus longimanus) are notched around its antennae.

Most insect species possess a fairly elaborate visual system that relies primarily on a pair of compound eyes. The term "compound" is used to indicate the aggregate nature of these visual organs. They are composed of a multitude of identical minuscule units called ommatidia, each possessing its own lens, pigments, and nerve cells with which to perceive a small portion of the visual field. The information coming in from all the ommatidia is combined in the brain, forming a mosaic image of what is being viewed.

The quality of eyesight in insects correlates with the number of ommatidia present in each eye. Dragonflies rely heavily on visual cues for hunting; they have up to thirty thousand ommatidia or more in each of their large, protruding, compound eyes. When ommatidia are so numerous, they take on a hexagonal shape and lie close together. When less abundant, they are round and separated by relatively large areas of cuticle.

Compound eyes are often accompanied by two or three simple eyes. These rudimentary visual structures, called ocelli in adult insects, develop when the wings do, and most wingless insects don't have them. Each simple eye has a single corneal lens that lies over a layer of vision cells, some of which contain photoreactive pigments that absorb light. The role of simple eyes is not yet fully understood, but they are believed to assist the compound eyes in detecting variations in light intensity. Experiments have shown that light falling on a locust's ocelli can stimulate it to move faster; when the center ocellus is covered, the insect moves more slowly. Furthermore, nocturnal insects, such as night-flying wasps, often have larger ocelli than diurnal insects.

Insects don't need eyes to respond to light; light-sensitive cells have been found deep in the head of blow-fly maggots, and cave-dwelling species, which are often blind, can detect light through their cuticle.

INSECT VISION

Although it is difficult to determine exactly what insects see, there is no doubt that, due to the fragmentary way they receive visual information, they distinguish images less clearly than we do. Insects also lack any mechanism for changing focus. On the other hand, they can detect movement much faster than we can. Insects such as house flies can process a "slide show" of up to two hundred separate images per second, enabling them to react swiftly. The human eye, although capable of rendering a sharp image, can perceive only about eighteen separate images per second.

Most insects can distinguish at least some of the colors of flowering plants. Bees and butterflies (among others) readily perceive colors at the blue end of the spectrum, as well as shades in the ultraviolet that are invisible to the human eye. Research using ultraviolet photography has revealed that many insect-attracting plants display patterns that can be seen only in ultraviolet. These patterns, called honey-guides, lead the

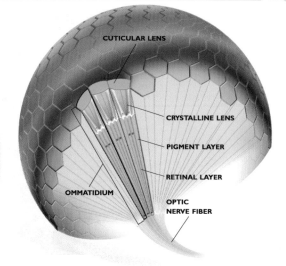

Compound Eye
When light is received by the eye, it passes first through cuticular lenses (part of the cuticle covering the insect's entire body) and then through crystalline lenses before falling on a group of retinal cells at the base of the ommatidia. The cells pass the message to the brain by way of optic nerve fibers. Each ommatidium is isolated from its neighbor by light-absorbing pigment cells.

insect to the flower's nectaries. Some species of butterflies have markings on their wings that are only visible in ultraviolet.

Another visual feat that is vital to insects is their ability to detect and orient themselves to the angle of the vibrating light waves coming from the sky. The atmosphere polarizes light from blue sky, setting most of the rays vibrating in the same plane. Insects can use this plane of polarized light as a navigational tool—an ability that is particularly useful for species, such as bees and wasps, that need to find their way to food or back to the nest.

The head of this narrow-winged damselfly shows the presence of three simple eyes between the much larger pair of compound eyes.

Antennae

Most nymphs and adult insects bear a pair of segmented, flexible antennae on their heads, usually between and slightly above their compound eyes. Equipped with a variety of sensory organs, or sensilla—including chemoreceptors, thermoreceptors, and mechanoreceptors—antennae can help an insect taste, touch, hear, detect pheromones (the chemicals involved in mate-finding), and locate food, water, and sites for egg-laying.

Antennae are composed of three basic segments: the scape, or basal stalk; the middle segment, or pedicel, which usually has a sensory organ, called the Johnston's organ, that is involved in perceiving antennal movement relative to the body; and the flagellum, a filamentous end piece—typically formed of subsegments (*below*)—that is modified in a variety of ways to suit insect needs.

Because sensitivity is proportional to the number of receptors on the antennae, these sensory appendages are often designed to maximize their

surface area. For instance, male silk moths have large, featherlike antennae, loaded with chemoreceptors that are able to detect food plants as well as the sex pheromone emitted by the female of the species from several miles away.

Many species show marked physical differences between the sexes, and in the case of antennae, the males often have the largest ones. A widespread exception is the female parasitic wasp (and other parasitoids in the order Hymenoptera), most of which have larger, more elaborate

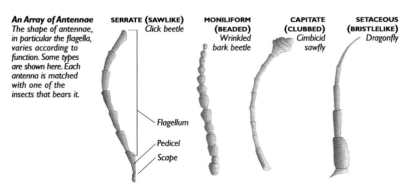

An Array of Antennae
The shape of antennae, in particular the flagella, varies according to function. Some types are shown here. Each antenna is matched with one of the insects that bears it.

SERRATE (SAWLIKE)
Click beetle

Flagellum
Pedicel
Scape

MONILIFORM (BEADED)
Wrinkled bark beetle

CAPITATE (CLUBBED)
Cimbicid sawfly

SETACEOUS (BRISTLELIKE)
Dragonfly

Microscopic sensilla in the form of hair. magnified ten times in the photo above, cover the feathery antennae of the polyphemus moth (Antheraea polyphemus). These sensory organs also come in the form of pegs, pits, or cones.

al cues are often scarce at this level, they must rely on their sense of touch to get around. In groups endowed with larger eyes, such as dragonflies and mayflies, the antennae are smaller and play less of a role in locomotion.

Sound can sometimes be "heard" via the antennae. In male chironomid midges, the Johnston's organ is modified to sense the sound of female chironomid wing vibrations. Their antennae are deaf to all other sounds.

antennae because they lay their eggs directly in the bodies of live insects and scent helps them to find the right hosts.

Some sensilla are minute bristles that cover the antennae and are sensitive to touch, vibration, and wind. Social insects, such as bees and ants, are often seen touching antennae in an exchange of information about the location of a flower patch or the invasion of an intruder in the nest. Tactile information is especially crucial among ground dwellers such as cockroaches and crickets. Since visu-

While antennae are essentially designed to function as multipurpose sense organs, they can also play a direct physical role in mating or feeding. Most male fleas, for example, have large numbers of adhesive discs on the inner surface of their antennae that are used to hold the female firmly in place during copulation. The aquatic larvae of the mosquito-like genus *Chaoborus* use their antennae as hunting accessories to grasp prey.

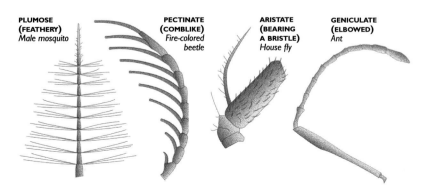

PLUMOSE (FEATHERY)
Male mosquito

PECTINATE (COMBLIKE)
Fire-colored beetle

ARISTATE (BEARING A BRISTLE)
House fly

GENICULATE (ELBOWED)
Ant

FROM EGG TO ADULT

Insects have adopted several routes to achieve adulthood, but they all need to escape their exoskeleton to grow.

Insects typically adopt a "lay-the-eggs-and-leave-them" approach to parenting. After mating, the female selects a location that will give her offspring the best chance to survive; plant stems conceal the eggs of tree crickets, underwater provides shelter for dragonfly eggs, and live insects become living larders for developing ichneumon wasps. Most females lay between fifty and a few hundred eggs, often using a long egg-laying organ, called an ovipositor, for hard-to-reach spots. Only rarely are eggs cared for until they hatch. One example of this

"You must behold insects when full of life and activity . . . practicing their various arts, pursuing their amours . . . the laying and kind of their eggs, their wonderful metamorphoses . . ."

— William Kirby and William Spence

practice is the female giant water bug. She glues her eggs to the back of the male, and he "egg-sits" until the offspring emerge.

Young insects may emerge by simply chewing their way through the egg. Others are equipped with "egg-bursters," spinelike protrusions on the top of the head that break through the hard shell. In some cases,

Life Cycles
About 85 percent of known insects undergo holometabolous, the life-cycle pattern that is proving to be most evolutionarily successful.

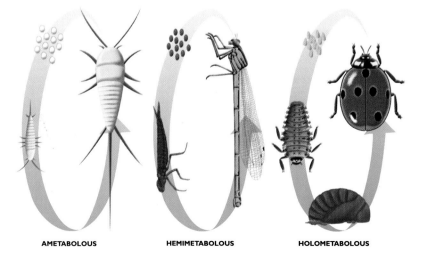

AMETABOLOUS   **HEMIMETABOLOUS**   **HOLOMETABOLOUS**

wriggling or applying pressure on the egg from the inside is enough to rupture the shell along lines of weakness.

Once hatched, a few groups of insects, including springtails and house-dwelling silverfish, are faithful replicas of their parents, except in size. They grow, but otherwise change little as they develop. This is called ametabolous. These insects may molt as many as fifty times during their life, continuing to molt even after mating and laying eggs.

An alternative route to adulthood is taken by the young grasshopper, called a nymph, which resembles its adult parents, but lacks wings, which form as it grows. This type of development is called hemimetabolous, or incomplete metamorphosis, and comprises three stages: egg, nymph, and adult. Other insects that develop this way include crickets, mantids, cockroaches, mayflies, dragonflies, and true bugs.

The young of more advanced insects, such as beetles, do not look like their parents. In a type of development called holometabolous, or com-

The eggs of this Colorado potato beetle (Leptinotarsa decemlineata) have been laid on the underside of a potato leaf. Fifteen to twenty days after hatching, the larvae reach full size and drop to the ground. Ten to fifteen days later, the development to adulthood is complete.

plete metamorphosis, the hatching insects change from larvae to pupae and then to adults. Butterflies, moths, flies, wasps, bees, ants, caddisflies, fleas, and lacewings also develop in this manner. During their final molt, the larvae enter a pupal, or "resting," stage—although at the cellular level, there is no resting involved. Their tissues are broken down and regrouped to form an adult's body.

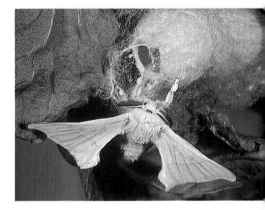

An adult Chinese silk moth (Bombyx mori) clings to its fibrous cocoon after emerging from its pupal stage.

The queen honeybee lays one egg per cell, the number of cells being determined by the hive's workers. Her unfertilized eggs become drones (males), her fertilized eggs workers (females) and queens. When the eggs hatch into larvae, those destined to be workers are fed honey, and, for the first three days, royal jelly—fortified bees' milk secreted by glands in the workers' heads. Larvae destined to become queens are fed royal jelly throughout their lives.

Holometabolous development allows adults and larvae to exploit different environmental conditions, often eating different foods as well. For these insects, feeding is generally concentrated in the larval stage, while the role of adults shifts to dispersal, courtship, mating, and, ultimately, production of offspring. In extreme cases, such as non-biting midges and giant silkworm moths, adults do not eat at all. This contrasts with their larval stages, when they consume tremendous amounts. Polyphemus moth caterpillars (*Antheraea polyphemus*) can eat 86,000 times their birth weight in leaves in just fifty-six days, expanding at a rate that, if it were matched in a human, would turn a baby into

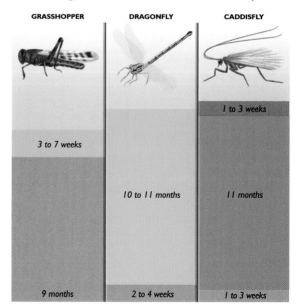

Perfect Timing
Each species of insects is genetically programmed to proceed at its own unique pace as it moves from egg to adult.

PUPAL STAGE

LARVAL STAGE

NYMPHAL DEVELOPMENT

EGG STAGE

GRASSHOPPER	DRAGONFLY	CADDISFLY
		1 to 3 weeks
3 to 7 weeks		
	10 to 11 months	11 months
9 months	2 to 4 weeks	1 to 3 weeks

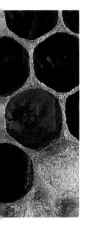

something the size of an elephant in less than two months.

Many insects go through their life cycle in a continuous manner, but sometimes unfavorable climatic conditions can cause them to go into diapause, a period of slowed development during which their metabolic rate is usually one-tenth or less of a normal active insect. A given species is likely to diapause in only one life stage. Some swallowtail butterflies, for example, go into diapause and overwinter as pupae. Periods of dormancy are typically triggered by short days and ended when warm temperatures return—generally only after a long bout of cold, which keeps the cocoons from responding fatally to a brief autumnal or winter warming.

OFF WITH THE OLD

To grow, insects must shed their exoskeletons periodically. Most molt four to eight times before adulthood, but some ametabolous insects molt after becoming adults. The molting process begins with the forming of a new "skin" under the old one. Then, under pressure exerted by blood, drawn-in air, or water, the old exoskeleton splits along lines of weakness. The new, lighter-colored exoskeleton is soft for an hour or two—long enough to give newly molted insects time to draw in air or water to enlarge

themselves to the size of the next stage, called an instar.

Molting is induced by hormones, chemical messengers that control a variety of morphological and behavioral changes, including diapause and reproduction. Only adult insects can reproduce, and the maturation of reproductive structures such as ovaries are all regulated by a complex cocktail of hormones.

Most insects mate before laying eggs. Some, however, have developed parthenogenesis, in which young are produced without the prelude of mating. The best example is the female aphid, which is literally born pregnant: She emerges live from the adult female with a female developing inside her. This reproduction is so quick that a single aphid can produce thirteen hundred descendants in just two weeks. The female bears only females until the need arises for a sexual generation to mate and lay eggs that will survive winter conditions and perpetuate the species.

In July and August, cicadas are often seen emerging from nymphal skins.

Mating Methods

Emerging from her cocoon, an adult female giant silkworm moth has no time to spare. Lacking mouthparts, she doesn't eat or drink, and is destined to die within a week or two. Before this happens, she must attract a mate, copulate successfully, and lay fertilized eggs—or her life will have been wasted. Perched on a tree limb, she begins to emit a pheromone from the tip of her abdomen. As the chemical wafts into the night breeze, a male of the species catches the scent with his huge, feathery antennae. Detecting even just a molecule or two, he follows the scent trail to its source and finds the signaling female. The two attach to each other, abdomen to abdomen, and the male uses his penis to ejaculate sperm into the genital opening of his mate. The moths remain united until well into the next day, when the male flies off to search for another mate. Later that night, the female begins to lay hundreds of eggs on tree leaves.

VERSATILE LOVERS

Besides emitting sexual pheromones, insects also use auditory and visual signals *(page 38)* to communicate their desire to mate. The males of some species, such as the scorpionfly (*Panorpa* spp.), offer freshly killed insects to the females to distract them so they will allow mating to occur. A male dance fly (*Empis* spp.) will also catch a small insect and give it to a female before he can mate. But sometimes he cheats; these insects have been observed offering a silk-wrapped inedible object or even an empty silken package.

While mating is often a one-on-one affair as it is for the giant silkworm moths, many insects mate in vast flying swarms. To attract females, males of chironomid midges and March flies (*Bibio* spp.), among others, congregate in groups that can number in the thousands. Females enter the swarm, and males compete vigorously for them. Up to ten males have been observed clinging to a single female, jostling and struggling to assume a mating position with her.

Insects mate in many positions—including front-to-front, end-to-end, and side-by-side—depending in part on the shape of the males' external genitalia. These short-horned grasshoppers (family Acrididae) are mating with the male riding on the female's dorsum, or back.

This may seem a rather inefficient technique, but it does ensure that females mate with the strongest and quickest males and pass on fitter genes to the next generation.

The male of the African species of flower beetle Cetonia polyphema *mounts the female in attempting to mate.*

FERTILIZATION

Once the species-specific mating pattern is concluded, the process of fertilization in most insects follows a similar path. The sperm travels by way of the vagina to the female's spermatheca, a storage unit connected to the vagina by a tubule. There, the sperm remains until the female is ready to lay her eggs. At that time—sometimes as long as a season later—the sperm is released to fertilize the eggs as they travel out of the insect and into the world.

Sperm Precedence

Being first to mate with a female does not necessarily mean that a male insect's sperm will fertilize her eggs. The last sperm into the female's spermatheca is generally the sperm that fertilizes the eggs. To prevent subsequent males from fertilizing her eggs, some male damselflies and dragonflies will hang on right through egg-laying. Others of the order employ a modified penis to push the sperm of previous suitors deeper within the spermatheca. Still others insert a plug in the female's vagina. With the damselfly genus *Calopteryx (left)*, the male employs his brush-tipped penis to scoop out the sperm of earlier couplings, thus ensuring that his sperm will fertilize her eggs.

Insect Clues

In criminology, success in cracking a case often depends on the work of forensic scientists—specialists in the collecting and analyzing of the physical evidence of a crime. Some of these experts focus on clues related to insects. The clues may be useful in solving a variety of criminal and civil cases, including murder, suicide, sexual assault, and drug trafficking.

SILENT STORYTELLERS

The field of forensic entomology is based on the fact that some arthropods, especially insects, are carrion feeders. They eat dead flesh, bones, and animal waste products—and in the process leave behind a trail of evidence that scientists can use to establish the time, manner, and location of an offense.

Forensic entomologists typically make a thorough visual observation of the possible crime scene, noting everything from the weather to the time of day. Then they examine insect specimens found on, around, and under other evidence. For a death, insects within the body are typically collected later during the autopsy.

The period between death and discovery of the body is estimated by determining what insects inhabit the cadaver and if possible, their age, or developmental stage. Insects will generally lay eggs on a corpse within two days of finding it. Temperature, time of day and year, and level of exposure of the corpse influence the speed with which they pass through the various species-specific developmental stages.

STEP BY STEP

When a mammalian carcass is left to rot, it undergoes a predictable series of stages as it decays. The stages include: initial internal decay of the cadaver; black putrefaction, when the cadaver's exposed flesh turns black; butyric fermentation, when the stomach area becomes moldy from fermentation; and finally, dry decay, when the cadav-

High Turnover

A rotting cadaver represents an attractive habitat for all kinds of arthropods, especially insects and mites. They move in and out following a fairly predictable order, as each colony feeds on what it can before moving on. While there are arthropods that feed off the soil under or near the carcass, those that first take up residence inside usually include blow flies (right) and their eggs, rove beetles and larvae, and hister beetles. Gamasid mites and parasitic wasps are among those that move in as the body continues to expel gases and liquids. Once the cadaver starts to dry out, colonies of dermestid beetles, tineid moths, and certain mites take over.

er's rate of decay slows down dramatically. Specific colonies of insects take up residence in the cadaver throughout the decay process *(box, opposite)*.

USING THE CLUES

Piecing together physical evidence can help to reconstruct a crime scene and convict the guilty. To figure out the origin of stolen goods, vehicles, or other items or to determine whether a body has been moved may be as simple as establishing whether the insects found on or near the pieces of evidence can be linked to the ecological community of the place of discovery.

Re-creating a crime scene may also depend on clues left by insects themselves. For example, blow flies commonly lay eggs in natural body openings, including the facial region. So, even if the cadaver is badly decomposed by the time it is found, infestation in other parts might indicate body trauma prior to death. For example, a knife attack might be suspected if blow flies are found on the lower part of the arm or hands, indicating the presence of wounds acquired in self-defense. In addition, blow fly eggs uncovered in the genito-anal regions can indicate sexual assault and trauma.

Many criminal cases have been solved with the help of forensic entomology. In one famous case in Scotland during the 1930s, dismembered human remains were found in a river near Edinburgh. The remains were even-

Forensic entomologists learn about the time and manner of death from the insects that have colonized a body. Here, maggots, one of the earliest colonizers, thrive on the decaying flesh of a seal carcass.

tually identified as belonging to two women, a Mrs. Ruxton and a Mary Rogerson, the Ruxton children's nurse. Investigators discovered blow fly larvae near the remains and employed them to estimate the date when the bodies were dumped in the river. This calculation was instrumental in leading to the conviction of Dr. Ruxton, husband and employer of the victims, respectively, although he never confessed to the murders.

Forensic entomologists work with evidence left by other arthropods besides insects. In 1982, in California's Ventura County, deputies noted that a suspect in the strangulation of a twenty-four-year old woman had bites made by chiggers (microscopic mites) similar to those suffered by crime scene investigators. When the bites were analyzed, it was determined that the chigger species responsible existed locally only near a eucalyptus tree under which the victim had been found. The suspect claimed that he had been nowhere near that area, but the bug bites exposed his lie. He was convicted of first-degree murder and sentenced to life without parole.

STAYING ALIVE

Whether adapting to new habitats, escaping predators, or joining in a fight against a common enemy, insect survival is an intricate art.

The life of insects is not an easy one. They expend their energies primarily on foraging for food, securing supplies for their young, and defending themselves against predators.

That insects not only survive but prosper is explained in part by their ability to adapt to so many different environments. Besides the advantages provided by their exoskeleton *(page 11)*, flexible life-cycle patterns and short generation times have led to quick radiation of insect lineages, with accompanying adaptations that support further insect survival. Linked to these advantages is their small size *(page 9)*, which allows insects to find more niches in a given environment than larger organisms. A single tree might support larvae of the gossamer-winged butterfly (family Lycaenidae) chewing on the leaves; hemipterans such as the oak lace bug (*Corythuca arcuata*) sucking

"The thing-in-itself, the will-to-live, exists whole and undivided in every being, even in the tiniest; . . ."

— Arthur Schopenhauer

the stem sap, and coleopterans such as longhorn beetle larvae (family Cerambycidae) boring into the bark. It might also sustain midges that eat the flower buds, bruchid beetles that consume the seeds, mealybugs that nourish on the root sap, and, to top it off, a number of wasp species that parasitize any one of these insects. A nearby tree of a different species may reveal an entirely different microcosm of insects.

HAPPY CAMPERS
Once ensconced in a particular habitat, insects are likely to remain until circumstances intervene, as

Diving into freshwater pools and ponds to pick off prey, this giant water bug (Lethocerus americanus) feeds on other insects, tadpoles, small fish, and salamanders. Because it trolls shallow waters, this water bug also goes by the name "toe biter."

Happy Together

When two species evolve in tandem, it is called coevolution. Sometimes the species end up benefiting from the interaction, as in the case of mutualistic symbiosis, a term for the type of relationship that has evolved between various species of ants and aphids, treehoppers, and certain types of caterpillars. The ants protect these insects from predators, and, in return, they supply the ants with nourishment in the form of honeydew *(page 74)*. Mutualistic symbiosis has also evolved between ants, such as the *Pseudomyrmex ferruginea*, seen at right, and acacia trees. In exchange for nutritious sap, the ants trim weeds and chase off pests, including leaf-cutting caterpillars, from the leaves of the tree.

sometimes occurs after a natural disaster or when humans invade their territories and they are forced to expand their range. They might do this in many ways, perhaps by crawling into a crevice next door, hitching a ride on a host, attaching themselves to crops that are marketed at great distances from where they are grown, or by being taken to non-endemic areas as agents of biological control *(page 49)*. Ladybugs, cockroaches, and parasites such as lice and fleas are just a few insects that have been widely dispersed in some of these ways.

QUICK-CHANGE ARTISTS

While longer-living, more developed vertebrates usually adapt to change by learning, then modifying their behavior, insects—short-lived and fecund—adapt by changes in their genes. This is one reason why *Drosophila melanogaster* has been so very successful as an experimental animal *(page 50)*. Rapid genetic adaptation has led many insects to become immune to pesticides, prospering in the face of this man-made adversity. Some insects, however, such as the monarch butterfly (*Danaus plexippus*), may not be able to keep up with human-introduced environmental changes quickly enough and so are at risk *(page 34)*.

When insects do adapt, other organisms in their habitat sometimes adapt with them, maintaining or enhancing the success of both. This process, called coevolution, which may spur or hasten evolutionary change and differentiation, is explained in the box above.

Ichneumon wasps are among the most successful of insect parasites, making a living from a wide variety of insects and spiders. Here a female Megarhyssa lumator drills into a branch with her ovipositor to deposit eggs in her host larvae. When the eggs hatch, they will feed on their hosts until they are adults, killing them in the process.

In contrast to the mutualistic symbiotic relationship that often underlies coevolution, parasitic relationships serve only one party. Insects, ever-opportunistic, frequently play the parasite, staying alive by feeding off other organisms such as vertebrates, some crustaceans, molluses, spiders, as well as other insects. Some species of insects are even hyperparasites—parasites of parasites.

Insects have mastered the parasitic lifestyle so well that there are more than 115,000 species—mostly tiny parasitic wasps, but some flies, beetles, moths, and butterflies—that live on or within other insects. These parasites, also known as parasitoids, usually kill off their hosts after feeding on or in the host's body as larvae. Parasitic wasps, for instance, feed off their host's blood, leaving vital organs intact and the host alive—until they grow to adults and finish the job by consuming the host completely.

Parasitism is only one of many feeding habits. Scavenging on plant debris was probably the practice of

Ripple Effect

Once confined to manufacturing sprays that destroy insect pests, the insecticide industry has begun to experiment with genetic engineering. Unfortunately new technologies don't always take into account the ecological ripple effects that may occur following their introduction. Nowhere is this more evident than in the case of the recently introduced Bt corn, a genetically altered plant exuding a chemical poisonous to corn-boring caterpillars. Recent laboratory experiments suggest that if enough of the corn's pollen blows onto nearby milkweed pods, it could kill feeding monarch larvae. If that is true, then the monarch *(left)* may be threatened.

the earliest terrestrial insects, fore-runners of the silverfish that today feed off book bindings and other household paper products. When thin-barked trees evolved during the Carboniferous period, insects that would give rise to the true bugs began to suck plant sap. Around the same time, insects developed the ability to fly, enabling them to extend their range and exploit more food sources, including those offered by other insects as host or prey.

The most important insect predators are insects themselves, rivaled only by spiders. They kill and eat their own kind by hunting, ambushing, or trapping. Robber flies wait for insects to soar by, then take off in pursuit, ultimately landing their prey and impaling it with their sharp mouth-parts. By contrast, tiger beetles wait for caterpillars in sandy areas such as beaches, then scurry after them. Still others, such as antlion larvae, dig sand pit traps and bury themselves in the bottom. Once an insect tumbles in, its downfall hastened by the antlion's flicking sand at it, the larva devours it.

Insects defend themselves in a variety of ways against such fierce attacks. Camouflage and mimicry are used *(page 36)*, and bright colors serve as widely understood warn-ings that worse will follow if a predator persists. The shield bug

Graphosoma italicum, for example, warns predators of its nasty flavor with its bold colors—black and red stripes across its head, its antennae, and its body.

Some insects resort to more aggressive means of defense, includ-ing poisonous sprays and venomous stings. Many employ several defense strategies. The predominantly green puss moth caterpillar (*Cerura vinula*)

To protect itself, a bombardier beetle (Brachinus *spp.*) squirts a high-temperature toxin containing quinones, a cor-rosive substance that is also used in tanning leather. The chemicals that produce this noxious gas—hydroquinone and hydrogen peroxide—are manufactured in separate abdomi-nal glands. When the beetle is disturbed, they are brought together in an explosive enzymatic reaction; the resulting spray can be aimed in a 360-degree radius.

first uses camouflage, then inflates its head to yield a pair of "horns," and then sprays a squirt of acid from a gland just below its head. Social insects, such as ants, bees, and wasps, rely on strength in num-bers, alarm-call pheromones *(page 40)*, and, finally, stingers, with their lethal cocktail of some fifty poiso-nous chemicals.

Camouflage & Mimicry

Look closely at the twigs above: One of them is actually a walkingstick insect, camouflaged so well that even sharp-eyed birds won't notice it.

The world of insects is filled with lush colors and highly individualistic behavior. But sometimes it's in an insect's best interest to forego its distinctiveness. Camouflage and mimicry can help an insect evade predators or coax prey into a false sense of security.

Birds, lizards, snakes, and even primates such as tropical-dwelling monkeys feed on insects. To avoid their keen eyes, some insects blend into their surroundings. The gray and white patches of the nocturnal merveille du jour moth (*Dichonia aprilina*) render it indistinguishable from lichen-covered bark. Many butterflies, moths, and katydids mimic dead and decaying leaves. Butterfly wings often have intricate markings that make it hard for predators to distinguish body outlines from the environment.

Other insects mimic the color or shape of inanimate objects. To keep competitors at bay, sap-sucking treehoppers take on the appearance and color of thorns. The color of some praying mantids allows them to blend in with the blossoms on which they sit, awaiting their insect prey. Bird droppings are mimicked by the early larval stages of the citrus swallowtail (*Papilio thoas*). And the larvae of the bagworm moth caterpillar (family Psychidae) imitate decaying organic debris by covering their cocoons with sand, bark, and plant parts.

ANIMAL LOOK-ALIKES

Insects that are otherwise defenseless can sometimes mimic the appearance of creatures that are naturally threatening or perhaps bad-tasting or poisonous. When disturbed, for instance, some moth caterpillars of the family Sphingidae flatten the front sections of their body and constrict the sections just behind to form a "head" and a "neck." False eyespots and a weaving motion complete the ruse of a venomous viper ready to attack. Birds avoid robber flies and syrphid flies because they look like stinging bumblebees and wasps, respectively; robber flies can even buzz like bees. Although most viceroy butterflies (*Limenitis archippus*) don't taste as nasty as the monarch (*Danaus plexippus*), which gets its bad taste from feeding on milkweed as larvae, their orange and black wings so resemble those of the monarch that they are usually safe from insect-eating birds.

Some insects warn off predators with a flash of unexpected color or pattern, giving them a moment to escape. Resting sweetheart underwing moths (*Catocala amatrix*), camouflaged on tree bark by their gray-and-brown forewings, startle potential attackers by exposing their brightly banded underwings when they fly off to escape.

Butterflies, in particular, utilize wing-tip eyespots to buy time, startling birds and other predators. When the otherwise camouflaged fulgorid bug (*Fulgora laternaria*) is disturbed, it spreads its wings for flight, revealing large hindwing markings strikingly similar to the eyes of an owl. To further confuse

This caterpillar combines body movement with false eyespots to mimic a viper's head, scaring off predators and competitors.

would-be predators, many species of hairstreak butterflies (family Lycaenidae) also possess fake hind-end antennae that they can wiggle.

DISINFORMING FOR DINNER

More rarely, insects can take on the behavior of other insects to deceive prey. The female lampyrid firefly of some *Photurus* species, for example, mimics the bioluminescent signal codes of as many as five other firefly species, including the *Photinus* species, to attract interested males, which she then eats.

The color and shape of the stone cricket (Stenopelmatinae) *makes it virtually indistinguishable among desert stones.*

Versatile Communicators

In a communal courtship display, thousands of Southeast Asian fireflies (Pteroptyx sp.) *gather on the boughs of the same tree and flash their lights synchronously.*

Insects can communicate an array of intents and fears related to territoriality, mating, safety, and food sources. They can pass on detailed directions *(box, page 41)*, call for help, and some can even relay disinformation *(page 37)*. To deliver such messages, they use a variety of media, including color, light, dance, sound, and pheromones.

The use of color to indicate mating eligibility is one of the most common visual signals. Male dragonflies, for instance, come in red, blue, green, and even violet, advertising their attractiveness in brilliant metallic hues that shimmer in the sunlight as they dart through the air.

Bioluminescence, light produced by living organisms, is used by a variety of insects, including several springtails, true flies, the fulgorid lantern bug, and the better known fireflies—coleopterans (beetles) from the family Lampyridae. Among fire-

flies, a roving male of *Photinus pyralis* lights up to engage the interest of sedentary females waiting below. He does this by setting off a complex chemical reaction in a light-making organ located at the hind end of his abdomen. The reaction converts chemical energy into light energy with little heat as a by-product. By varying the frequency and duration of the pulse, he lets the female know he is interested; she flashes her readiness in response. The code they use is only known to members of their species. All larvae of these lampyrids produce light in this manner. Most adults do the same; their luminescent abdominal segment appears ivory or glazed when not glowing. Even eggs of some species glow slightly.

SOUND LANGUAGE

Besides the visual signals of color and light, insects signal with song by rubbing one part of the body against another part—wing against wing, wing against back, leg against leg. Insects that make chirping, rasping, and squeaking sounds are said to stridulate. Grasshoppers, crickets, katydids, cicadas, true bugs, ants, and beetles stridulate. Each species has a characteristic call, and typically it is the males who sound off, either to attract mates or keep other males at bay. Some crickets have three different songs in their repertoire: a loud, belligerent song, a song of advertisement, and a courtship song. The mole cricket (*Gryllotalpa* spp.) emits the loudest insect mating call of all; it can be heard more than a half mile (0.8 km) away. Some insects make sounds to warn others or to summon help. One of the most common leafcutter ants (*Atta cephalotes*), for example, issues high-pitched squeaks when buried in soil.

For all the effectiveness of sound as a long-range tool of communication, there is always the danger that it will alert predatory insects to the signaling insect's whereabouts. That's how parasitic flies, for instance, track their cricket prey. They follow the crickets' stridulations to their source; then, they exploit the crickets as food for their larvae.

SCENT OF AN INSECT

Pheromones, an additional tool in the insects' communication kit, can also be picked up by species other than those for which they are intended. Even humans can detect the scents of certain moths and butterflies (some of which are said to smell like chocolate). When parasitic wasps catch the scent of the sex-attractant pheromones belonging to their moth or butterfly prey, they follow it back to its source.

The source of the scent is a collection of glands, derived from epidermal cells, located in various spots on an insect's body, depending on the species. These glands are exocrine glands, meaning they excrete their secretions directly outside the body. Female aphids, for instance, have the glands on their hind tibiae. Cockroaches sometimes have them on their backs. Small, silvery pyralid moths have them on their hind ends; when

The horned passalus beetle (Odontotaenius disjunctus) lives in communities made up of a mating pair and their larvae, all of which communicate by stridulating almost constantly. They are believed to have a repertoire of fourteen different sounds.

Soon after emerging from the chrysalis, a female luna moth (Actias luna) is ready to mate. She releases sex-attractant pheromones into the air and a male, downwind from her, picks up the scent with the thousands of chemoreceptors on his large featherlike antennae. Once he deciphers the scent, he heads out in her direction to mate.

gilippus), for instance, dusts pheromones directly on the female's antennae with his abdominal brushes as the courting pair are in flight.

Receiving insects detect the scents with specialized cells called chemoreceptors *(page 22)*, found on the antennae and the mouthparts, but also elsewhere on the body, such as on ovipositors. Only a minute amount of pheromone is needed to produce a reaction. Male cecropia moths (*Hyalophora cecropia*) can sense as little as a few thousand molecules of a female's love per-

they wag their abdomen, scent scales release the mate-luring scent, which spreads in the wind.

Although the pheromones of different species may be made up of some of the same chemicals, each species (with a few exceptions) has its own blend—and sometimes more than one. Some insects, for example, manufacture a particular formula to signal their location and another one to arouse their mates to copulate.

Pheromones are usually volatile, which means they are dispersed through the air as individual molecules, traveling far and wide. But sometimes they are deposited directly on items commonly found in the environment, such as soil, plants, and even the target insect. The male queen butterfly (*Danaus*

Smelling Good
Some cockroaches secrete an aphrodisiac pheromone, aptly named seducin, on their backs to attract mates. Females nibble the seducin during copulation and won't let the mating begin until after they have ingested some of it.

fume in a cubic inch of air. Usually it is the female that emits the sex-attractant pheromone, but the males of some species, including boll weevils, hangingflies, and the queen butterfly, can manufacture and excrete them as well.

Pheromones are used by virtually all eusocial insects *(page 42)*, their complex societies depending on a full spectrum of communication tools. Honeybees, when injured, release pheromones to rouse the troops, triggering the attack and stinging behavior of nest mates. This type of pheromone differs from sex attractants in that it disperses quickly and persists only long enough to sound the alarm.

To alert colony mates to the location of food, tropical stingless bees of the genus *Trigona* mark

Vienna-born Karl von Frisch studied the hearing and vision of fish before he began his famous experiments on bee communications (box, below). In 1973 he shared the Nobel prize for physiology/medicine with animal behaviorists Konrad Lorenz and Nikolaas Tinbergen.

their nest entrance with chemicals. Wandering scout ants lay trails with pheromones for their fellow colony members; after feeding at a new location, the scouts drag their distended abdomen along the ground as they head back to their nest. Hungry ants then trace along the trail with their antennae, following it to the food.

Dance of the Bees

In the busy world of a beehive, some of the inhabitants can be seen executing a series of dances. Called the round (or circle) dance and the waggle dance, these actions were first described by Austrian biologist Karl von Frisch *(above)*. They are performed by worker honeybees (*Apis mellifera*) within the wax honeycomb to communicate the location of nectar and pollen. Other bees stand by, taking in the information by sensing the air vibrations and touching the dancer with their antennae. When a bee dances the round dance, she is indicating that there are supplies within 80 feet (25 m). In the waggle dance *(right)*, the bee dances out a figure-eight shape to indicate food beyond 320 feet (100 m). The number of waggles indicate distance; the angle of the waggles indicate the direction relative to the sun. Later research has uncovered a third dance, the vibration dance, in which a worker vibrates her abdomen while in contact with other bees. This dance recruits the bees to the waggle dance area and rallies them to increase food foraging.

Truly Social

Although most insects are solitary creatures, certain species share life's burdens. Some are what entomologists call subsocial, meaning their societies are fairly simple. Subsocial species include earwigs that nest together, butterflies that congregate, and beetles that excavate galleries in trees where they can feed their young. Others are called eusocial, meaning "truly" social, indicating a higher level of organization. All work is performed by a sharply defined caste system and two or more generations live in the same

Termite workers tend the queen Macrotermes in her royal cell. As she produces her eggs, the queen's abdomen becomes enormously distended, making movement virtually impossible and her dependency on others complete.

A WORKING CLASS SYSTEM

Insect caste systems are typically divided into a sterile caste and a reproductive caste. Among ants, bees, and wasps, the sterile caste is made up of female soldiers and workers. Soldiers defend the nest by stinging, spraying, or biting intruders, while workers enlarge and repair the nest, care for the eggs, larvae, pupae, and queen, or forage for food. Workers may do one job for life, or may change jobs from time to time. Some ants even rely on workers from other species to do the jobs instead. Amazon ants, for example, have mandibles that are too curved for them to feed themselves or dig their own nests, so they capture other types of ants to do these tasks for them.

This tropical army ant is one of 8,804 known ant species, according to Edward O. Wilson. A foremost authority on the classification and behavior of social insects, Wilson himself has described some three hundred ant species.

nest, tending to the young. Termites and some hymenopterans (including ants, bees, and wasps) dominate the eusocial, each group having its own unique approach to living together.

The reproductive caste among hymenopterans is made up of the queen and drones (males), the sole purpose of which is to reproduce. In the case of some ant queens, this means laying several million eggs over the course of a twenty-year life span. The drones live just long enough to fertilize the queen's eggs.

Termite males get to stick around after mating. In fact, there are male workers and soldiers, as well as a king or two to mate with the queen as required. In these societies, if the queen or king dies, one of the sterile workers can develop the necessary hormones needed to become reproductive and take over the role.

Communication is an integral part of colony life. Honeybees use different dances—the waggle and the round *(page 41)*—to tell others the location of a food source. Some ants communicate by tapping on the sides of the plant that houses their nest. And many species of eusocials communicate by emitting pheromones *(page 39)* for various reasons: to warn of danger or to create a scent trail leading to food.

SELF-SERVING SACRIFICE

Such cooperative behavior has sometimes been explained in terms of biological altruism: Eusocial insects will give up their life to defend a nest so that the colony—and thus its gene pool—survives. But why do female work-

ers give up their reproductive potential? The explanation—at least for hymenopterans—may lie in genetics. A hymenopteran male has only half the normal complement of genetic material in his cells. When the sperm and an egg unite, a female offspring will have exactly the same 50 percent donation of her father's genes in common with her sisters, but only, on average, 25 percent of her mother's donation in common with them. Though mothers pass on 50 percent of their genes to their daughters, sisters share 75 percent of their genes (50 percent from their father, plus 25 percent from their mothers). Thus hymenopteran sisters are closer genetically than mother and daughter. This means that the insect has better odds of propagating her genes by staying in the nest to help raise sisters than by reproducing herself.

The nest of the honey pot ant (Myrmecocystus spp.) sometimes includes as many as fifteen hundred repletes, workers that act as food reservoirs, storing the colony's nectar in their crop, a storage area located behind their esophagus.

Insect Architects

Working with materials that range from leaves and wood fibers to wax and mud, insects build a wide assortment of shelters. Some of the more unusual are produced by larvae. The leaf roller moth larva rolls a leaf around itself each morning, sealing the ends with a silken thread ejected from its mouth. There the larva remains until evening, when it breaks out to hunt for food. The caddisfly larva builds a casing of pebbles or sticks around itself, which it then pulls along as it moves around.

Many shelters are built underground. When constructed by solitary insects, they may consist of a simple vertical cavity, such as that of the tiger beetle larva *(page 76)*, or more elaborate structures, such as the horn-shaped burrow of the mole cricket (*Gryllotalpa major*), which acts as an amplifier to enhance the male's stridulation.

Eusocial insects, spared the distraction of survival chores that solitary insects must pursue, channel their energy into constructing complex structures that may house millions of insects. Termites build vast networks of chambers and passageways in their nests. At the center are several stacked chambers, each with a specific function; the king and queen mate in the royal cell at the core, and the several thou-

sand eggs she lays every day are transported by workers to adjacent nurseries. In the nests of the fungus-farming termite *Macrotermes natalensis,* there are cells for the insects to raise a unique species of fungus, used as a digestive aid and heat source. Helix-shaped passages run through the nest and toward the top; chimneys vent the warm, moist air created by the termites and their gardens of fungi.

Some mounds built by tropical termites reach as high as twenty-three feet (7 m)—six hundred times the size of the average termite worker. Others are huge underground structures.

A variation on this design is constructed by the compass termites of northern Australia (*Amitermes meridionalis*). They build tall mounds that are wide but not deep. The wide sides face east and west to soak up heat from the rising and setting sun, while the sides facing north and south have a much smaller surface area, minimizing exposure to the hot noonday sun.

The nests of social bees and wasps are composed of combs, parallel rows of adjoining cells. Typically begun by the overwintering queen, the hive is expanded and repaired by the workers. The combs of bumblebees are fairly simple, untidy arrangements of cells made of wax secreted by the queen's epidermal glands. The honeybee has a more complex social structure and thus a more elaborate hive. Between its tenth and sixteenth day of life, a honeybee worker takes over making wax by chewing flakes produced by its abdominal pores. It then fashions the wax into the familiar six-sided cells organized into combs. Each comb is made of three concentric rings. The eggs and developing bees are posi-

The larval cells of the Polistes species of social wasps lack a protective envelope and are left open to the elements.

tioned at the center and surrounded first by a circle of pollen-filled cells, then by a honey storage area, and finally by an outer wall. The same cells can be used for various purposes, depending on the time of year. In spring, the colony focuses on procreation; in autumn, food storage.

Social wasps use masticated wood pulp rather than wax to construct combs on a similar hexagonal plan. An outer envelope, applied in layers with air spaces in between, provides excellent insulation that helps regulate the temperature in the combs. The wasps leave an opening to get in at the bottom of the nest; it traverses successive combs, allowing wasps to move from floor to floor. A common sight in North America is the nest of the bald-faced hornet (*Vespula maculata*), which may be as large as a basketball and can often be seen hanging from trees in autumn and winter, or attached to shrubs, utility poles, or house siding. Because the adult hornets cannot survive the winter, a new brood builds its own nest from scratch each year.

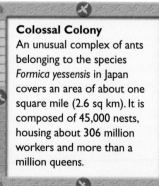

Colossal Colony

An unusual complex of ants belonging to the species *Formica yessensis* in Japan covers an area of about one square mile (2.6 sq km). It is composed of 45,000 nests, housing about 306 million workers and more than a million queens.

ALLIES & ENEMIES

*Insects play starring roles in maintaining our planet's ecosystem,
but sometimes their very success threatens our own.*

Imagine a world without insects. Although there would be no mosquito bites, bee stings, or half-eaten food in the pantry, the world would also lack flowering plants and be drowning in organic waste. And many predators of insects, including most birds, would soon die off.

All told, insects provide great service to humankind. Pollinators keep fruit, vegetables, flowers, and cattle-grazing fields thriving. Scavengers act as garbage crews, feeding on dung and decomposing plants and animals. Insects improve the quality of the soil, aerating it as they burrow, enriching it with the nutrients of their excretions and carcasses, and providing entrance points for fungi that enhance animal decomposition. In addition, insects have

"It is a common saieng: A lion feareth no bugs. But in our childhood . . . they have so fraied us with . . . the fierdrake, the puckle, Tom thumb, hobgoblin, Tom tumbler, boneles, and other such bugs, that we are afraid of our owne shadowes."

— Reginald Scot

proven to be of enormous benefit to science. For example, the fruit fly *Drosophila melanogaster* is used by developmental biologists to help fathom human genetics *(page 50)*, and a variety of scavenging bugs are studied by forensic entomologists in order to establish the

More than 80 percent of pollination is carried out by insects, primarily bees, wasps, beetles, flies, moths, and butter-flies such as this gray pansy (Precis atlites), resting on a blossom in Malaysia. Insects have determined both the evolution and distribution of most angiosperms and without them many plants would disappear from the planet for good.

Parasitic insects, such as these chalcid wasps (Spilochalcis mariae), are valuable allies in the biological control of insect pests. Here, the ravaged cocoon of a Cynthia moth (Samia cynthia) reveals wasps that have grown from larvae, feeding extensively on moth pupae.

time, place, and even manner of deaths *(page 30)*.

FOLLOW THE MONEY

Humans have long recognized the economic importance of some insects. Products such as honey, candles, cosmetics, and furniture waxes were once possible only because of the honeybee. And raw silk is still a gift of the silkworm moth's modified salivary glands.

Medicine has also benefited from insects. For centuries, military surgeons noted that untreated wounds, when allowed to become infested with certain species of Diptera larvae, would heal better than treated wounds. It was later learned that allantoin, a natural antibiotic secreted by the maggots, stimulates healing and growth of tissue.

Scientists have also used insects to help control the proliferation of mammal populations in non-native habitats. For example, the European rabbit, brought to Australia in the 1950s from Great Britain (presumably by trappers hoping to expand the fur trade), propagated so successfully that it competed with livestock for the grasslands. When attempts to control its numbers with poisoning and fumigation failed, Brazilian fleas infected with the myxomatosis virus were released to control it.

TOO MUCH OF A GOOD THING

When insects breed too rapidly and become competitors for our food and resources or bring disease, they become known as pests. It has been estimated that pests rob the world of up to one-quarter of its food supply. Major culprits include the Hessian fly (*Mayetiola destructor*), which ravages wheat, the chinch bug (*Blissus leucopterus*), which attacks corn, and the Colorado potato beetle (*Leptinotarsa decemlineata*), which has spread through North America and Europe, feeding on potatoes and related garden vegetables.

Since there is little that insects as a group won't eat, it's not surprising that they have also made substantial in-roads in attacking many non-food crops. Notably, American cotton crops have been repeatedly devastated by the boll weevil (*Anthonomus grandis*), which causes cotton to turn yellow and drop off the plants. Finally, an inventory of household pests includes innumerable

Picky Layers

When a female dung-feeding scarab beetle is ready to lay eggs, she forms a ball of dung, places an egg in it, and buries the ball in the ground. In this way, dung beetles are beneficial, helping turn dung into fertilizer. When Europeans colonized Australia, the wet cow pats of their imported cattle accumulated dangerously because indigenous dung beetles were interested in laying eggs only in the dry dung of native marsupials. The solution was to bring species of scarab beetles from Europe and Africa that prefer wet dung.

Seemingly insignificant because of their size, these insects have wreaked more havoc on the human condition than both world wars combined. Carriers of sleeping sickness, malaria, and the plague, respectively, the tsetse fly, the Anopheles *mosquito, and the rat flea are among the world's most deadliest insects.*

species from half a dozen orders. Some attack clothes and carpets, others damage wood furniture, and still others, such as cockroaches, feed on any foods that are lying around.

Insects that transmit diseases—including malaria, African sleeping sickness, elephantiasis, river blindness, and yellow fever, to name just a few—are clearly among the most dangerous insects. Typically the so-called disease vectors are biting flies, parasitic lice, and fleas, which host a disease-causing organism, then pass it on when they bite a mammal or a bird. Mosquitoes are the most feared, particularly the various species of *Anopheles* mosquito that transmit the amoeba-like protozoa *Plasmodium*, responsible for the four types of human malaria. Each year there are an estimated 2.7 million casualties (mostly children), with another 300 to 500 million infected.

Originally confined to the tropics, malaria is now on the rise around the world, partly because travelers and goods exportation have spread *Anopheles* to non-endemic areas, partly because global warming has increased the areas that are warm enough for the mosquito to thrive, and partly because DDT and related insecticides, once considered the miracle preventatives, are no longer effective.

CONTROL ALTERNATIVES

Insecticides often exacerbate the pest problem in the long run. Not only do they sometimes pollute the environment and even poison humans, they also kill off many beneficial parasites and predators that can keep the target pest in check. Furthermore, insects are quick to evolve a resistance to insecticides; more than five hundred species of insects are now resistant to one or more insecticides, including most of the *Anopheles* species. So instead of insecticides, various other methods are being explored. These range from genetic controls, such as releasing sterile males to reduce the population of screwworm flies, to cultural controls, which include rotating crops and growing varieties resistant to pests. Biological controls—the use of parasitic and predatory insects to keep a pest in check—have also been successful in many cases. One of the most famous cases involved the 1880 introduction of the ladybird beetle in California to control rampant cottony cushion scales in the state's citrus groves.

Black and Dreadful

In fourteenth-century Europe, repeated occurrences of a plague killed about 25 million people, close to one-quarter of the population. Called the Black Death, the disease was caused by the bacillus *Yersinia pestis* and transmitted to humans by the rat flea (*Xenopsylla cheopis*), which acquired it from infected rats. When an infected flea bites, it regurgitates the undigested plague bacteria into the wound. Although the name Black Death is generally thought to stem from the appearance of dark blotches on victims' skin, it is more likely a mistranslation from the Latin *atra mors* for "dreadful death," *atra* meaning "black" as well as "dreadful." Epidemics of the Black Death have recurred several times since the Middle Ages, but the threat has diminished as sanitary conditions around the world have improved.

D. Melanogaster

The science of genetics owes much of its progress to a tiny fruit fly known as *Drosophila melanogaster*. Measuring a mere one-tenth inch (3 mm) in length, the yellowish, stout, two-winged *Drosophila* flies can be found congregating around spoiled fruit—like so many "animal weeds," in the words of one biologist.

These "weeds" are the most studied organisms in biology, and they have contributed to critical breakthroughs in our understanding of genes and

Drosophila melanogaster *has been a very useful test animal, illuminating the mechanics of genetics and inheritance.*

chromosomal inheritance. Scientist Thomas Hunt Morgan first proposed using *Drosophila* in 1909 to study the gene, which had been given its name earlier that year. He realized that laboratory observation of the evolutionary process was possible with these flies because the life span of a generation is less than two weeks and each female yields some two thousand eggs. As test animals, they had the further advantage of being easily reared on rotting bananas.

Morgan set out to create enormous numbers of visible mutations in the fruit fly, searching for how physical traits are inherited. In little time, he was able to demonstrate that genes are located on chromosomes, jump-starting the new field of genetics. Advances in everything from gene therapy for treating human disorders to bioengineered crops that can fight insect attacks *(page 34)* were made possible by research based on this fly.

Of late, studies of *Drosophila* have added a great deal to the understanding of how a complex organism arises from a simple fertilized egg. In 1997, scientists at Duke University Medical Center inserted a glowing jellyfish protein tag into one of the *Drosophila*'s key cell-structure proteins in order to observe the fly in its transformation from embryo to larva and to adult. Employing high-resolution microscopes and time-lapse cameras, the researchers monitored reactions of the glowing jellyfish protein tag during the fly's development. From such research, they hope to gain insight into the occurrence of human birth defects, such as spina bifida, a condition caused when the spinal column does not develop properly in the embryo.

CHOICE AND COMPETITION

D. melanogaster also has added to knowledge about mating and male competition: The offspring of fruit flies live longer as adults when the female has a choice of mates than when only one male is available. For their part, males engage in sperm wars. To try to ensure that a female's eggs are fertilized only by his sperm, a male *Drosophila* emits a toxic seminal fluid that disables the sperm of other males that have previously mated with the females—a variation of the sperm displacement practiced by male dragonflies and damselflies *(page 29)*. Besides its DNA—which if uncoiled would measure more than twenty times the length of the fly's entire body—the fly's seminal fluid carries hormones that make the female less sexually receptive, reducing the likelihood of her mating again. Biologists are now finding that other male animals engage in similar practices.

In a letter to a friend, Thomas Hunt Morgan wrote, ". . . no funds for rearing larger animals . . . [so] I got some [Drosophila] to see if I could find characters suitable for genetic work, which turned out, as you know, to be the case."

Some researchers hope *Drosophila* can offer lessons about the role of genetics in alcoholism among humans. Existing as they do on the alcohol and yeast of fermented fruit, fruit flies are peerless tipplers; they even can survive on the ethanol fumes of alcohol. This is because their bodies produce abundant supplies of the enzyme alcohol dehydrogenase, which converts toxic alcohol to more benign aldehydes and ketones. To determine how genes control susceptibility to intoxication, researchers at the University of California, San Francisco, placed genetically engineered flies into a glass cylinder containing a miniature staircase and piped in ethanol vapor. Within a matter of minutes, the flies became "punch drunk" and stumbled from step to step. The researchers then measured which types of mutant flies were most likely to be influenced by the alcohol. They hope that their results will eventually yield applicable benefits for humans.

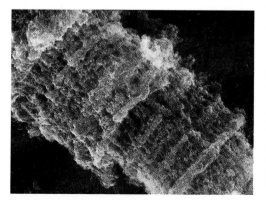

High-resolution scanning electron micrographs of Drosophila *chromosomes, such as this giant chromosome from the fly's salivary gland cells, help scientists in the mapping of genes.*

Spider silk, magnified forty times.

SPIDERS

SPIDERS UP CLOSE

Equipped with deadly venom and super-strong silk, spiders are the chief predators of insects, consuming an estimated 200 trillion of them each year.

Of the more than 34,000 species of spiders named so far (with another estimated 136,000 yet to be named), all are predators, their bodies designed to catch and consume their prey: insects.

Contemporary taxonomy *(page 178)* locates spiders along with insects in the phylum Arthropoda; both have jointed legs and a hard exoskeleton. The spider order Araneae is found in the class Arachnida, which also includes ticks, mites, scorpions, and harvestmen (more familiarly known

"To praise the spider as I ought, I shall first set before you the riches of its body, then of its fortune, lastly of its minde."

— Thomas Mouffet

as daddy longlegs). Taxonomists also divide spiders into three suborders and more than a hundred families. In general, however, spiders fall into two basic categories, the so-called "primitive" spiders, or mygalomorphs (including trap-

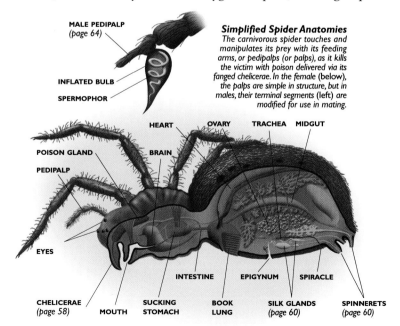

MALE PEDIPALP
(page 64)

INFLATED BULB

SPERMOPHOR

Simplified Spider Anatomies
The carnivorous spider touches and manipulates its prey with its feeding arms, or pedipalps (or palps), as it kills the victim with poison delivered via its fanged chelicerae. In the female (below), the palps are simple in structure, but in males, their terminal segments (left) are modified for use in mating.

HEART   **OVARY**   **TRACHEA**   **MIDGUT**

POISON GLAND   **BRAIN**

PEDIPALP

EYES

INTESTINE   **EPIGYNUM**   **SPIRACLE**

CHELICERAE
(page 58)   **MOUTH**   **SUCKING STOMACH**   **BOOK LUNG**   **SILK GLANDS**
(page 60)   **SPINNERETS**
(page 60)

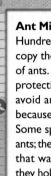

Ant Mimics
Hundreds of spider species copy the shapes and colors of ants. In this way, they gain protection from birds, which avoid ants, presumably because of their bitter taste. Some spiders even move like ants; there are jumping spiders that walk on six legs while they hold up their forelegs to resemble antennae.

door spiders, purse web spiders, and tropical tarantulas, or bird spiders), and "true spiders," or araneomorphs, which account for most spiders in the world today.

SPIDER ANATOMY

Spiders are generally differentiated from insects by having eight legs (rather than six), no antennae, and two body sections (rather than three). Unlike insects, their head and thorax are joined as one body part, called a cephalothorax, which is connected to their abdomen by a slender waist. Arachnologists examine a variety of anatomical features in their effort to distinguish among spider families. One of the most obvious is the arrangement and size of eyes. Most spiders possess eight simple eyes (as opposed to the compound eyes of insects) lined up in two rows, sometimes three. But the variety is great, ranging from the ogre-faced spider (*Deinopis spinosa*), which possesses a pair of enormous eyes resembling headlamps, to the male midget spider (*Walckenaeria acuminata*), which has its eyes perched on the top of stalks. Certain cave-dwelling species, such as *Anthrobia mammouthia,* have no eyes at all.

Other features used for identification purposes because they are unique from family to family include the spinnerets (or silk-spinning organs); the female's epigynum (or genital opening) on the underside of the abdomen; the male palp (or sexual organ) on the leglike pedipalps attached to each side of the spider's mouth; and the position and number of the ventral openings to the breathing organ called book lungs. Mygalomorphs have only book lungs for breathing, but true spiders also have a second breathing organ, the tubular tracheae. One handy way to

Like the wolf spiders (family Lycosidae), with which it is often confused, the nursery-web spider (family Pisauridae) has two rows of four eyes; the anterior row is in a straight line, the posterior row is U-shaped. Here a female Pisaurina mira *carries her egg sac in her chelicerae. Once the eggs are ready to hatch she will suspend the sac in an intricate silken "nursery web," and diligently stand guard nearby until the spiderlings disperse about a week after hatching.*

The spiderlings of the garden spider (Araneus diadematus) remain in an egg sac attached to a leaf or stick by their mother's web until first molt, when they are released to survive on their own.

A number of spiders, including the species of bolas spider (Mastophora spp.) shown here, are able to mimic bird droppings as a protective measure against their enemies, which regard such substances as inedible.

distinguish between these two groups is by the presence of air holes, also called spiracles, leading to the tracheae. They can be seen in front of the fingerlike spinnerets at the rear end of the abdomen. In some cases, there is only a single hole.

GROWING UP

Like every animal with an exoskeleton, spiders must shed their casing in order to grow. Increased blood pressure in the body forces the old exoskeleton to crack, and the growing spider carefully pulls itself out. Even the legs are removed from the old casing, leaving a perfect husklike replica of the spider. Many true spiders hang acrobatically from a thread of silk or a web during molting, while mygalomorphs lie on their back throughout the entire exhausting process. A spider may shed its exoskeleton between four and ten (occasionally twelve) times before it reaches maturity.

Strength in Numbers
Although most spiders live solitary lives, at least thirteen species are known to live together and attack large prey as a group. Two of those species, *Agelena republicana* and *Anelosimus eximius*, cooperate to weave single, huge webs, much larger than they could achieve on their own. They then proceed to cohabit, ganging up on any insect or spider that lands on their shared web.

Once a spider is mature, reproduction becomes a top priority. Many male spiders develop a wanderlust, leaving their web or territory in search of a mate. Before they set off, they exude sperm through a ventral opening onto sperm webs *(page 62)* spun for this purpose. Then, they suck the sperm into their spermophors, ducts within the enlarged tips of their palps. Once they find a mate, they insert the spermaphors in the female's epigynum and release the stored sperm. Contrary to popular opinion, most male spiders do survive the mating process, although elaborate courtship rituals may be essential to reduce the risk of being preyed upon by mates *(page 64)*.

Once her eggs are fertilized, the female wraps them in a silken cocoon *(page 60)*. Later, when the eggs hatch, the females may guard them; some, such as the wolf spider and the nursery-web spider, actually carry both eggs and spiderlings everywhere.

Most males live only weeks; they die soon after mating. Females live longer, often until the first heavy frosts hit in cold areas. Male tarantulas, however, live for about a year after mating. The females are extremely long-lived; Some have been known to live up to thirty-five years in captivity.

A huntsman spider (family Heteropodidae) discards its old skeleton in order to grow to full size: The typical male reaches ¾ inch (19 mm) long, the female one inch (25 mm).

Top-notch Predators

Hanging head-down from the hub of her web, the silver argiope (*Argiope argentata*) feels her trap begin to quiver, indicating the presence of prey. Determining direction by the vibration of the radial web spokes, she scrambles toward a grasshopper that is frantically struggling in a sticky thread. Working quickly, she wraps her victim in silk. Then she gives it a paralyzing bite with her jaws, or chelicerae, and regurgitates digestive enzymes that begin to liquefy the insect. Leaving her mummified meal suspended from the web, the spider returns to her control post to wait for more victims.

INGENIOUS HUNTERS

Few creatures have developed more varied techniques to capture their prey than the spider. Although 60 percent of spiders, including the orb-weaving *A. argentata*, fashion some sort of aerial trap with silk *(page 60)*, the rest do not spin webs at all but pursue their prey in other deadly ways.

A jumping spider (family Salticidae) can leap on its prey from a distance, impaling it with venom-delivering fangs. Its leaping prowess is astonishing, especially considering that it has no enlarged muscular hindlegs to propel it. Researchers suggest that hydrostatic pressure builds up in the legs, suddenly releasing and popping the spider forward—as much as forty times its own body length.

Jumping spiders are stalkers like cats, but some spiders simply run down their prey. Wolf spiders (family Lycosidae) have earned their name for their speedy pursuit of

Spiders' Chelicera
Individual spider species use their chelicerae for a variety of purposes—among them to subdue prey, defend territory, dig burrows, transport bound prey, and carry egg sacs. The hairy mygalomorphs have chelicerae that stab downward to impale their prey; most other spiders, however, have chelicerae that pinch together like a finger touching a thumb.

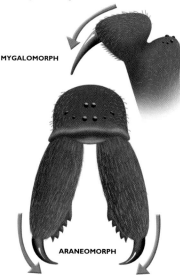

MYGALOMORPH

ARANEOMORPH

Jumping spiders prefer to eat flies, bugs, beetles, and, as shown here, leafhoppers. Large frontal eyes and acute eyesight make them excellent hunters.

prey. The much larger tarantulas are also generally runners, often lurking in underground burrows until they detect vibrations of prey on the soil outside their lair.

Bolas spiders (family Araneidae) do their hunting with a short silk thread tipped with a drop of glue; they hold one end of the thread and fling the sticky end at passing prey.

To improve their chances, these spiders emit a pheromone that mimics that of female moths; approaching male moths looking for a mate are likely to become lunch instead.

A pirate spider (family Mimetidae) preys on other spiders. It invades a web, then paralyzes the weaver by biting and sucking it dry through its legs, one after another. The pirate spider *Ero* adds deception to its aggression: It plucks on the web of its prey of choice, *Metellina segmentata* (family Tetragnathidae), like a courting male to gain entrance.

Dolomedes, the fishing spiders (family Pisauridae), venture right onto the water surface to hunt, sometimes diving to capture insects and small fish. The surface of the water acts as their web. By touching the water with their legs, these spiders detect vibrations of passing insects. Supported by surface tension, they dash out to subdue prey. The king of the fishers is the water spider (*Argyroneta aquatica*); it weaves an air-filled diving bell out of silk and can remain submerged in the water inside it for weeks.

This goldenrod crab spider (Misumena vatia) *feeds on a hackberry butterfly. Crab spiders (family* Thomisidae) *don't spin webs; instead they catch their prey through speed and through the art of camouflage, changing color to match the blossom on which they sit.*

Spider Silk

The silvery strands of spider silk are woven into almost every aspect of a spider's life. Only by unraveling the mysteries of this silk does it become clear how spiders have secured a place among the most successful predators on Earth.

Spider silk is made of fibroins, proteins manufactured in the creature's abdominal glands. There are eight kinds of glands (though no single spider possesses them all) and each type produces a unique silk. Spiders that weave orb-shaped webs have the largest variety of silk glands, but even ground-dwelling spiders produce at least four kinds of silk. The glands lead to tiny, movable spigots on the spinnerets on the rear underside of the abdomen. Spigots can be extended, withdrawn, or compressed to manipulate the silk as it leaves the spider's body.

The best-known use of silk is to construct traps for insects. Experts hypothesize that spiders developed silken traps in order to compete suc-

cessfully with airborne insects in the invertebrate arms race. Trap designs vary tremendously. Sheet-web weavers (family Linyphiidae) and funnel-web weavers (family Agelenidae) make platforms suspended from vegetation, overhung with a mass of silken "guylines." Jumping insects and flying insects blunder into the tangle of silk, eventually falling on the woven platform. Sheet-web weavers bite their prey from beneath the gauzy platforms. Funnel-web weavers lurk at the bot-

Constructing an Orb Web
The orb-weaver spider has a modified foot with an extra claw and serrated hairs to grasp the silk. Orb webs can extend as much as three feet (1 m) or more across and be strong enough to catch small birds.

MAKING A BRIDGE LINE
The spider begins with a line created either by casting a dry silken thread into the air to catch onto something suitable or by traveling with it to a second anchor point.

LAYING DOWN FOUNDATION LINES
Once the spider has made a basic Y-shaped frame, it spins sets of dry thread around the outside and sets of radial threads, also dry, from the center out.

As a spider weaves its web (left), liquid silk extrudes from the tiny spigots that protrude from the spider's spinnerets, tubelike organs linked to the silk glands housed in the abdomen. To draw the silk out of its spinneret (above), a spider may use the modified claws of its hindlegs or it may secure the silk to something and then walk away, pulling the silk from its abdomen.

ing. It may contain sixty-five feet (20 m) of silk and have from one thousand to fifteen hundred connections, yet it is usually spun in less than thirty minutes by its master weaver. Extremely fine and light, the web may support a spider that weighs more than a thousand times as much as the silk used in its fabrication.

Most web weavers begin by securing a thread of dry (not sticky) silk to objects at the endpoints and complete a structure with three main parts: a strong, reinforced frame of support threads; radial threads, like spokes on a wheel, converging at a hub; and a spiral, made of paired silken threads. This silk is covered with a gluey substance to catch prey.

tom of their aptly named traps, rushing out to attack once their prey drops on the platform. Cobweb weavers (family Theridiidae) employ a similar technique, minus the platform, to temporarily confuse and immobilize an intruder. Some cobwebs feature support strands with sticky ends, leaving the luckless bug dangling in midair.

CHARLOTTE'S WEB

The most renowned web in the arsenal, the orb, is a marvel of engineer-

An airborne grasshopper that blunders into the sticky spiral is held by a substance with far greater tensile strength than steel and twice as elastic as nylon. Some threads can stretch to more than four times their original length without snapping. Moreover, when an insect collides with the web, the energy that could otherwise rip and tear the web is

SPINNING DRY SPIRALS
Still working with dry silk, the spider spins a temporary spiral that is tight near the center and open at the rim.

WEAVING THE CATCHING SPIRAL
Working from the outside in, the spider eats the temporary dry-silk spiral and lays down a pair of sticky threads, plucking the thread with its back legs to break up the silk into droplets.

Different Uses of Silk
Spiders use silk for different purposes.

SPERM WEB
When a male spider reaches maturity, he spins a small triangular web and deposits a drop of sperm from his genital opening on its surface. Then the spider dips his palps in the semen until it is all absorbed. With his palps thus charged with sperm, the spider is ready to mate.

EGG SAC
The shape of the silken egg sac woven by the female to enclose her fertilized eggs varies from species to species. Once the spiderlings hatch, they usually spin draglines of silk and swing free of the sac.

TRAP DOOR
Trapdoor spiders line their tubelike burrows with silk, then cut out an opening, leaving one side of the door attached as a hinge. The nocturnal spider holds the silken door ajar with its head and front legs, waiting for an unwary insect to pass by.

BURROW EXTENSIONS
The silken tube of the purse web spider is built into its burrow, leaving a small length protruding—like the finger of a glove. When a passing insect treads on the exposed portion of the tube, the spider spears the target through the wall with its chelicerae, saws a hole in the wall with its teeth, and drags the insect inside to be eaten.

transformed into heat, which serves to strengthen the silk. The trapped insect thus seals its own fate.

Some insects, however, would escape were it not for the vigilance of the web weaver. Alerted by vibrations of the web, the spider rushes to its victim and again uses silk to subdue its prey. Before or just after delivering a paralyzing bite, the spider binds the insect in swathes of silk, a straitjacket from which there is little chance of escape.

Orb webs, quickly covered with dust and pollen, must be renewed regularly. Conservationists by necessity, orb weavers consume their old webs and convert up to 90 percent of the old silk into new silk.

VERSATILE FIBER

Many spiders do not spin webs, but nonetheless live and die by silk. As jumping spiders and wolf spiders prowl for prey, they pay out a silken safety line behind them, gluing it every so often to the surface on which they are moving. Burrowing tarantulas strengthen their tunnels by lining them with silk. Protective egg cases are fashioned from silk. When spiderlings hatch, they may trail out a strand of silk that catches the wind and carries the "ballooning" traveler to new territory. Researchers have collected ballooning spiders

*The silken web of the water spider (*Argyroneta aquatica*) is used to encase its air bubble, permitting it to eat, molt, mate, and raise young underwater. The spider makes its home by spinning a sheet of silk and anchoring it to plants in a quiet stream or pond. Then, the spider swims to the surface and catches a bubble of air on its abdominal hairs. On returning to the silken platform, the spider scrapes off the air bubble and traps it beneath the silk. The spider keeps adding air until the bubble is a comfortable size.*

at elevations as high as 16,500 feet (5,000 m) in the air; one was found on Mount Everest at 22,000 feet (6,700 m), the highest-altitude land animal that has ever been encountered.

In spite of spider silk's tremendous elasticity, strength, and durability, humans have made little use of the material. Historically, spider webbing was used as dressings for wounds; its medical merit was later traced to its antibiotic properties. The holy grail of spider-silk research, however, has been to produce clothing from this remarkable product. However, even the most effective efforts to extract silk from spiders have produced only about half of the silkworm moth's output, and estimates are that it would take five thousand spiders to make a single silk dress. Also, the predatory nature of spiders renders them difficult to raise domestically.

Researchers are hopeful that someday the silk-producing gene will be inserted into bacteria or another organism, which will then churn out the fibroins even faster than spiders do. Potential products, aside from clothing, include antibiotic surgical sutures, helmets, high-strength cables, and aircraft "skin."

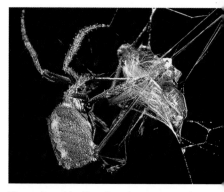

The garden spider, like other orb weavers, usually wraps its prey in silk before giving it a quick venomous bite. Then, the spider cuts the victim from the web, carries it to the hub, secures it with thread, and proceeds to eat.

Spider Courtship

Mating is a risky endeavor for most male spiders. Usually their prospective mates are considerably larger and more powerful than they are, programmed to interpret any nearby movement as a potential meal. Thus male spiders approach copulation in a very careful fashion—their aim being to become an object of romantic, rather than gastronomic, desire.

Mating Positions
Spiders display a variety of positions to mate. To ensure the most efficient transfer of sperm from male palp to female epigynum, the female usually remains in a trancelike state while the male does most of the work. The length of time required to complete the transfer can vary from a few seconds to more than six hours.

FRONTAL APPROACH
The female rises up on her hindlegs and the male advances frontally. Primitive wandering spiders typically adopt this approach.

UPSIDE DOWN
The mating pair hangs upside down from the web. The male inserts first one palp and then the other. Orb weavers typically copulate in this fashion.

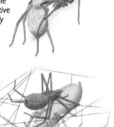

WRAPAROUND
The male climbs on the back of the female and reaches underneath with his palps.

HEAD TO TOE
In what is perhaps the most dangerous position, the male moves under the female.

DIFFERENT STROKES

When he reaches sexual maturity, a male orb-weaver spider goes in search of a mate. Finding a web woven by a female of his own species, he reaches out and touches a silken thread. Detecting the chemical composition of the web's silk from this single touch, he can distinguish both the sex and the sexual maturity of the web weaver. If the female is immature, he may wait patiently by the web until she has completed her last molt. Usually the male attaches a mating thread to her web, plucking it in a special rhythm that carries his message to the female. Gradually, she is enticed to move onto the mating thread, where they touch repeatedly with their forelegs before copulating. Orb weavers typically mate while hanging upside down from the web *(left)*.

With their superior vision, wolf spiders employ a type of flagging code to signal their mating desire. When he encounters a female, a male wolf spider crouches low and begins to wave his palps, raise and lower his front legs, and vibrate his abdomen up and down. Soon, he drums with his palps, making a stridulating sound that is audible to humans. After all of this activity, he pauses for about fifteen seconds, then continues his display. During pauses, the female may respond by waving her forelegs. This encourages the male to repeat and intensify his performance until she eventually

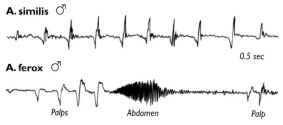

A. similis ♂

0.5 sec

A. ferox ♂

Palps   Abdomen   Palp

Tapping on the Web
Male spiders sometimes lure females by drumming on their webs. For each species, the vibratory signal is different. For example, Amaurobius similis taps with only his palps; Amaurobius ferox vibrates his abdomen and drums with one or two palps.

touches him and signals her readiness for copulation.

Possessing even better vision than that of wolf spiders, jumping spiders use body movements and a zigzag type of dance to approach mates. Without the exact, species-specific dance and movement, a female will withdraw from the male's advances.

Some male crab spiders bind the female while they mate. The silken ties are strictly symbolic, though, since after mating the female has no trouble freeing herself.

Although females rarely eat their mates, cannibalism does occur in some species. For example, when the male Australian red-back spider (*Latrodectus hasselti*) mates, he turns a 180-degree somersault to fall directly in front of his mate's jaws. In most cases she begins to feed on him immediately, while he injects his sperm into her. It is believed that this suicidal maneuver increases the male's chances of paternity by distracting the female and thus extending the time period for sperm

transfer. Also, those females that eat their mates do not tend to mate again.

The male nursery-web spider is known to use bribery to reduce his mate's predatory instincts. He wraps an insect in silk and carries it to the female. If she feeds on it, he begins to copulate; sometimes, though, her meal doesn't end with the insect.

Sexual Dimorphism

In almost every case, male spiders are much smaller than females; some orb-weaver males are so tiny they are considered dwarfs. The female golden-silk spider (*Nephila clavipes*) shown here typically measures about one inch (25 mm), the male, about one-eighth inch (4 mm). Although this would seem to heighten the risks of mating, males gain some advantages from their size: They are more agile and some can even balloon on silken threads just like young spiders.

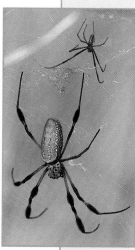

BACKYARD
& BEYOND

BACKYARD BUG PRIMER

*The study of insects and spiders offers an eye-opening
view of the fascinating dynamics of the natural world.*

Night and day, insects and spiders provide a stupendous range of natural drama right in your own backyard. In a single patch of lawn, there can be thousands of them, congregating beneath stones, building underground cities, attacking interlopers, and locked in the elaborate rituals of courtship.

A good place to begin training the eye and developing an understanding of individual species and families is by studying the photographs and reading the accompanying profiles on pages 86 to 173. For more in-depth information, consult a reputable comprehensive field guide. In addition, universities and natural history museums often exhibit wide-ranging collections. To find out what other amateur entomologists and arachnologists are up to, check the various clubs and associations listed on the Internet. A variety of other useful addresses are listed on page 175.

Books, exhibits, and clubs will contribute to your education, but nothing is more rewarding than direct observation. Take the time to watch a spider spin a web, a honeybee perform the waggle dance, or mayflies molt around the water's edge. If you need to capture an insect or spider for further study, it's generally easiest to use a net with a long mesh sack for flying insects, a long-handled dip net for aquatic life, or a sweep net for insects and spiders that are found on vegetation. A kitchen strainer also serves as an effective scoop and is handy for separating insects from mud and algae.

Handy Equipment
Catching nets, aquaria, and wooden cages are available through your local nature supply store, museum shop, or science hobby shop.

> *"So there was more in science than the arranging of pretty beetles in a cork box and giving them names and classifying them; there was something much finer: a close and loving study of insect life..."*
>
> — Jean Henri Fabre

Once you have caught a flying insect in an aerial net, give the handle a quick half twist to bring the netting over the opening and prevent escape. Moving an insect from net to container for better observation can be tricky. Try slipping a plastic jar into the net and trapping the insect between the jar and the net.

For a vivarium, use a quart-sized plastic container, a terrarium, or a shoe box. Make sure that the container is big enough and well ventilated, and that it closes securely. Research the creature's basic needs and re-create its habitat as much as possible in the container.

Plant eaters will prefer particular plants and can derive most of the water they need from the leaves. Many terrestrial insects can make do—for a short time—with a crumpled, damp paper towel, which also offers places to hide. To keep aquatic insects healthy, you should fill an aquarium with the same water in which you found the insect.

Supply spiders with live insects to eat and, of course, a source of water; a moistened piece of cotton wadding works well.

Tick Alert

Before setting off to study bugs in woods or tall grasslands, find out from local public health officials if the area is home to ticks that carry Lyme disease. A tick is a tiny, wingless, eight-legged arachnid. Those tick species of the family Ixodidae known to carry the corkscrew-shaped bacterium *Borrelia burgdorferi*, which causes the severe rashes and nerve damage associated with Lyme disease, include *Ixodes dammini* (in the northeastern United States), *I. pacificus* (in the West), and *I. ricinus* (in Europe). When walking in tick country, wear long sleeves and long pants, socks and shoes, and a hat, and apply bug repellent. Throw your clothes into the laundry on your return and check your body for ticks. To remove a tick, use tweezers and take care not to squeeze the body, thereby releasing the bacteria.

Once the captive has settled into its temporary home, you can study it at your leisure, using a 10x magnifying lens to get a closer view. If you are unfamiliar with the insect, consult the identification flow chart *(page 70)* to help you place it in its proper taxonomic order—the first step toward the often complex business of insect identification. For suggestions of things to observe when studying insects, see pages 72 to 83; for spiders, see page 84.

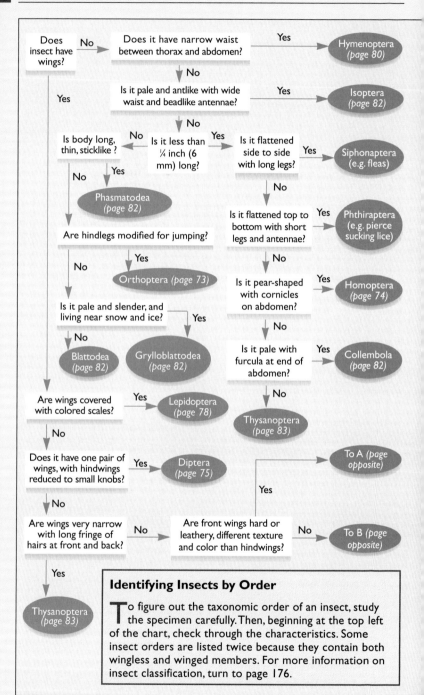

Does insect have wings? — No → **Does it have narrow waist between thorax and abdomen?** — Yes → Hymenoptera *(page 80)*

No ↓

Is it pale and antlike with wide waist and beadlike antennae? — Yes → Isoptera *(page 82)*

No ↓

Is body long, thin, sticklike? ← No — **Is it less than ¼ inch (6 mm) long?** — Yes → **Is it flattened side to side with long legs?** — Yes → Siphonaptera *(e.g. fleas)*

Yes ↓ / No ↓

Phasmatodea *(page 82)*

Are hindlegs modified for jumping?

No ↓ / Yes ↓

Is it flattened top to bottom with short legs and antennae? — Yes → Phthiraptera *(e.g. pierce sucking lice)*

No ↓

Orthoptera *(page 73)*

Is it pear-shaped with cornicles on abdomen? — Yes → Homoptera *(page 74)*

No ↓

Is it pale and slender, and living near snow and ice? — Yes →

No ↓

Blattodea *(page 82)* / Grylloblattodea *(page 82)*

Is it pale with furcula at end of abdomen? — Yes → Collembola *(page 82)*

No ↓

Thysanoptera *(page 83)*

Are wings covered with colored scales? — Yes → Lepidoptera *(page 78)*

No ↓

Does it have one pair of wings, with hindwings reduced to small knobs? — Yes → Diptera *(page 75)*

To A *(page opposite)*

Yes

No ↓

Are wings very narrow with long fringe of hairs at front and back? — No → **Are front wings hard or leathery, different texture and color than hindwings?** — No → To B *(page opposite)*

Yes ↓

Thysanoptera *(page 83)*

Identifying Insects by Order

To figure out the taxonomic order of an insect, study the specimen carefully. Then, beginning at the top left of the chart, check through the characteristics. Some insect orders are listed twice because they contain both wingless and winged members. For more information on insect classification, turn to page 176.

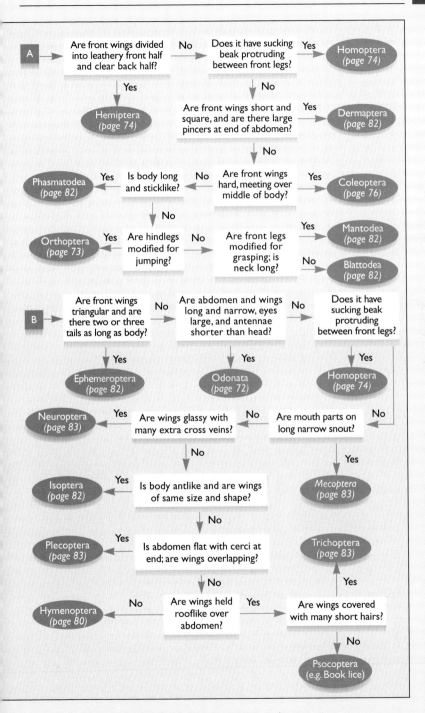

A Are front wings divided into leathery front half and clear back half? — No → Does it have sucking beak protruding between front legs? — Yes → Homoptera (page 74)

↓ Yes
Hemiptera (page 74)

↓ No
Are front wings short and square, and are there large pincers at end of abdomen? — Yes → Dermaptera (page 82)

↓ No
Are front wings hard, meeting over middle of body? — Yes → Coleoptera (page 76)

Is body long and sticklike? — Yes → Phasmatodea (page 82)

↓ No
Are hindlegs modified for jumping? — Yes → Orthoptera (page 73)

↓ No
Are front legs modified for grasping; is neck long? — Yes → Mantodea (page 82) / No → Blattodea (page 82)

B Are front wings triangular and are there two or three tails as long as body? — No → Are abdomen and wings long and narrow, eyes large, and antennae shorter than head? — No → Does it have sucking beak protruding between front legs?

↓ Yes
Ephemeroptera (page 82)

↓ Yes
Odonata (page 72)

↓ Yes
Homoptera (page 74)

Are wings glassy with many extra cross veins? — No → Are mouth parts on long narrow snout? — No →

↓ Yes
Neuroptera (page 83)

↓ No
Is body antlike and are wings of same size and shape? — Yes → Isoptera (page 82)

↓ Yes (snout)
Mecoptera (page 83)

↓ No
Is abdomen flat with cerci at end; are wings overlapping? — Yes → Plecoptera (page 83)

↓ No
Are wings held rooflike over abdomen? — No → Hymenoptera (page 80) / Yes → Are wings covered with many short hairs? — Yes → Trichoptera (page 83) / No → Psocoptera (e.g. Book lice)

7 1

Taking a Closer Look

Begin your insect and spider studies with creatures that live in habitats around your home; bear in mind that knowing a lot about a few is often more rewarding than knowing a little about many. Record what you see in a field notebook. Since these creatures are small, their habitats are small, too—in leaf litter, under a log or a paving stone, by railroad track

DRAGONFLIES & DAMSELFLIES (ODONATA)

Like helicopters on patrol, adult dragonflies and their cousins, damselflies, are often seen hovering over water in the summer. Both have slender bodies three-quarters to five inches (18 to 27 mm) long topped by two pairs of wings that move independently. Neither can fold its wings flat against its body: At rest, the dragonfly's wings remain outstretched; the damselfly holds its wings together over its back. The dragonfly is the stronger flier: It can beat its wings as many as a hundred times per second, propelling itself at speeds of up to sixty miles (100 km) per hour. It also can reverse direction in midair within one body length.

Odonatans have acute vision. The compound eyes of the dragonfly, which almost cover its entire head, are made up of about ten thousand to thirty thousand facets. Those of the smaller damselfly bulge to the side of the head.

Mating often takes place midflight. After depositing his sperm capsule in a cavity in his abdomen, the male grasps the female by the neck while she curls the tip of her abdomen up to retrieve the sperm. Afterward, the female lays her fertilized eggs on or just below the surface of the water. It takes a nymph one to five years to mature, yet the adult lives only a few weeks to a few months.

VIOLET-TAILED DAMSELFLY
(*Argia violacea*)

WHITE-TAILED SKIMMER
(*Plathemis lydia*)

Field Tips

Observe these accomplished aerialists near the water's edge around noon.
• Note how they grab other insects (such as mosquitoes, gnats, and bees) in midflight, caging them in their six legs until their jaws can grasp them.
• Dragonflies usually keep their distance, whereas damselflies often fly right up people.
• To catch one, use an aerial net. Place the net in front of the insect as it rests in the path of its forty-five degree takeoff. Startle it, then move quickly; they are quite adept at evading capture.

sidings. Many are associated with particular plants, either as feeders or indirectly as predators of plant pests, so if you find the plant, you are likely to find what you're looking for. Although the creatures are most active in the warm summer months, they are easier to catch in cool weather when they slow down. For night viewing of insects, use a flashlight covered with red cellophane; red light isn't seen by insects.

GRASSHOPPERS, KATYDIDS, & CRICKETS (ORTHOPTERA)

Famous for the chirping songs produced by the males of the species in late summer and fall, orthopterans are found throughout the world. Many are plant eaters; others live underground, burrowing in soil or ants' nests and feeding on other invertebrates and roots. Champion jumpers, they are all equipped with powerful jumping legs as well as two sets of wings. At rest, the thicker and smaller forward pair folds over to protect the delicate rear wings. Although typically camouflaged in brown or green, some orthopterans, such as Australia's red- and blue-striped mountain grasshopper (*Acripela reticulata*), sport flashy colors. Short-horned grasshoppers (which include grasshoppers and locusts) have antennae that are less than half as long as their bodies, and their tympanic organs (for hearing) are on their abdomen. Long-horned grasshoppers (which include crickets and katydids) have long antennae, sometimes longer than their own bodies and their "ears" are located on the tibia of their front legs.

Each species has a distinct song or stridulation that the male uses to attract females. For example, male crickets create a musical sound (akin to trills or whistles) by rubbing their front wings together. Grasshoppers

Field Tips

In cool weather, catch these insects with a jar. Check under rocks and logs. Or, use a sweep net in tall grass and weeds along paths and trails.
• Use a terrarium as a temporary abode. Stock it with a damp sponge and small leafy branches from the area where the insect was found.

move the bumps on their hindlegs against their front wings like pieces of sandpaper being rubbed together. All twenty thousand species of the order undergo hemimetabolous development *(page 24)*: Eggs hatch into wingless young in the spring and they take forty to sixty days—and up to fifteen molting sessions—to reach adulthood.

RED-LEGGED LOCUST
(*Melanoplus femurrubrum*)

NORTHERN MOLE CRICKET
(*Gryllotalpa hexadactyla*)

73

TRUE BUGS (HEMIPTERA)

A handy catch-all for insects, the term "bug" is used by entomologists to describe the approximately twenty-three thousand species of the order Hemiptera. They can be recognized by the way they fold their wings flat over their bodies, forming an X-shape. Their forewings, called hemelytra, are leathery-thick in front and membranous in back; hence their name Hemiptera, which means "half wing." True bugs have sucking beaks, which they use like straws to slurp up juices; some feed on insects and small invertebrates, but most (from the family Miridae) feed on plants. Look for terrestrial species, such as plant bugs and assassin bugs, under bark or sweep vegetation with a net. Less common, but equally fascinating to watch, are the aquatic species: water boatmen, which spend much of their life clinging to underwater vegetation; backswimmers, which swim on their back on a shimmering film of air; and long-legged water striders.

GREEN STINK BUG
(Acrosternum hilare)

APHIDS, CICADAS, & HOPPERS (HOMOPTERA)

Homopterans, once considered to be a suborder of Hemiptera, are now recognized by some taxonomists as being sufficiently different to form their own order, one which includes some forty-five thousand species of terrestrial insects. They are all juice lovers par excellence, none more so than the tiny aphids. Aphids are small, less than one-eighth inch (3 mm) when fully grown, and usually wingless and green—although some are brown, white, or pink. Living on plant buds where sugary sap is easy to reach, aphids use their tube-shaped mouths to pierce stems and leaves and feed. (If you look closely, you'll see their distinctive pointed snouts.) They then produce a sweet fluid called honeydew, which pours out of specialized organs, or cornicles, at the tip of their bodies, and it is lapped up by waiting ants and bees. In a classic display of natural cooperation and coevolution *(page 33)*, ants often guard aphids, moving them around to ensure a good supply of food.

Cicadas are among the largest species of plant-sucking insects. Some have wingspans of more than 8.5 inches (216 mm). But the cicada's true claim to fame is the raucous buzz produced by the male, which swells and then tapers off. The sound

ROSY APPLE APHIDS
(Dysaphis plantaginea)

FLIES (DIPTERA)

Although they are despised for spreading disease and hounding hikers, flies are second only to wasps and bees as pollinators. They make up the order Diptera, which means "two wings." All other insects have four. Many species have a mesothorax packed with flight muscles, giving them great speed and the ability to perform dazzling aerial acrobatics. For example, a house fly can zip into a room and, just as quickly, alight belly-up on a ceiling. The maneuver involves flying close to the ceiling, reaching back over its head until its feet touch the ceiling, and then somersaulting upside down into position.

Their vestigial hind wings, or halteres, act like gyroscopes, helping them keep balance.

Among the 120,000 known species of Diptera are the primitive and delicately-winged mosquito and the more developed and sturdy bluebottle. Lacking biting jaws, flies suck or sponge up liquid food, such as nectar and blood. Some flies salivate over their meal with enzymes that dissolve solids. Others, such as the three-inch- (8-cm-) long robber fly, are daytime hunters that catch other insects midflight.

PROGRESSIVE BEE FLY
(*Exoprosopa* spp.)

CRANEFLY
(*Tipula* spp.)

is made when the male uses his muscles to rapidly vibrate two drumlike membranes, or timbals, at the base of its abdomen. In North America the Dog-day group of cicadas appears in July and August. They are large and often sport greenish markings. It takes four to seven years for them to develop from egg to adult. Members from another group of cicadas known as the Periodical cicadas (*Magicicada* spp.) can take up to seventeen years to develop.

Like other homopterans, treehoppers carry their uniform wings like a tent over their back. They run sideways when young and only begin hopping in adulthood. Some have developed camouflage; the thorn-mimic treehopper (*Campylenchia latipes*) has a spike sticking up from its back that makes it appear to be a thorn on a branch. Like aphids, treehoppers from the family Membracidae gain the protection of ants because of their production of honeydew.

17 YEARS PERIODICAL CICADA
(*Magicicada septendecim*)

THORN-MIMIC TREEHOPPER
(*Campylenchia latipes*)

BEETLES (COLEOPTERA)

BLACK OAK ACORN WEEVIL
(*Curculio rectus*)

EUROPEAN STAG BEETLE
(*Lucanus cervus*)

There are 360,000 known species in the order Coleoptera, comprising 40 percent of all insect species and one-third of all known animal species. They live in all kinds of habitats, from mud puddles and mountain lakes to deserts and polar regions. They also vary by diet, life cycle, shape, color, and size, ranging from the long and slender firefly that lights up the sky to the dome-shaped tortoise beetle that pulls in its antennae when threatened. Despite their amazing diversity, however, they have a number of features in common. All possess biting mouth parts and antennae used for touch and smell. As with other insects, their mouths are specifically adapted to their diets. For example, carnivorous beetles have sharp, sickle-shaped jaws, while plant feeders have a long "snout" with biting jaws at the tip.

Another feature shared by all beetles is the way their closed wings meet in a straight line down the back. The leathery front pair of

Catching Tiger Beetle Larvae (Family Cicindelidae)

The adult sun-worshipping tiger beetle is too quick to catch easily, so this insect is best observed when it is still in the larval stage. The larvae live in vertical tunnels dug in hard-packed sandy soil, as shown here, along shady paths or by streams. The burrow opening is flat, unlike earthworm burrows, which have castings around them. On spotting the flat top of the larva's sand-colored head, move quickly, shoveling beneath the burrow and lifting it out. Place the larva in a glass jar packed with damp sand at least six inches (15 cm) deep. Use a pencil to poke a hole through the sand to the bottom of the jar and lay the larva, hind-end first, near the hole. It will probably crawl into the hole, but in a day or two you may notice its head peeking out. Keep the sand moist and the jar out of the sun. Feed the larva live insects and watch how it lifts its head to grab them with its jaws. If the prey is too large and begins pulling the larva out of the hole, tiny hooks on the fifth abdominal segment will anchor the larva in the hole.

SIX-SPOTTED TIGER BEETLE
(*Cicindela sexguttata*)

wings, or elytra, cover and protect the fragile membranelike flying wings. Most beetles are able to fly, but generally just short distances.

Coleopterans are both pests and allies. Crops, trees, seed stores, fabric, and dried animal products all fall victim to beetles. Some of the worst transgressors are the boll weevil (*Anthonomus grandis*), the bane of American cotton growers, and the elm bark beetle (*Scolytus* spp.), which carries the fungus that devastated the American and European elm population in the 1970s. Other members of the order, however, serve as scavengers and recyclers while tending to their own food needs. Some are excellent pollinators, while others, such as the ladybird beetles, help control the population of insect pests. Then there is the dung beetle, which makes balls out of dung for its eggs and buries them, thereby clearing the ground surface of animal droppings. Similarly, the carrion beetle buries small dead animals to create a suitable repository for its eggs.

Collecting beetles is very popular among amateur entomologists. In Japan the pastime has become so widespread that food vending machines have been converted to sell live stag beetles—a sleek, black beetle

with antlerlike jaws. Of special interest to some collectors are those beetles that use chemical defenses. Some ground beetles ward off predators by spraying a potent brew of formic acid, acetic acid, benzaldehyde, decane, butyric acid, and phenols. Other beetles use their legs to smear their toxins evenly over the abdomen. And in the arid regions of the southwestern United States, when darkling beetles are disturbed, they stand on their heads and emit a foul-smelling dark liquid from the tip of the abdomen.

Field Tips

Since beetles inhabit practically every habitat, they're easy to observe in the wild.

• Watch the shiny and almond-shaped whirligig beetles in spring and fall as they move over slow-moving waterways. When disturbed, they furiously whirl around in small curves, remaining in a tight group. Somehow they manage to avoid bumping into one another.

• When gardening in the spring, keep an eye out for the white larvae of the common June beetle (*Phyllophaga* spp.) of the scarab family, found all over North America. The grubs are distinguished by a double row of hairs at their rear end. As adults, June beetles are attracted by light and will congregate on porch screens and windows during warm summer months. Like other scarabs, they have well-developed hindwings. When the beetle lands, it can take up to a minute for it to fold these wings under the elytra.

MOTHS & BUTTERFLIES (LEPIDOPTERA)

Among insects, moths and butterflies are unique in that their bodies are covered by minute scales that overlap like shingles on a roof *(page 17)*. (The order name, Lepidoptera, comes from the Greek words "scaled wing.") It is from these scales and from the pigments stored in the wings that butterflies often derive protection; dull wing colors provide camouflage, eyelike markings startle attackers, and brilliant colors may serve as a warning to would-be predators that they taste foul.

Moths are more numerous than butterflies, but because many are night flyers, they often go unnoticed (studies suggest that as many as 25 percent of flowers are pollinated at night by moths). When trying to distinguish between the two, keep in mind that a moth's wings are held flat against the abdomen when at rest, while a butterfly's wings fold together and stand up. Furthermore, unlike butterflies, moths tend to have heavy, furry bodies and feathery antennae. Butterfly antennae are smooth, with knobs at the tip.

It is more difficult to distinguish moth from butterfly caterpillars, which are of various shapes and may or may not have scales or hair. Caterpillars are essentially eating machines. Most feed off a single type of plant and thus can sometimes be identified by what they are eating when found. Others eat a variety of leaves. During this stage, a caterpillar molts two to four times, experiencing three to five growth stages (or instars). After about a month of feeding and skin-shedding, it creates a silky pad from a liquid it deposits on the stem of the food plant or on the ground. Its skin then falls off, revealing the pupa, or chrysalis. Inside the

OLD WORLD SWALLOWTAIL
(*Papilio machaon*)

Watching Metamorphosis

Watching a caterpillar metamorphose *(page 24)* into a butterfly or moth is one of the most exciting shows on Earth. You can purchase caterpillars at a biological supply company or collect your own. You'll need to know the species of caterpillar in order to provide it with the right food and to know how long each stage will last. If you are uncertain, refer to a field guide with photographs or illustrations of the species in both adult (winged) stage and larva (caterpillar) stage. When catching a caterpillar, handle it gently. (Wear gloves to hold a fuzzy caterpillar; it may give you a rash). Place it in a large, dry, well-ventilated container with a lid and add the right plants, potted or freshly cut, keeping their stems moist. For example, add milkweed for the monarch butterfly caterpillar (*Danaus plexippus*), violets for the great spangled fritillary (*Speyeria cybele*), cabbage leaves for the European cabbage white (*Pieris rapae*). Keep the pupal case, during a stage that can last any-where from a few days to more than a year, larval structures break down and new tissues develop: Abdominal legs wither, thoracic legs grow longer, mouth parts change to nectar feeders, and wings grow. When it is ready to emerge, the adult emits a fluid that cracks the case, allowing it to exit head first. It uses its muscles to pump air and blood through the body and wings. When they are rigid—typically after several hours—the insect is ready for flight.

CECROPIA MOTH
(*Hyalophora cecropia*)

Field Tips

A light touch is essential when handling butterflies or moths. To capture one with a net, approach the creature from behind. Never carry one in a jar; that might dam-age its wings. Place the insect care-fully in a glassine envelope (available at biological supply stores) with its wings in the proper resting position. Keep it out of the sun and return it to the wild once your observations are concluded.
• The best place to observe butter-flies is in a meadow of wildflowers on a warm, sunny day. Butter-yellow sulphur butterflies alighting briefly on leaves are likely to be females laying their eggs.
• In winter, examine the seed-heads of swamp-dwelling fluffy cattails for cattail moth larvae wrapped in silk.
• In the morning sun, butterflies and moths vibrate their wings to heat their muscles for flight. In cold regions, butterflies are darker in color to trap the radiant heat they need for flight.

plants fresh; they provide the caterpillar with essential moisture. Clean out the frass (caterpillar droppings) every day. Make sure that there is foliage or a screen near the top of the container to which a butterfly caterpillar can secure itself before its final molt to become a chrysalis. Most moth caterpillars spin a cocoon or form a chrysalis in the soil. Do not disturb the insect once it is in the pupal stage *(right)*. When the adult emerges, release it into its appropriate natural habitat.

ANTS, BEES, & WASPS (HYMENOPTERA)

Order Hymenoptera, which includes ants, bees, wasps, and their kin, is the second-largest order after Coleoptera (beetles). More than 130,000 species have been described. Most of the adults are characterized by their wasp waist, a narrow constriction between the thorax and the abdomen, which allows them to move their back end freely to sting, to lay their eggs just so, and to turn around in a nest or burrow.

Since ants don't fly (except during one stage in their life cycle), they are easier to observe—in the wild or in a homemade farm *(box, below)*—than bees and wasps. They are eusocial insects *(page 42)*, living in highly organized colonies (as do some bees and wasps). After mating, the female progenitor of a colony sheds or bites off her wings as she develops into a queen. With enough sperm to last for years, she spends the rest of her life (up to fifteen years) laying eggs, which become larvae, then pupae, and finally workers. The workers are sterile females that have the job of caring for the young and maintaining and guarding the nest. To observe ants' all-for-one behavior, keep an eye out for masses of them crawling over one another on the sidewalk. This is likely to be a territorial battle over a nest site. The combatants, all sterile females, will battle individually, using their pincers to dismember rivals, or in gangs, as in a tug of war. When the dust clears, the ground may be scattered with ant body parts.

GOLDEN NORTHERN
BUMBLEBEE
(*Bombus fervidus*)

Setting Up an Ant Farm

Instead of buying a commercial ant farm, which is likely to be made up of workers only, set up your own. One way to locate an underground nest is to follow a line of marching ants back to where they came from. Dig out the nest with a shovel and lay it onto newspaper. Note that the queen is usually twice as large as the workers, the eggs are round, and the pupae are oval. You may also notice soldier ants—worker ants with big heads and jaws. To build the farm, place a large sealed can in a slightly larger transparent jar. Fill the space between the can and the jar with sand or soil from the area around the ant nest. Spoon the ants into the jar, taking along at least fifteen workers with the queen. The thinness of the layer of soil next to the glass will allow you to observe the ants building their tunnels. Keep the sand or soil moist, not soggy. Ants will eat almost anything: sugar grains, bread crumbs, freshly killed insects, a tiny piece of vegetable or fruit. Keep the top of the jar sealed with cotton wool or muslin secured with a rubber band. Once you have finished observing the ant colony, return the ants and the soil to where you found them.

RED ANT
(*Formica* spp.)

and plant crops; pollen is caught, transported, and redistributed by the bee's featherlike body hairs. Many ichneumon and vespoid wasps serve as pollinators, too, carrying grains of pollen on their antennae as well as on their smooth, branchless body hairs.

YELLOW JACKET
(*Vespula* spp.)

Observing bees and wasps is best done carefully because their stings can cause an allergic reaction. Watch from a distance and, if necessary, use binoculars. The buzzing sound that warns of their presence is created by wings moving at some two hundred beats a second. Although the best known species of bees and wasps are the black-and-yellow striped varieties, there are species that are black and white, black and red, metallic blue, red, yellow and blue-black. Like all hymenopterans, they undergo total metamorphosis *(page 24)*.

Parasitoid wasps lay their eggs on or in the bodies of other insects or spiders. When the eggs hatch, the larvae feed off the tissue around them until the host dies.

Bees are strict vegetarians, feeding on plant pollen and nectar. In so doing, they are unwitting pollinators of food

Africanized Bees

Popularly known as the killer bee, the African honeybee traces its lineage to bees that were brought from southern Africa to Brazil in the 1950s to improve honey production. In time, some queens escaped and mated with local drones. By the spring of 1999, the Africanized bee had spread north as far as Texas, Arizona, New Mexico, and California and south as far as Argentina. Similar in size and appearance to a European honeybee, the Africanized bee nests in places its European cousins do not, such as small cavities near the ground. Its nickname comes from the vigorous way in which the bees defend their colonies. They are easily disturbed, and many will participate in stinging and continue an attack over a long distance.

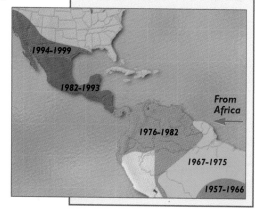

1994-1999

1982-1993

From Africa

1976-1982

1967-1975

1957-1966

MINOR INSECT ORDERS

There are at least twenty-five insect orders, depending on the system used to classify them *(page 176)*. To help identify the order in which an insect belongs, use the flow chart on page 70. The eight major orders *(pages 72 to 81)* embrace seven of every eight known insect species. Prominent members of some of the remaining orders are listed below.

SPRINGTAILS (COLLEMBOLA)

These tiny, wingless plant scavengers are recognized by the forklike jumping organ on the underside of their body, which can propel them four inches (10 cm) into the air. They reach maturity after five molts and continue molting until they die.

MAYFLIES (EPHEMEROPTERA)

The most primitive of all winged species, mayflies usually die within twenty-four hours of becoming adults. They spend their brief time alive mating midair over lakes and streams.

STICK AND LEAF INSECTS (PHASMATODEA)

Superb mimics, these insects resemble sticks, twigs, and leaves. They even have a swaying stride to imitate wind-blown vegetation. They can regenerate lost limbs.

ROCK CRAWLERS (GRYLLOBLATTODEA)

These soft-bodied, wingless, and often eyeless insects live on rocks and ice. The females have a short ovipositor and the nymphs look like small pale adults.

EARWIGS (DERMAPTERA)

Characteristic features are the large pincers at the end of the abdomen. Found in crevices and under stones and logs, they build nests in the ground. Nymphs resemble adults except for their lack of wings.

TERMITES (ISOPTERA)

These insects are characterized by a soft, whitish or tan body and strong biting mouthparts for chewing on wood. The only eusocial insects outside Hymenoptera, they have variable shapes according to caste.

COCKROACHES (BLATTODEA)

Loathed by humans, these nighttime scavengers are very common in rainforests. Their flat body enables them to slip into cracks; though winged, they escape by running.

MANTIDS (MANTODEA)

Praying mantids are recognized by their long, slender bodies and slow movements—except when they hunt. Masters of camouflage, they impale their prey, from bees to butterflies, between clawed front legs.

WEBSPINNERS (EMBIIDINA)

These rare insects live in a community of tunnels dense with silk, usually on tree trunks. Females use their mouths for chewing, the males for grasping females during mating. Their silk glands are found on the front legs.

LACEWINGS & ANTLIONS (NEUROPTERA)

These net-veined beneficial predators usually have transparent wings distinguished by branched veins. They have a weak fluttering flight and are often attracted to lights at night.

CADDISFLIES (TRICHOPTERA)

Resembling moths that have lost their proboscis and scales, caddisflies have fine hairs covering their wings. Eggs are placed on branches overhanging fresh water; larvae drop into the water when they hatch.

STONEFLIES (PLECOPTERA)

Featuring long antennae and equal-sized wings held flat over the abdomen, these insects mature in freshwater streams. Poor fliers, they are generally seen crawling on vegetation and rocks.

THRIPS (THYSANOPTERA)

Thrips generally live on flowers, sucking on plant juice. Most species measure about one eighth inch (3 mm) in length and, when flying, they are obliged to go wherever the wind takes them.

ALDERFLIES (MEGALOPTERA)

Alderflies are known for large, densely veined hindwings that, at rest, sit rooflike over their abdomen. Larvae are accomplished aquatic predators, targeting blackfly larvae.

SCORPIONFLIES (MECOPTERA)

These reddish brown insects resemble large flies. The tip of the abdomen of some males is curved like a scorpion's tail. Some hang by their legs on the underside of leaves. They are sometimes seen flying in fields or open areas of forests on sunny days.

SPIDERS

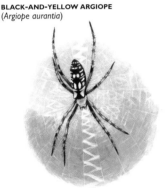

DESERT TARANTULA
(Aphonopelma chalcodes)

BLACK-AND-YELLOW ARGIOPE
(Argiope aurantia)

Spiders are easy to find. Although their numbers are greatest in tropical rainforests, the flowery meadows and woodlands of temperate climates are rich with them as well. Some of the best places to look are buildings, inside and outside. Attics, garages, basements, and even main living areas are home to many species, particularly webspinners. Since spiders don't need to eat often to survive, they can inhabit areas such as caves and cellars where food is relatively scarce. Some have been known to live for a year without food or water.

When observing spiders in their habitat, move carefully; they often have highly acute eyesight and will scamper away if they perceive a threat. If you decide to touch one, keep in mind that they might nip your hand if you handle them roughly. All spiders are venomous, but few are harmful to humans *(box, opposite)*.

WEBSPINNERS

To find webspinners in action, look for cobwebs in seldom-used areas. However, if the webs are coated with dust, they have probably been abandoned. On dewy mornings, check out orb webs strung from eave to siding. Because of the coating of water droplets, you'll be able to see the marvelous detail of their designs. To discover how a web works, try touching its various components; parts of it may be sticky, such as the spiral part on an orb web *(page 60)*. Place a small grasshopper, fly, or other insect on the sticky part of the web and observe what happens.

Other places to look for webspinners include bathtubs and sinks; male webspinners often get trapped inside as they search for mates. Instead of the brushy pad at the tip of the feet that allows some spiders to climb right up the smooth surface of windows and tubs, the feet of webspinners are equipped only with hooks.

NON-WEBSPINNERS

Spiders that do not spin webs are more difficult to find. During the summer months, examine flowers for crab spiders waiting in ambush—they're the ones with the two front pairs of legs that are longer and stronger than the back pairs. An insect lying immobile on a blossom may be captured prey belonging to a spider or an insect predator such as an ambush bug.

Death by Venom

Spiders may bite when threatened but only about twenty to thirty species have venom harmful to humans. A variable mixture that includes amino acids and neurotoxic peptides, spider venom is designed to paralyze—not kill—prey. Widow spiders, of which the North American black widow *Latrodectus mactans* is best known, have dangerous, but rarely fatal bites; their venom attacks the central nervous system, causing fear and panic as well as severe muscular pain, breathing difficulty, and nausea. All recluse spiders (*Loxosceles* spp.) are poisonous, including the brown recluse (*L. reclusa*) common in the midwestern United States. Although the Sydney funnel-web spider (*Atrax robustus*) is extremely poisonous, chances of death are slight if a bite is treated quickly. By contrast, the spider most commonly feared, the hairy mygalopmorph tarantula, is docile and rarely bites.

Some spiders, such as wolf spiders, prefer to hunt at night. To spot one on the prowl, wear a headlamp; you may be able to see the spider's large eyes glowing like amber jewels.

Spiders are around all the time—in temperate climates, they typically take a year to pass through their life cycle. But they're usually more common when their insect prey is flourishing in summer and autumn. To catch spiders outdoors in tall grass and along pathways, use a sweep net *(page 68)*. Indoors, a domestic house spider can sometimes be captured by sliding a piece of paper under it, bending the paper into a U-shape, and tipping the spider into a plastic jar. Jumping spiders, with their huge, catlike eyes, are speedy. One way to catch them is to get hold of the silken safety line they use to move around. Drag your finger on the ground around the spider until you touch the line. Lift it and the spider may clamber up the line to your hand.

Keep captured spiders supplied with moisture in a well-ventilated container *(page 68)* and return them to the wild after observation. Some species, such as the tarantula, should be protected in their proper habitat because they are frequently caught and sold as exotic pets.

Field Tips

If you spot a web, you'll know that a spider is probably nearby.
• An orb-shaped web indicates an orb weaver, possibly a black-and-yellow argiope, a garden spider, or a golden orb weaver.
• Silken platforms with attached hiding tunnels indicate a sheet web weaver, such as a hammock-web spider. The spider may be hanging upside down from the bottom of its web.
• A real tangle of silk is the work of a cobweb weaver, such as the domestic house spider. Watch carefully when the spider approaches its prey and you may notice it suddenly stop and begin rocking from side to side as it repeatedly moves first one rear leg forward, then the other. To spin silk to wrap prey, cobweb spiders pull thread from their spinnerets using tiny combs on the end of their rear legs.

Insects & Spiders: An International Biome Guide

This section contains photographs of more than 160 insects and spiders from around the world. Most of the descriptions are of a particular species. Some, however, are of the genus and a few are of the family or order. Genus and species names are italicized; family and order names are in roman. When referring to all the species of a genus, the genus name is followed by "spp."—as in the case of *Phricta* spp., the rain-forest katydids *(page 90)*. When referring to an insect or spider, where the genus is known, but the species name is not, the genus name is followed by "sp."

The selection is organized according to the biome in which the insects and spiders live, a biome being defined as a major community of plants and animals that share similar environmental conditions. Biogeographers organize the world into as many as ten or more biomes, each based on the prevailing vegetation. However, for the purposes of this guide, the biomes have been grouped into seven types, covering most of the world's dry land: rain forest *(page 88)*, woodlands and forests *(page 108)*, taiga *(page 128)*, grasslands and meadows *(page 140)*, arid lands *(page 149)*, tundra *(page 162)*, and desert *(page 168)*.

The habitats of insects and spiders— those ecological niches where they prefer to live—range from specific homes, such as the bark of a particular tree species or the blossom of one type of flower, to more general areas, such as in rain-forest ponds, leaf litter, and burrows deep in the desert sand. Since every habitat requires certain adaptations, knowing where an insect or spider lives can tell you a lot about its biology, life cycle, and behavior.

Because many habitats occur in a variety of biomes, the insects and spiders one finds in one biome may also be seen in another. For example, black flies (*Simulium decorum*) are abundant in Alaska and the Northwest Territories, but they are also found in other forested areas of North America, wherever there are animals on which to feed and rivers in which to lay their eggs.

MAJOR INSECT ORDERS

 ODONATA

 HOMOPTERA

 HEMIPTERA

 LEPIDOPTERA

 ORTHOPTERA

 COLEOPTERA

 DIPTERA

HYMENOPTERA

SYMBOL FOR ORDER
For the symbols of the eight major insect orders, see opposite; for those of the minor orders, see page 82. For spiders, the symbol represents the order Araneae.

COMMON SPECIES NAME

LATIN SPECIES NAME

ATLAS MOTH / *Attacus atlas*

Moths in the family Saturniidae are occasionally referred to as "the kings of the moths" because of their size and striking appearance. *Attacus atlas* has forewings that are strongly hooked at the front margins; the wings are brightly colored brown, beige, and orange, with some transparent spots in the middle of each wing where the colored scales are absent. Like many other members of the family, *A. atlas* is nocturnal. Although this moth has the greatest wing surface area of any moth in the world, it is not the largest in body size—that record belongs to the giant owlet moth *(below)*.

HABITAT
Rain-forest trees
RANGE
Southeast Asia
SIZE
Wingspan up to 9.5 inches (240mm)
LIFE CYCLE
Holometabolous

KEY FACTS

BRIEF DESCRIPTION

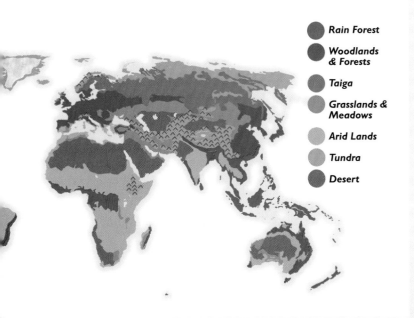

- **Rain Forest**
- **Woodlands & Forests**
- **Taiga**
- **Grasslands & Meadows**
- **Arid Lands**
- **Tundra**
- **Desert**

Rain Forest

Titanus giganteus *(family Cerambycidae), one of the rain forest's nocturnal denizens, measures about seven inches (180 mm) and is considered to be one of the world's largest insects.*

It rains every month of the year in a tropical rain forest, reaching an annual amount of about eighty inches (200 cm). Days and nights are warm, averaging around eighty degrees Fahrenheit (27°C), which, combined with the moist air, produces a dense canopy of tall trees so thick that very little sunlight can penetrate to reach the ground. Because of the shade cast by the trees, relatively few plants grow on the forest floor, although a rich variety thrives in clearings and along the rivers that cut through the forest.

Found near the equator, primarily in parts of South and Central America, central Africa, Southeast Asia, and northern Australia, tropical rain forests once covered more than four billion acres (1.6 billion ha). They have been reduced in this century by almost half. Rain forests also occur in some temperate regions, including the northwest coast of North America.

This life zone contains the greatest number of plant and animal species on Earth, and of these, insects are the most abundant:

Among the millions of insect species yet to be discovered, most will undoubtedly be found in the rain forest. More than three hundred different species of butterflies have already been identified in a single square mile (2.6 sq km) of African rain forest. As a comparison, only 429 species of butterflies occur in all of eastern North America. Some fifty species of ants have been found in a single tree in Peru, and there may be as many as eighteen thousand species of beetles in 2.5 acres (1 ha) of rain forest in Panama.

ZONE OF GIANTS AND BEAUTIES

Many of the largest and most striking insects and spiders live in the rain forests, including brilliant morphos, large birdwings, hairy tarantulas, giant beetles such as the goliath and the hercules, and countless mantises, cleverly hidden by their ability to imitate flowers, leaves, and branches. Most of these forest creatures live in the canopy, where there is more light and they can feed on leaves, fruits, flowers, and other insects. Some, however, scavenge in the understory and on the forest floor, devouring decaying leaves and dead animals.

HELICOPTER DAMSELFLY / *Megaloprepus coerulatus*

The largest and one of the most common species in the family Pseudostigmatidae, the damselfly *Megaloprepus coerulatus* beats its wings more slowly than any other insect. The females lay their eggs in the pools of water that collect in crevices and holes of large rain-forest trees, and so are threatened as rain-forest trees are cut down. Unlike dragonflies, the adults of this species are most commonly found not near water, but in sunlit gaps in the forest, where they hunt insects.

HABITAT
Larvae in tree holes filled with water; adults in openings of rain forest
SIZE
Wingspan 7.5 inches (190 mm)
RANGE
From Guatemala to Amazon basin
LIFE CYCLE
Hemimetabolous

PYRGOMORPH GRASSHOPPER / Pyrgomorphidae

The pyrgomorphs are colorful grasshoppers closely related to the family Acrididae. One difference between the two families is that the pyrgomorphs are often sluggish and slow-moving, and so have other ways than speed to protect themselves. Some species of African pyrgomorphs release an irritating fluid to discourage predators and some are poisonous. Others rely on bright aposematic color patterns as a warning that they taste bad. When disturbed, some species raise the forewings to display brightly colored hindwings. Many species cannot fly and spend most of their time feeding on low-lying vegetation. The pyrgomorphs vary greatly in size, from some of the smallest known grasshoppers to some of the largest.

HABITAT
Rain-forest floor
RANGE
Family Pyrgomorphidae found worldwide; African species shown
SIZE
0.6 to 2.8 inches (15 to 70 mm)
LIFE CYCLE
Hemimetabolous

RAIN-FOREST KATYDID / *Phricta* spp.

The katydids and their relatives in the family Tettigoniidae are diverse and common in the tropics. The genus *Phricta* includes some very large species of katydids that live in the rain forests of Australia. The adults are rarely seen because they spend most of their lives in the canopy feeding on leaves and flowers. During big storms they sometimes move to the lower vegetation to protect themselves from the rain. Other than this, the only way that they can be seen is by climbing up into the canopy or, late in the rainy season, by waiting for the females to come down to the rain-forest floor to lay their eggs. The nymphs hatch and are abundant on the lower vegetation by mid-October. They have disruptive coloration, which helps camouflage them as they feed on vegetation. The adults have long spines on their hindlegs; when they are disturbed, they flick these spiny legs toward the intruder.

HABITAT
Rain-forest canopy
RANGE
Eastern Australia
SIZE
0.75 inch (19 mm)
LIFE CYCLE
Hemimetabolous

TOAD BUG / Gelastocoridae

Most species of toad bugs are associated with muddy or sandy banks of rivers and ponds, where their mottled brown or yellow color mixes almost perfectly with the background. But many species of toad bugs in the family Gelastocoridae also live in wet debris on the rain-forest floor, where they hunt small insects. Their common name comes from the way both nymphs and adults jump on their prey, as well as from their shape, which resembles a tiny toad. They have big, bulging eyes, and their antennae are small and hidden under the eyes. The thorax is large and convex and partly conceals the head and eyes. Their front legs are adapted for grasping prey, while their hindlegs are adapted for jumping. At rest, they are often mistaken for small rocks. Female toad bugs lay eggs in moist mud or sand and under stones. The emerging nymphs look like the adults, but are much smaller.

HABITAT
Damp soil
RANGE
Family Gelastocoridae found worldwide; many species restricted to tropical regions
SIZE
0.3 to 0.4 inch (8 to 10 mm)
LIFE CYCLE
Hemimetabolous

CICADA / *Tacua speciosa*

The family Cicadidae contains the noisiest animals in the rain forest. The loudest insect ever recorded is an African cicada that sings at over 106 decibels—about as loud as a jet plane just after takeoff. Only the male cicada sings, his song playing a role in mating and possibly in defense. Two sound-making organs come into play, one on each side of the abdomen. Small depressions covered with membranes act as drums; when the cicada contracts its muscles, the membranes vibrate. The membranes themselves are covered with semicircular plates, and by raising or lowering the plates, the cicada increases or decreases the sound. Many of the world's largest and most colorful cicadas, such as *Tacua speciosa*, are found in southeast Asian rain forests. Although they can be clearly heard, they are often difficult to see since they inhabit the upper reaches of tall trees.

HABITAT
Tree trunks and branches; nymphs near tree roots
RANGE
Southeast Asia
SIZE
Body 1 to 2 inches (30 to 50 mm); wingspan up to 7.5 inches (190 mm)
LIFE CYCLE
Hemimetabolous

PEANUT-HEADED PLANTHOPPER / *Laternaria phosporea*

The family Fulgoridae includes many species of planthoppers, ranging from smaller species in northern forests and fields to large, spectacular tropical species. This latter group includes the so-called peanut-headed planthopper, a plant-sucking insect with a large, hollow projection at the front of the head that resembles a peanut. The head was once believed to be luminous; hence its second common name, lanternfly. The insect's head also resembles that of a lizard when seen from the side—and this seems to scare off predators. Its dull-colored front wings, conceal large red and black spots on the hindwings. These eyespots, when suddenly revealed, startle would-be attackers.

HABITAT
Rain-forest foliage
RANGE
South America
SIZE
Body 2.8 inches (70 mm); wingspan 6 inches (150 mm)
LIFE CYCLE
Hemimetabolous

TREEHOPPER / *Heteronotus glandiguler*

The family Membracidae includes some of the world's most bizarre-looking insects. Their pronotum (the dorsal plate of the front part of their thorax) extends forward over their head and back over their abdomen like a shell. These extensions may have spines, ridges, horns, or balls, such as *Heteronotus glandiguler,* shown here. Other species,

known as thorn bugs, have pronotums shaped like thorns that help camouflage their presence on thorny branches. Occasionally many of them sit together in groups or rows, rendering their camouflage even more effective. In numerous tropical species, the pronotum has developed to such a degree that the treehopper doesn't look like an insect anymore.

Even when the extension of the pronotum rises two to three times their height, the insects are still remarkable jumpers.

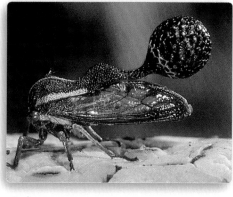

HABITAT
Rain-forest vegetation
RANGE
South America
SIZE
0.2 to 0.3 inch (5 to 8 mm)
LIFE CYCLE
Hemimetabolous

HUMAN BOTFLY / *Dermatobia hominis*

This stout-bodied fly in the family Oestridae has a dull black thorax, a metallic-blue abdomen, and a triangular yellow head. The larvae are parasites of large mammals, including livestock, and humans. When an adult female botfly is ready to lay her eggs, she catches a live mosquito and lays fifteen to thirty eggs on it. When the mosquito later lands on a human or another animal to feed on blood, the botfly eggs hatch and one larva penetrates the skin through the mosquito bite. There it remains, in the skin near the entrance hole, which it needs for breathing, and feeds on its host's body tissues. The feeding irritates the skin and, as the larva grows, a large lump forms. The larva lives in the host's skin for four to fourteen weeks until it is mature. It then crawls out through the breathing hole, falls on the ground, and pupates in the soil.

HABITAT
Adults along or near rain-forest rivers and streams; larvae parasitic
RANGE
Mexico and Central and South America
SIZE
0.5 to 0.7 inch (12 to 18 mm)
LIFE CYCLE
Holometabolous

MALARIA-CARRYING MOSQUITO / *Anopheles freeborni*

Several species of mosquitoes within the family Culicidae in the genus *Anopheles* transmit malaria, mostly in the tropical parts of Africa, South and Southeast Asia, and South America. The larvae develop very quickly in pools of water and take only about three weeks to complete their life cycle. When an adult female bites someone who has malaria, she picks up the disease-causing parasite, *Plasmodium*, and passes it along to the next person she bites. The abundance and ubiquity of these mosquitoes have made them particularly hard to target. As well, they've grown immune to most insecticides and the parasite developed resistance to most anti-malaria drugs. Adults are active at night, a time when it is safer to cover up or, better still, stay inside in areas with a high incidence of malaria.

HABITAT
Adults around rain-forest vegetation; larvae in pools of water
RANGE
Anopheles widespread throughout world; disease-carrying *A. freeborni* most common in tropical regions
SIZE
0.2 inch (4 mm)
LIFE CYCLE
Holometabolous

SOUTH AMERICAN FRUIT FLY / *Anastrepha fraterculus*

The abundant South American fruit fly (family Tephritidae) causes considerable damage, including distinct swellings or galls, when it feeds on citrus trees as well as other fruit trees, nuts, and vegetables. Like other members of *Anastrepha*, *A. fraterculus* is a yellowish brown fly the size of a housefly; its wings are clear, except for a characteristic yellow-brown pattern. The female lays her eggs just under the surface of fruit and the larvae tunnel into the fruit and feed there until ready to pupate. Other family members are yellow, brown, or orange, with complicated patterns on the wings that vary among species. When the flies rest on vegetation, they slowly pump their wings up and down, and thus are often called peacock flies.

HABITAT
On fruits and wherever food plants grow
RANGE
From Mexico south to South America
SIZE
0.5 inch (12 mm)
LIFE CYCLE
Holometabolous

ATLAS MOTH / *Attacus atlas*

Moths in the family Saturniidae are occasionally referred to as "the kings of the moths" because of their size and striking appearance. *Attacus atlas* has forewings that are strongly hooked at the front margins; the wings are brightly colored brown, beige, and orange, with some transparent spots in the middle of each wing where the colored scales are absent.

Like many other members of the family, *A. atlas* is nocturnal. Although this moth has the greatest wing surface area of any moth in the world, it is not the largest in body size—that record belongs to the giant owlet moth *(below)*.

HABITAT
Rain-forest trees
RANGE
Southeast Asia
SIZE
Wingspan up to 9.5 inches (240mm)
LIFE CYCLE
Holometabolous

 GIANT OWLET MOTH / *Thysania agripina*

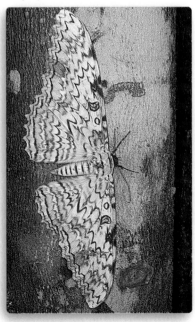

The Noctuidae, sometimes known as the owlet moths, is by far the most numerous family of the order Lepidoptera. The size of these nocturnal moths is extremely variable. At one end of the spectrum, there are species with a wingspan of less than 0.8 inch (20 mm); at the other end, there is *Thysania agripina*, with its wingspan of 11 inches (280 mm), the largest wingspan among the world's known moths and butterflies. The wings of *T. agripina* are patterned with whitish gray and brown stripes and spots on the upper side, offering it excellent camouflage as the moth rests sideways on the bark of a tree.

HABITAT
Rain-forest tree trunks
RANGE
Central and South America
SIZE
Wingspan up to 11 inches (280 mm)
LIFE CYCLE
Holometabolous

MORPHO BUTTERFLY / *Morpho rhetenor*

Belonging to the family Nymphalidae, butterflies of the genus *Morpho* are known for brightly colored wings, displayed primarily by the males, that range from pure white to an intense iridescent blue *(box, page 17)*. The

different species vary greatly in size, with the largest reaching a wingspan of almost 6 inches (150 mm). *M. rhetenor* is a medium-sized species. The adults feed on the juices of rotting fruits as well as nectar and pollen; the larvae feed on the leaves of plants. The upper side of the male's wings are almost entirely deep blue, while the female's wings have white spots with large brown margins. As in other morphos, the undersides of the wings are not nearly as colorful. When feeding, the butterflies hold their wings upright with only the undersides showing, thus making themselves less visible to predators.

HABITAT
Low vegetation and open areas of rain forest
RANGE
Central America and northern South America
SIZE
Females 3.2 to 3.4 inches (81 to 87 mm); males 2.9 to 3.1 inches (73 to 78 mm)
LIFE CYCLE
Holometabolous

PRIAM'S BIRDWING / *Ornithoptera priamus*

The birdwing butterflies (family Papilionidae) include some of the world's largest and most colorful butterflies. Those of the genus *Ornithoptera* show strong dimorphism, the male being much more colorful, the female

being much larger. The world's biggest butterfly is the Queen Alexandra birdwing (*O. alexandrae*), which is restricted to a small area of rain forest on Papua New Guinea; the females have a wingspan of up to 10 inches (260 mm). The Queen Alexandra birdwing has been so popular among collectors that it is endangered and is now protected. Another reason for its rarity is the competition for food with a more common and widespread species, Priam's birdwing.

HABITAT
Larvae on vines in rain-forest canopy; adults in flight in rain-forest openings
RANGE
Papua New Guinea, Solomon Islands, and northern Australia
SIZE
Females 7 to 8 inches (175 to 205 mm); males 5 to 6 inches (125 to 155 mm)
LIFE CYCLE
Holometabolous

ZEBRA BUTTERFLY / *Heliconius charitonius*

Nymphalid butterflies belonging to the genus *Heliconius* spend their entire life of up to nine months—quite long for a butterfly—within a small area. *Heliconius charitonius* has yellow and black wings with a characteristic zebra-striped pattern. The larvae feed on the leaves of passion flowers, including some species that are poisonous to most other insects, even other species of *Heliconius*. Typically, insects mate soon after emerging from the pupae, but the males of this and many other species in the genus will often mate with females at an earlier stage. It is believed that the female releases a sex-attractant pheromone while pupating. When a male finds the pupa, he tears a small hole in the case to reach the female. After mating, the female is ready to lay eggs almost as soon as she emerges.

HABITAT
Open areas of rain forest on or close to passion flowers
RANGE
Southern United States and throughout Central and South America; West Indies
SIZE
3 to 3.3 inches (75 to 85 mm)
LIFE CYCLE
Holometabolous

AFRICAN GOLIATH BEETLE / *Goliathus goliatus*

This beetle of the family Scarabaeidae is one of the heaviest insects in the world. A large male can measure four inches (100 mm) long and weigh a little more than 3.5 ounces (100 g). The elytra are brown and covered with a short velvet coating that rubs off easily. The thorax and head are white with curved black lines. Many other species of goliath beetles are similar in appearance but smaller. Some have short projections on the front of the head. Despite their large size, goliath beetles are strong fliers and good climbers. The adults are plant feeders and drink the juices out of vines that they pierce with their long claws. In Africa these beetles are often used as toys. Children tie the beetles to sticks with string and watch as they fly around the end of the sticks.

HABITAT
Adults on rain-forest vines; larvae in rotten logs
RANGE
Africa
SIZE
Body 2 to 4 inches (55 to 100 mm); wingspan up to 8 inches (200 mm)
LIFE CYCLE
Holometabolous

AUSTRALIAN STAG BEETLE / *Phalacrognathus muelleri*

The stag beetle (family Lucanidae) gets its name from the male's huge mandibles, which are often shaped like deer antlers. These mandibles can vary greatly in size even within the same species. When two males fight, they use their mandibles to grasp each other and try to turn each other over. Most species of stag beetles are tropical, and the larger species can reach a size of up to almost four inches (100 mm). Although they look like voracious predators, these coleopterans feed on leaves, bark, sap, fruit juices, and aphid honeydew *(page 74)*. Most species are dark brown or black, but a few species are more colorful; one, *Phalacrognathus muelleri*, an Australian species that lives in the rain forests of North Queensland, is metallic-green, bronze, blue, red, or violet.

HABITAT
Leaf litter and low vegetation
RANGE
Northeastern Australia
SIZE
2 inches (55 mm), including mandibles
LIFE CYCLE
Holometabolous

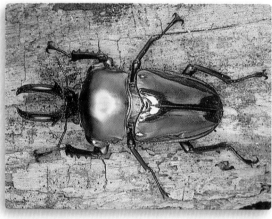

GIANT METALLIC WOOD-BORING BEETLE / *Euchroma gigantea*

The metallic wood-boring beetles of the family Buprestidae have a characteristic stout-bodied oval shape and, as the common name suggests, they are often metallic in appearance. Most species are under an inch (25 mm) long,

but the South American species *Euchroma gigantea* can reach a length of two inches (55 mm). It is the largest buprestid in the world and also one of the largest tropical insects. Because of its size and its iridescent elytra, it is very popular among collectors, some of whom use the elytra to make jewelry and ornaments. However, the adults are fast runners and strong fliers, making them difficult to catch. Like other buprestids, the larvae feed on living and dying trees and freshly cut logs and branches. They bore into the wood to feed in tunnels; they also excavate galleries where they then pupate. When their numbers are high, they can cause damage to trees and shrubs.

HABITAT
Larvae in trees; adults on or near trees
RANGE
Central and South America
SIZE
Up to 2 inches (55 mm)
LIFE CYCLE
Holometabolous

HARLEQUIN BEETLE / *Acrocinus longimanus*

This long-horned beetle of the family Cerambycidae has orange, beige, and black patterns on its body. Like most other cerambycids, it has very long antennae. Its front legs are so long and slender that the muscles are not strong enough to move them. Instead, the beetle pumps body fluids into its legs, extending them like hydraulic pistons. It is believed that these unusual legs might make it easier for the beetles to crawl from branch to branch along the floor and lower vegetation in the rain forest. Like many other cerambycids, the larvae of harlequin beetles bore into the wood of freshly cut logs or dying trees, where they feed and pupate.

HABITAT
Rain-forest floor
RANGE
Central and South America
SIZE
Body 2 inches (55 mm); twice as long when antennae and legs included
LIFE CYCLE
Holometabolous

HERCULES BEETLE / *Dynastes hercules*

The male *Dynastes hercules*, the largest species of scarab beetle (family Scarabaeidae), has large horns that project forward from the head and the thorax. He uses these horns to fight other males for the smaller, hornless females. The larger the horns, the more chance the male has of finding a mate. Adult hercules beetles are attracted to light at night and are very impressive when seen in flight. The larvae feed on roots and decaying plant material in the soil. The adults feed on decaying fruits.

HABITAT
Rain-forest floor
RANGE
Central and South America
SIZE
2 to 6 inches (55 to 150 mm)
LIFE CYCLE
Holometabolous

METALLIC LEAF CHAFER / *Plusiotis chrysargyrea*

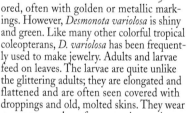

There are many different species of leaf chafers (family Scarabaeidae) worldwide. Adults feed on the leaves and fruits of plants; the larvae feed on plant roots and decaying plant material. Because they attack live plants, some species of leaf chafers are major pests. Adults are often colorful, and some of the best known and most brightly colored ones belong to the genus *Plusiotis*. These species, the jewels of the leaf chafers, have bright metallic colors and are very popular among collectors. The metallic and iridescent colors are produced by the structure of the beetle's exoskeleton, which is composed of very thin layers of chitin that break up or refract the light. *Plusiotis chrysargyrea* is metallic silver or metallic gold; the silvery form is fairly common, but the golden form is very rare.

HABITAT
Rain-forest foliage and fruit
RANGE
Panama and Costa Rica
SIZE
0.8 to 1 inch (20 to 25 mm)
LIFE CYCLE
Holometabolous

TORTOISE BEETLE / *Desmonota variolosa*

Tortoise beetles are among the most unusual and colorful members of the very large family Chrysomelidae, also known as leaf beetles. Their elytra and thorax are expanded out into flat plates that make them look like small turtles. These plates cover their head and legs and are very effective protection against both predators and parasites. Most tortoise beetles are small and brightly colored, often with golden or metallic markings. However, *Desmonota variolosa* is shiny and green. Like many other colorful tropical coleopterans, *D. variolosa* has been frequently used to make jewelry. Adults and larvae feed on leaves. The larvae are quite unlike the glittering adults; they are elongated and flattened and are often seen covered with droppings and old, molted skins. They wear these for protection against predators, as a source of food when supplies are scarce, and as a way to attract mates as soon as they become adults.

HABITAT
Rain-forest foliage
RANGE
South America
SIZE
0.2 to 0.3 inch (6 to 8 mm)
LIFE CYCLE
Holometabolous

ARMY ANT / *Eciton hamatum*

The species *Eciton hamatum* (family Formicidae) earned its common name from the way the ants march in huge swarms, all arranged in columns. Eusocial insects *(page 42)*, they live in colonies that range from 25,000 to one million ants. They are voracious creatures, eating other insects and attacking any small animal in their path. All worker ants are blind. Scouts forage for food by smell, laying down a scent trail to find their way back. Because of the large size of their colonies, they don't make a permanent nest like most other ants, but must continually move around in search food. They bivouac at a different place every night; workers link their bodies together to surround and protect the queen.

HABITAT
Rain-forest floor
RANGE
Central and South America
SIZE
Workers 0.5 to 1 inch (13 mm to 25 mm)
LIFE CYCLE
Holometabolous

FIG WASP / *Agaonidae*

Female fig wasps (family Agaonidae) pollinate tropical rain-forest fig plants, which in turn provide food and shelter for the wasp larvae. Each species of fig plant is pollinated by a different species of Agaonidae. As a female leaves the fig plant after mating, she becomes covered with pollen, which she then transfers to another fig plant when she stops to lay eggs in a growing fig. The larvae develop and feed on parts of the figs. As adults, they mate inside the fruit. The males then eat a hole in the fig so the females can leave to lay more eggs, thus pollinating another fig tree. The males are wingless and blind, living only long enough to mate.

HABITAT
Adults near tropical fig plants; larvae inside figs
RANGE
Tropical regions worldwide
SIZE
0.04 to 0.08 inch (1 to 2 mm)
LIFE CYCLE
Holometabolous

LEAFCUTTER ANT / *Atta cephalotes*

Leafcutter ant workers (family Formicidae) spend most of their life cutting circular pieces of leaves with their sharp mandibles and then carrying the pieces back to the nest. They use the leaves to grow fungi, which they eat. They can travel more than 650 feet (200 m) from the nest to cut the leaves, and each fragment can take two to three minutes to cut. Back in the nest, they prepare the leaves by chewing off any protec-

tive wax covering. Then, they place the fungus on the leaf to grow. Despite the size of their colonies—sometimes as many as ten million workers—these eusocial insects *(page 42)* can live in permanent nests because they grow their own food. When a queen leafcutter ant starts a new colony, she takes some fungus with her to begin a new fungus garden. Leafcutter ants are aggressive and will bite anything that gets in their way.

HABITAT
Rain-forest floor
RANGE
Central and South America
SIZE
0.08 to 0.5 inch (2 to 13 mm) depending on caste
LIFE CYCLE
Holometabolous

ORCHID BEE / *Euglossa* spp.

Orchid bees from the genus *Euglossa* are shiny and brightly colored, often a brilliant blue or green. They have very long tongues, sometimes twice as long as their bodies. Excellent fliers, they live in many areas of the tropics, including rain forests, polli-

nating the flowers of certain species of orchids. Male orchid bees are attracted to the orchid blossoms, where they collect a strong smelling substance that they use to attract females. While the male bee visits the flower, a small package of pollen becomes stuck to his body. When he visits the next flower, the pollen is transferred. Many orchid bees build their own nests, but some parasitize the nests of other *Euglossa* species and lay their eggs there. They are stingless—like their relatives, the stingless bees—but they can bite.

HABITAT
Open areas of rain forest
RANGE
Mexico to Argentina
SIZE
0.3 to 1 inch (8 to 30 mm)
LIFE CYCLE
Holometabolous

STINGLESS BEE / *Trigona nigerrima*

The stingless bees (family Apidae) are a common group of bees in the tropics, including rain forests. As their common name suggests, the various *Trigona* species do not have the pointed sting that most bees use to defend themselves. Instead, they protect their colonies by such methods as swarming into an intruder's eyes, ears, or nose or biting with their mandibles—they have poison glands in their head. Eusocial *(page 42)*, they live in complex colonies of between 80,000 to 180,000 bees. To show colony mates where to find food, they communicate in a variety of ways, including scent trails and a buzzing, zig-zag "dance."

HABITAT
Near flowering plants
RANGE
Genus *Trigona* widespread in tropical regions worldwide
SIZE
0.08 to 0.5 inch (2 to 13 mm)
LIFE CYCLE
Holometabolous

GOLIATH STICK INSECT / *Eurycnema goliath*

Stick insects (family Phasmatidae) belong in the order Phasmatodea. These plant-feeders are mostly nocturnal. All have a sticklike appearance; some have lost their wings, further emphasizing their resemblance to twigs. The insect that holds the world record for length is a Southeast Asian stick insect about 12 inches (300 mm) long. A runner up is Australia's *Eurycnema goliath*, which measures around 8 inches (200 mm). The females are so cumbersome they cannot fly. The males, however, are good fliers. Most stick insects are completely brown or green, but the wings of *E. goliath* are green on the upper side and bright red underneath. When at rest, these insects show only the green portion of their wings, but they raise their wings to show the bright underside when they are disturbed. The flashing color often scares predators away.

HABITAT
Rain-forest tree branches
RANGE
Northern Australia
SIZE
8 inches (200 mm)
LIFE CYCLE
Hemimetabolous

LEAF INSECT / *Phyllium siccifolium*

Leaf insects are the only members of the order Phasmatodea that do not look like sticks. Instead, they are almost perfect mimics of various types of leaves. Species in the genus *Phyllium* (family Phyllidae) are the best leaf imitators of all. Their body is flattened, their wings are leaflike, and their legs have broad leaflike expansions. They even have "veins" on their body that look like the veins on a leaf. Some species are brown and yellowish; they resemble dead leaves. Others are various shades of green and they blend perfectly with live foliage. The females are much larger than the males and lack hindwings so they cannot fly. Herbivorous, they are all very slow-moving, relying on their camouflage for protection from predators and parasites.

HABITAT
Rain-forest foliage
RANGE
Southeast Asia, New Guinea, and Australia
SIZE
Females up to 4 inches (100 mm); males smaller
LIFE CYCLE
Hemimetabolous

RAIN-FOREST EARWIG / Dermaptera

The rumor that earwigs crawl into the ears of careless campers may be untrue, but it has certainly tarnished the reputation of these pincer-tailed insects. Members of this family are slender and elongated; some grow to a length of 2.2 inches (55 mm). Most are

nocturnal. They feed on living and dead plants and small dead animals. The female lays eggs in a burrow that she digs beneath debris on the ground. There she will remain, guarding the eggs, then caring for the young nymphs. The male uses the pincers, or cerci, at the end of his abdomen to hold the female while mating. These pincers are also used in defense, and larger species can give a painful pinch when handled.

HABITAT
Rain-forest floor
RANGE
Widespread worldwide; tropical earwig pictured
SIZE
Up to 2.2 inches (55 mm)
LIFE CYCLE
Hemimetabolous

NASUTE TERMITE / *Nasutitermes corniger*

Termites are eusocial insects *(page 42)* that live in large colonies with different castes playing different roles; sterile and wingless workers find the food and bring it back to the nest; soldiers, also sterile and wingless, defend the colony; and the queen and the king—reproductive individuals—perpetuate the colony. Nasute termites got their common name from the Latin word *nasus*, meaning "nose:" Members of the soldier caste spray

a sticky fluid from their pointed snouts onto intruders. When a queen starts a new colony, her abdomen becomes greatly enlarged and her only function is to lay eggs. In some tropical species ,the queen can grow to 4.3 inches (110 mm) in length, laying some thirty thousand eggs a day. Among the common tropical species *Nasutitermes corniger* (family Termitidae), there are sometimes two or more queens in a colony that grow to 1.2 inches (30 mm). The colony makes its nest in a tree or in the center of a rotting log. The nest is made of a mixture of digested wood, soil, and other materials that are chewed up and cemented together by the workers.

HABITAT
Rain-forest trees
RANGE
Central America and northern South America
SIZE
Queen 1.2 inches (30 mm); king up to 0.4 inch (10 mm)
LIFE CYCLE
Hemimetabolous

MADAGASCAR HISSING COCKROACH / *Gromphadorina portentosa*

This member of the family Nauphoetidae (order Blattodea) is a large, wingless species of cockroach that contributes to the rain-forest ecosystem by consuming the leaf litter and other decaying debris on the forest floor. To communicate, it makes a loud hissing sound by forcing air out through its spiracles. Males, distinguished by two large bumps on the thorax, hiss to attract the larger

females, to express their aggression when they fight over them, and to scare off enemies. Females and nymphs only produce this sound when disturbed. Females don't lay eggs; instead, they are ovoviparous, meaning they give birth to live young hatched from eggs retained within their body. They carry their eggs for about sixty days. When the nymphs are born, they are a smaller version of their parents. It takes seven months for the nymphs to become adults and they can live for two to five years.

HABITAT
Under rotting wood and leaves on forest floor
RANGE
Madagascar
SIZE
Up to 3 inches (75 mm)
LIFE CYCLE
Hemimetabolous

PRAYING MANTIS / *Chaeradodis rhombicollis*

Mantids in the family Mantidae are excellent mimics. Some imitate flowers, others resemble dead leaves, and some change their color to match their background. *Chaeradodis rhombicollis* is distinguished by its greatly enlarged thorax that is flattened into a wide plate. Like other mantids, it is carnivorous, preying primarily on other insects, including ones larger than it—such as big butterflies. The female often consumes the male after they mate.

HABITAT
On low-lying rain-forest vegetation
RANGE
South America
SIZE
3 to 4 inches (80 to 100 mm)
LIFE CYCLE
Hemimetabolous

WEBSPINNER / Oligotomidae

Webspinners of the family Oligotomidae are small, slender insects that are usually pale brown or yellow. The males have a somewhat flattened body, while the females and the young are more cylindrical in shape. In most species, the males have wings; the females are always wingless. Webspinners are not very common and are primarily a tropical group. Although many insects make silk, most have the silk glands near their mouth or in their abdomen. Webspinners, however, have them on their front legs. They use the silk to make nests and tunnels under leaves, in moss, on trunks of trees, or in cavities in the ground, where they live in colonies. The colonies are made up of a female and her young. The female protects the eggs and the nymphs from predators and parasites. Webspinners rarely leave their nest, preferring instead to expand the silk tunnels to find new food sources. They have the unusual ability of being able to run backward very rapidly in their tunnels. Female webspinners feed mostly on dead leaves or other plant materials; males feed on other insects.

HABITAT
Rain-forest vegetation and floor
RANGE
Tropical regions worldwide
SIZE
0.1 to 0.4 inch (3 to 10 mm)
LIFE CYCLE
Hemimetabolous

SPIDERS

OGRE-FACED SPIDER / *Deinopis longipes*

Spiders in the family Deinopidae go by the common names of stick spiders and ogre-faced spiders. The former name refers to their long, thin body and very long legs; the latter comes from the fact that two of their eight eyes are very large and project forward like spotlights. After sunset, the spider builds a rectangular silken web the size of a postage stamp, then hangs upside down less than an inch or so above the ground, its front legs holding the corners of the sticky web. When an insect passes below, the spider throws the web over the prey like a net. Since the web is elastic, it can be stretched to wrap even large moths.

HABITAT
Near forest floor in tropical regions
RANGE
Central and South America, Africa, and Australia
SIZE
Abdomen 0.8 inch (20 mm); leg span 3 inches (80 mm)

GOLIATH BIRD-EATING TARANTULA / *Theraphosa blondi*

Theraphosidae is the family name for tarantulas, the world's largest spiders. Common in tropical or subtropical regions, they possess stout bodies that are covered with short, needlelike hairs. They live in burrows in the ground and do not construct webs. The largest of all of them is *Theraphosa blondi*, a

species that normally feeds on insects, but has been known to eat small birds, mice, frogs, and snakes. When it is disturbed or threatened, *T. blondi* (like other tarantula species), uses its hindlegs to brush off the small body hairs in the direction of the intruder. The hairs are very irritating and can cause an allergic reaction, which may appear as an itchy skin rash, almost like poison ivy. This species will also not hesitate to bite if provoked. Although the bite can be painful, the venom generally will not kill people.

HABITAT
Rain-forest floor
RANGE
Northern South America
SIZE
Leg span 10 inches (250 mm)

SILVER ARGIOPE / *Argiope argentata*

The black and silver striped *Argiope argentata* belongs in the family Araneidae—commonly known as orb weavers—which includes most spiders that construct orb webs *(page 60)*. *A.*

argentata makes a large web with a distinctive thick cross of white silk in the center, where it can sometimes be seen resting. The large cross may help to camouflage the spider, but some researchers have suggested that the large cross makes it easier for birds to see the web and avoid flying into it by mistake. These spiders are not harmful to humans.

HABITAT
Webs in open, sunny places, especially in tall grass or gaps in rain forest
RANGE
Southern United States to American tropics
SIZE
Females 0.8 inch (20 mm), excluding legs; males up to 0.2 inch (5 mm)

SYDNEY FUNNEL-WEB SPIDER / *Atrax robustus*

The Sydney funnel-web spider (family Dipluridae) is the most dangerous spider found in Australia. Large, black, and aggressive, it produces a highly toxic venom that can kill humans. When disturbed, it rears up on its hindlegs, lifts its front legs straight over its head, and exposes its chelicerae, tipped with forbidding fangs. During an attack, it sometimes grips its prey with its hindlegs . Male funnel-web spiders are a little smaller than the females, but their venom is five times more toxic. Unfortunately for humans, the males are often the ones encountered because they leave their burrow during the breeding season in search of a mate. The females are shier, usually staying at the entrance of the burrow awaiting insects and other prey to pass by. The burrow is lined with silk, and the spider spins trip lines that radiate out from the entrance, helping it to detect insects close by.

HABITAT
Rain-forest floor
RANGE
Eastern Australia
SIZE
Leg span 2.4 to 2.8 inches (60 to 70 mm)

Woodlands & Forests

Deciduous trees, such as oak, maple, elm, and birch, and evergreen trees, such as spruce and fir, make up the woodlands and forests of the world's temperate zones. These forests occur between approximately 25° and 50° latitude in both hemispheres, with deciduous trees predominating in the lower latitudes, evergreens in the higher, and mixed forests of both types of trees flourishing in between.

The climate of the temperate forest is generally characterized by relatively warm summers and cold winters, and a high level of rainfall and humidity. Although insect diversity is considered very high here, it is not as high as in the rain forests, due in part to the colder winter temperature, which means that there are fewer species of plants for the insects to feed on, and in part to the inability of some insects to survive the winter in a resting (diapause) stage. Even so, many of the insect groups that are found in tropical rain forests also occur here. Examples of these shared insects include stick insects, mantids, and stag beetles.

A WORLD OF MANY LAYERS

Like the rain forest, temperate forests are divided into many different layers—soil, leaf litter, small plants, shrubs, and the bark, roots, and foliage of various trees—all of which provide different environments where insect species can become specialized and thrive. Many forest insects are scavengers, feeding on the decaying debris on the ground, preyed on by tiger beetles and wolf spiders. Wood borers and fungus eaters attack dying trees and fallen logs. Flies, grasshoppers, and beetles feed on shrubs and smaller plants. Immature dragonflies and mayflies develop in woodland ponds, where aquatic bugs can be found. And a single flowering tree can be home to a highly diverse population, with cicada nymphs sucking sap from the roots, caterpillars eating the leaves, butterflies taking pollen from the flowers, and jumping spiders hunting down insects on the bark.

Scorpionflies (Harpobittacus sp.), inhabitants of temperate forests, engage in nuptial feeding. The female eats an insect brought to her by the male as a distraction to allow him to mate.

GREEN DARNER DRAGONFLY / *Anax junius*

Aeshnidae, the darner family, includes some of the largest and the fastest dragonflies in North America. Among them is *Anax junius*, which has a wingspan of almost 4.5 inches (115 mm) and is distinguished by a greenish thorax and bluish abdomen. It is often seen flying over ponds hunting other insects. The naiads, which can measure up to 2 inches (48 mm), live at the bottom of ponds and streams and are voracious predators, feeding on aquatic insects and animals, such as tadpoles and small fish. They usually

sit and wait for their prey to come close enough to grab in their mouth, but they can also pursue a potential meal by squirting water out of their abdomen. North America has both a migratory population and a resident population. The migratory population arrives from the tropics in the spring to lay eggs in streams and ponds. The naiads grow rapidly in the summer and emerge in the fall to fly back to the tropics and start another generation. The resident green darners have only one generation a year and spend the winter as naiads under the ice. The next

spring or summer, when the naiads are mature, they crawl out of the water and rest until they molt to become adults.

HABITAT
Near ponds and slow-moving streams
RANGE
Canada to Panama
SIZE
Body 2.8 to 3 inches (70 to 80 mm); wingspan 4.5 inches (115 mm)
LIFE CYCLE
Hemimetabolous

WHITE-TAILED SKIMMER / *Plathemis lydia*

Male white-tailed skimmers are distinguished by a large dark band in the middle of each wing. The females have spotted wings and a narrower brown abdomen with a row of yellow spots. One of many species of common

skimmers (family Libellulidae), these dragonflies are abundant throughout the summer, when they are often seen in the throes of mating in the so-called "wheel" position. The females lay eggs by hovering just above the surface of a pond, the tip of their abdomen touching the water to wash off the eggs, which sink to the bottom and hatch in about five days.

HABITAT
Near ponds and slow-moving streams
RANGE
Widespread in United States and in southern Canada
SIZE
Body 1.7 to 1.9 inches (42 to 48 mm); wingspan 2.6 to 3 inches (65 to 75 mm)
LIFE CYCLE
Hemimetabolous

BROAD-WINGED KATYDID / *Microcentrum rhombifolium*

The katydids, known for their singing on warm summer nights, are the most familiar members of the family Tettigoniidae. The male broad-winged katydid makes a song that is also sometimes heard during the day. It consists of two sounds, "lisps" and "ticks." Only the male lisps, and he does so to attract females and advertise his territory. Both males and females make the tick sound. Usually the male begins by ticking, the female responds within a second, and then the male moves closer to the answering female. The female has a short, strong, curved ovipositor that is toothed at the end. She chews on the surface of small twigs to roughen the area and lays her eggs in double rows on each side of the twigs.

HABITAT
In bushes and at top of deciduous trees
RANGE
New York to northern Florida, northwest to Oregon; British Columbia
SIZE
1 to 1.2 inches (25 to 30 mm)
LIFE CYCLE
Hemimetabolous

EUROPEAN MOLE CRICKET / *Gryllotalpa gryllotalpa*

The European mole cricket (family Gryllotalpidae) was introduced to the United States from Holland and Belgium early in the twentieth century. Pale brown insects, they are covered with short hairs and equipped with short antennae and strong front legs adapted for digging. They spend most of their life in burrows consisting of tunnels dug in moist soil to a depth of about eight inches (20 cm). The female lays one hundred to three hundred eggs in a burrow chamber and visits regularly to remove fungus and mold from the eggs with her mouthparts. After hatching, the nymphs stay in this chamber and eat plant roots and soil under their mother's guard. On warm summer nights, males sing a low, grinding song to attract females.

HABITAT
Moist soil
RANGE
Northeastern United States and Europe
SIZE
1.2 to 1.6 inches (30 to 40 mm)
LIFE CYCLE
Hemimetabolous

GIANT WATER BUG / *Lethocerus americanus*

Lethocerus americanus is the largest member of the Belostomatidae family found in North America. Its hindlegs are flattened and fringed with hairs for swimming. The front legs are clawed for grasping prey. These predators feed on other aquatic insects, as well as tadpoles, salamanders, small fish, and snails. Once they've caught their prey, they suck its fluids with their short beak. If han-dled carelessly, they can give a painful bite. Although they spend much of their time among the aquatic vegetation, swimming up to the surface regularly to breathe, these hemipterans often leave the water at night, flying to other ponds to feed or find mates. On these trips, they sometimes veer off course and bang into walls and windows because of their attraction to bright lights—hence their other common name: "electric light bugs." Females lay their eggs on the back of the males, obliging them to look after the eggs until they hatch.

HABITAT
Ponds and lakes
RANGE
Widespread in North America
SIZE
1.8 to 2.4 inches (45 to 60 mm)
LIFE CYCLE
Hemimetabolous

BUFFALO TREEHOPPER / *Stictocephala* spp.

Treehoppers (family Membracidae) have modified pronotum, which covers most of their body like a shell. They also have sucking mouthparts for feeding on the sap of trees and shrubs. Those belonging to the genus *Stictocephala* possess a pronotum shaped like the horns of a buffalo—hence their common name. Although most membracids don't damage vegetation, some *Stictocephala* spp. harm apple trees, in particular, when they make slits in the twigs to lay eggs. The twigs may break and the slits allow viruses and fungi to attack the tree. The eggs overwinter in the slits and hatch in the spring. The nymphs fall to the ground and feed mostly on low plants before moving back into the trees as adults to lay eggs later in the year.

HABITAT
On trees and low vegetation in woodlands, orchards, and meadows
RANGE
Widespread in United States and southern Canada; south and central Europe
SIZE
0.4 inch (9 mm)
LIFE CYCLE
Hemimetabolous

PERIODICAL CICADA / *Magicicada septendecim*

When all the young of a species in a given location become adults in the same year, the species is referred to as "periodical." The nymphs of the periodical cicada become adults after seventeen years living underground, feeding on fluids from tree roots. In late spring of their seventeenth year, when they are ready to molt for the last time, they dig their way to the surface and climb up a tree trunk. The adults live for only about a month, just enough time to mate and lay eggs in twigs. The egg-laying can cause serious damage to young trees. The long life spent underground may be an adaptation that evolved to escape predation. By emerging in huge numbers at the same time, many cicadas will escape being eaten by birds and other predators.

HABITAT
On tree trunks and branches in deciduous and mixed forests
RANGE
Eastern United States
SIZE
1 to 1.2 inches (25 to 30 mm)
LIFE CYCLE
Hemimetabolous

CALLIDUS DEER FLY / *Chrysops callidus*

The deer fly and its cousin, the horse fly, belong to the family Tabanidae. The deer fly is the smaller and often more brightly colored of the two, but both are known for their painful bites. *Chrysops callidus*, a common North American species, is a little larger than a house fly, with a yellow abdomen and dark patterns on the wings. The eyes are green, purple, and yellow, but these colors fade quickly after the fly dies. Adults are abundant in June and July. The females feed on blood, which they obtain for their eggs by cutting open animal skin with sharp mandibles. The males don't bite; instead, they eat pollen and flower nectar. Deer-fly eggs are shiny black and are laid in groups of a hundred or more on vegetation close to or in the water, where the larvae develop after they hatch. The larvae are predators of other aquatic organisms and take about a year to develop before they pupate in the ground. After one or two weeks, the next generation of adults emerges and starts to feed.

HABITAT
Open woodlands close to water
RANGE
British Columbia to Maine, south to Texas and Florida
SIZE
0.4 to 0.6 inch (9 to 14 mm)
LIFE CYCLE
Holometabolous

CECROPIA MOTH / *Hyalophora cecropia*

This well-known member of the Saturniidae family is the largest moth in North America. Only one day after emerging from a pupa, the female begins to emit a sex-attractant pheromone. She has to act quickly because these moths live as adults for only a week or two. The caterpillars are greenish with two rows of large, yellow projections along the back and two pairs of large, red projections on the thorax. They can reach almost six inches (150 mm) in length, feeding voraciously on the leaves of a variety of trees and shrubs, including ash, birch, maple, and wild cherry. They overwinter in a cocoon formed on a twig and the adults emerge in May or June. They have one generation a year.

HABITAT
Open areas around temperate woodlands
RANGE
Widespread in United States and in southern Canada east of Rocky mountains
SIZE
5 to 6 inches (120 to 150 mm)
LIFE CYCLE
Holometabolous

GYPSY MOTH / *Lymantria dispar*

The caterpillars of the gypsy moth (family Lymantriidae) are serious defoliators of deciduous and evergreen trees. Native to Europe, the moths were introduced to North America in the 1860s as part of an effort to produce a hardier strain of silk worms. The plan was unsuccessful and some escaped. The females are large and stout-bodied, with

white wings marked by black patches. They cannot fly and so stay close to where they emerge from their pupae. The brown and gray males are smaller. Good fliers, they spend much of their adult life flying around looking for females. The female lays her eggs on tree trunks, rocks, or other objects—including cars and tents—in masses of about four to five hundred, covering them with hairs rubbed off her body. The eggs overwinter and hatch the following spring. The caterpillars feed at night, attacking a variety of shrubs, deciduous trees, and evergreen trees, although their preference is for oak trees. When abundant, they can strip the leaves from entire trees in a matter of days.

HABITAT
Deciduous and mixed forests: larvae on trees and shrubs; adults on ground or in flight
RANGE
Northeastern United States, southern Canada, and northern Europe
SIZE
Female wingspan 1.6 to 2 inches (40 to 50 mm); male wingspan 0.8 inch (20 mm)
LIFE CYCLE
Holometabolous

GREAT SPANGLED FRITILLARY / *Speyeria cybele*

The fritillaries (family Nymphalidae) are medium-size to large butterflies, usually brownish or orange with black markings on their wings. Most of the larger fritillaries, commonly known as the greater fritillaries, belong to the genus *Speyeria*. The adults are very strong fliers, stopping only for short periods to suck flower nectar. Because of their mobility and their variety, fritillaries can be hard to identify. Adults are most common in July, but can be seen in flight from early June to September. The caterpillars, which feed on violets, are not seen as often as adults because they feed at night and hide during the day. The most common North American species of fritillary is *Speyeria cybele*. The males are bright orange with black veins on the upper surface of the wings; the females are yellow-brown with black markings. They are becoming less abundant, possibly because of the destruction of suitable habitats.

HABITAT
Deciduous forests and moist meadows: larvae on violet flowers; adults on flowers or in flight
RANGE
Most of United States and southern Canada
SIZE
2.6 to 3.5 inches (65 to 90 mm)
LIFE CYCLE
Holometabolous

 LUNA MOTH / *Actias luna*

The luna moth is a very large pale green moth that has two long tails on the hindwings and a transparent eyespot on each wing. The front wings have a dark brown or purple front margin. The larvae—green with a yellow stripe on each side—feed on the leaves of walnut, hickory, birch, and other trees. They

pupate for the winter on the ground in the leaf litter of deciduous forests. In the northern part of its range, the luna moth has one or two generations a year, the adults appearing in May. In the southern part of the range, they have two or three generations a year and the first adults come out around March. Like the other members of the family Saturniidae, adult luna moths do not feed and they live for only a short time, usually no more than a week. Their brief life span and their nocturnal habits explain why they are so rarely seen.

HABITAT
Larvae in trees in deciduous forests
RANGE
Eastern North America
SIZE
Wingspan 3 to 4.5 inches (80 to 115 mm)
LIFE CYCLE
Holometabolous

MOURNING CLOAK / *Nymphalis antiopa*

Although the wing pattern of the mourning cloak (family Nymphalidae) is distinctive when flying, it serves as excellent camouflage when the butterfly sits on tree trunks. The mourning cloak is one of the few butterfly species that overwinters as adults, and so they are the first to be seen in the spring; they even come out on warm days late in the winter. There are two generations per year; early-spring adults mate in June or July and a second generation emerges in August, staying until late October before moving to sheltered areas for the winter. The adults vary in size; larger ones reside in the southern part of their range, smaller ones in the north. The caterpillars feed in large groups on the leaves of willow, elm, and poplar. When their numbers are high, they defoliate entire trees.

HABITAT
Deciduous and mixed forests and meadows: larvae on trees; adults resting on tree trunks or flowers or in flight

RANGE
Europe, Asia, and North America southward into northern Central America

SIZE
1.8 to 3 inches (45 to 80 mm)

LIFE CYCLE
Holometabolous

PAINTED LADY / *Vanessa cardui*

The painted lady (family Nymphalidae) is probably the most widespread of all butterflies. In North America, the adult butterflies overwinter in northern Mexico and the southwestern United States. Around March they start to migrate north to colonize the rest of the continent. Usually by late spring they have moved into Canada. This butterfly goes through population cycles and in some years is exceptionally abundant in the northern part of its range. Eggs are laid on vegetation in the early summer. The caterpillars feed on a variety of plants, although they seem to prefer thistles. They are not usually considered pests, except in California, where they sometimes attack cotton plants.

HABITAT
Most abundant in wooded areas, present in desert and tundra; larvae on vegetation

RANGE
Everywhere except South America, Australia, and Antarctica

SIZE
1.7 to 2.6 inches (42 to 66 mm)

LIFE CYCLE
Holometabolous

BLACK OAK ACORN WEEVIL / *Curculio rectus*

Voracious plant feeders, some weevils (family Curculionidae) are considered serious pests. The acorn weevils in the genus *Curculio* feed inside the acorns or nuts of different species of trees; *C. rectus*, for instance, specializes in the acorns of black oaks, white oaks, and red oaks. This oval-shaped weevil has a long slender snout. A basic brown, it has small brown or yellow spots on its exoskeleton, which is also covered in pale brown scales that look like tiny hairs. The female's snout is longer than the rest of her body; she uses it to chew small holes in the side of acorns, where she lays her eggs—one egg per hole per acorn—sealing them off with small pellets of droppings. When the eggs hatch, the larvae develop by feeding on the nut. They emerge as adults by chewing their way out through the shell.

HABITAT
In acorns and near oak trees in deciduous forests
RANGE
Western coast of United States
SIZE
0.4 inch (9 mm)
LIFE CYCLE
Holometabolous

CONVERGENT LADY BEETLE / *Hippodamia convergens*

Most lady beetles, or ladybird beetles (family Coccinellidae), are useful predators that feed on aphids and other pest insects. *Hippodamia convergens* is a common orange species with six small black dots on each elytron. It is sometimes called a "convergent" lady beetle because of the two white lines that converge on the pronotum just behind the head. Both larvae and adults feed not only on aphids and other insects, but also on insect eggs and larvae. They have a short life cycle and produce many generations per year. Their bright yellow eggs are laid in masses on leaves or twigs and they hatch in three to four days. The black and orange larvae resemble tiny alligators. They feed for about two weeks, then pupate on the leaves of the plants where they have been feeding. The adults emerge in about a week.

HABITAT
On leaves in deciduous forests, meadows, and gardens
RANGE
Widespread in North America and Mexico
SIZE
0.2 to 0.3 inch (6 to 8 mm)
LIFE CYCLE
Holometabolous

ELDER BORER / *Desmocerus palliatus*

Like the other long-horned beetles of the family Cerambycidae, the elder borer is an elongated and cylindrical insect with lengthy antennae; it is distinguished by its metallic blue and yellow-orange elytra. Unlike dull-colored cerambycids, which are active at night, more colorful ones like the elder borer favor the day. Adults feed on the pollen of elderberry flowers, but cause little damage. The larvae, however, are wood borers and they are more destructive. Once hatched from eggs deposited on the lower stems of elderberry bushes, the larvae bore into the stems and tunnel downward toward the roots as they feed. When they reach the soil, they pupate, emerging as adults in June. They live until September.

HABITAT
Adults on flowers; larvae in elderberry bushes
RANGE
Eastern North America west to Kansas; Canada
SIZE
0.7 to 0.9 inch (17 to 24 mm)
LIFE CYCLE
Holometabolous

EUROPEAN CATERPILLAR HUNTER / *Calosoma sycophanta*

This brilliant greenish European beetle (family Carabidae) feeds on caterpillars such as the gypsy moth—which is why it was introduced to America in 1905. The larvae live for about two weeks, during which time each one can eat up to fifty caterpillars. They pupate in the soil, spend the winter there, and emerge early the next spring to mate and lay eggs. The adults live up to four years, overwintering in the soil, and will eat several hundred caterpillars during their life.

HABITAT
On trees in open woods
RANGE
Northern Europe and northeastern United States
SIZE
0.9 to 1.4 inches (24 to 35 mm)
LIFE CYCLE
Holometabolous

EUROPEAN STAG BEETLE / *Lucanus cervus*

Lucanus cervus (family Lucanidae) has a shiny, reddish brown body with black antennae and black legs. Like all other large stag beetles, *L. cervus* males have large branched mandibles that are used for fighting other males. These mandibles cannot inflict a painful bite on humans because they are too large to get a good grip. However, the shorter and unbranched mandibles of the females are more powerful and can give a hard nip. They use them to carve a cavity in decaying wood where they lay their eggs. Larvae feed on the wood and pupate in the soil close by. Adults emerge during the middle of the summer and usually live a year or two, feeding on plant secretions and aphid honeydew *(page 74)*. They are attracted to lights and may fly toward them at night.

HABITAT
On floor and fallen logs in deciduous forests
RANGE
Europe
SIZE
1.8 to 2.4 inches (45 to 60 mm)
LIFE CYCLE
Holometabolous

EYED CLICK BEETLE / *Alaus oculatus*

Click beetles (family Elateridae) acquired their common name from the way they get back on their feet when they are upside down: They bend their body at the junction of the thorax and abdomen and snap themselves straight with a loud clicking sound. This launches them into the air, sometimes up to six inches (150 mm) high. If they land upside down again, they will repeat this clicking until they land right side up. *Alaus*

oculatus is one of the largest click beetles in North America and the easiest to recognize: It is dark gray with small white dots on the elytra and two large black spots on the thorax that look like eyes. The adults are plant feeders and are found on flowers, on leaves, or under the bark of trees. The larvae live in the soil and feed on small soil animals and on the roots of a variety of plants. They can cause serious damage to plants.

HABITAT
Adults on vegetation or under bark of trees in deciduous and mixed forests; larvae in soil
RANGE
Widespread in North America east of Rocky Mountains
SIZE
1 to 1.8 inches (25 to 45 mm)
LIFE CYCLE
Holometabolous

HORNED FUNGUS BEETLE / *Bolitotherus cornutus*

Members of the family Tenebrionidae, commonly known as the darkling beetles, vary in appearance. Most are dark; some are smooth and shiny and resemble ground beetles (family Carabidae), while others are dull and rough-bodied, such as the horned fungus beetle, a black or dark brown beetle covered with small bumps. Male horned fungus beetles have two horns that project forward over the head from the thorax. Adults feed on the bracket fungus that grows on dying or dead tree trunks. The eggs are laid on the fungus and the larvae burrow into the fungus and feed on it. If the fungus is hard and offers good protection, the larvae pupate inside it; if the fungus is too soft, they pupate in the soil. When an adult is disturbed, it becomes immobile and looks like a piece of rotten wood on the ground.

HABITAT
Fungus on tree trunks in forests
RANGE
Eastern United States; Ontario
SIZE
0.3 to 0.5 inch (8 to 12 mm)
LIFE CYCLE
Holometabolous

JUNE BEETLE / *Phyllophaga* spp.

June beetles are scarab beetles (family Scarabaeidae) and most belong to the genus *Phyllophaga*. They are smooth-looking herbivores, reddish brown to black, and possess long spiny legs. The adults are active in late spring and early summer and are often seen in large numbers congregating around lights at night. In June the females lay eggs in the soil and the larvae emerge within two weeks. The larvae, called white grubs, are pale with a light brown head. At rest, they have a C-shaped body and are found close to the surface. They feed on the roots of grass, shrubs, and trees for three summers and overwinter deep in the soil. They pupate in the third summer for a few weeks and the adults overwinter to emerge the next spring. Capable of causing serious damage to plants, they are considered serious pests.

HABITAT
Larvae in soil; adults on vegetation in open areas of deciduous forests
RANGE
Widespread in North America and into Central America; Europe
SIZE
0.7 to 1.4 inches (18 to 35 mm)
LIFE CYCLE
Holometabolous

PYRALIS FIREFLY / *Photinus pyralis*

The pyralis firefly is a dark brown beetle, with some dull yellow on the elytra. The large and flat pronotum that covers its head is pink, with some dull yellow and a black spot in the middle. The beetle belongs to the family Lampyridae and is one of many species that produces flashes of light at night. The male flies about three feet (1 m) off the ground and produces a yellow flash about half a second long every seven seconds. About three seconds after the male flashes, the female, which cannot fly, answers with a half-second flash from the grass. The pair continue flashing back and forth until the male finds the female. The larvae are predators that eat other insect larvae, slugs, and snails. The adults do not eat and have a brief life.

HABITAT
Open meadows in forest clearings and at edges of forests
RANGE
Widespread in North America east of Rocky Mountains
SIZE
0.4 to 0.6 inch (10 to 14 mm)
LIFE CYCLE
Holometabolous

RED MILKWEED BEETLE / *Tetraopes tetraophthalmus*

The red milkweed beetle is one of the most colorful long-horned beetles (family Cerambycidae) in North America. It is mostly red, with some black markings on the elytra and four black spots on the pronotum. Its compound eyes are divided by long antennae, making it appear to have two eyes on each side of its head. As its common name suggests, it feeds on milkweed, a plant poisonous to most animals. The beetles are immune to the milkweed's poison and store it in their body, which gives them protection against birds and other predators. The bright red color is probably a warning to would-be attackers. Adult females lay eggs on milkweed stems close to the ground and the larvae bore into the stem, spending the winter inside the roots. They pupate in the spring and the adults emerge on the milkweed plants at the beginning of the summer. The adults make a squeaking sound when threatened.

HABITAT
On vegetation in open meadows and along roadsides
RANGE
Eastern United States and Canada
SIZE
0.4 to 0.6 inch (9 to 14 mm)
LIFE CYCLE
Holometabolous

SIX-SPOTTED TIGER BEETLE / *Cicindela sexguttata*

running legs make them excellent hunters. They are also agile flyers; if predators get too close, a short, rapid flight keeps them out of reach. The larvae are also predators; they live in vertical burrows in the soil, positioning themselves at the entrance with their jaws wide open, waiting for insects to pass by. In the fall, the larvae pupate in the soil. The adults overwinter there, appearing in the forest early the next spring.

The six-spotted tiger beetle is a bright, shiny blue-green beetle with small white spots on its elytra. Despite its common name, the number of spots ranges from six to ten. Most other species of Cicindelidae are found in dry, open areas, such as beaches, but the six-spotted tiger beetle lives in woodlands, where it feeds on other insects and spiders. The beetles' large eyes, powerful mandibles, and

HABITAT
Woodland paths and open forests
RANGE
Northeastern United States and Canada
SIZE
0.5 to 0.6 inch (12 to 15 mm)
LIFE CYCLE
Holometabolous

AMERICAN PELECINID / *Pelecinus polyturator*

Pelecinus polyturator is the only North American species of pelecinid wasp (family Pelecinidae). The females are large and shiny black, with long legs and a long, slender abdomen. Despite their dangerous look, pelecinid wasps do not sting. They fly slowly and are usually seen close to the ground. The males are smaller than the females, but they are extremely rare and so are almost never seen. Because males are so rare, some entomologists think that the females are parthenogenetic, meaning that the eggs can develop without being fertilized by males. This

species is a parasite of June beetles *(page 119)*. The female wasp uses the tip of her abdomen to locate June beetle larvae in the soil, laying one egg on each beetle larva she finds. As soon as the egg hatches, the wasp larva burrows into the host and grows there, eating the beetle from the inside and killing it in the process. The larva continues to feed inside the dead body, pupating there until emerging as an adult in late summer. Pelecinids go through population cycles and every few years they are more plentiful than usual. Still, spotting a pelecinid wasp is a rare event.

HABITAT
Adults close to ground in moist deciduous forests; larvae in June beetles
RANGE
Southeastern Canada, United States, and south to Argentina
SIZE
Up to 2 inches (50 mm)
LIFE CYCLE
Holometabolous

BLACK CARPENTER ANT / *Campanotus pennsylvanicus*

The black carpenter ants (family Formicidae) are so-named because they dig galleries out of decaying wood for their nests. They always start in decaying wood because it is easier to dig, although later they sometimes spread into healthy wood or into the ground below. Like termites *(page 104)* and other ants, *Companotus pennsylvanicus* is a eusocial species *(page 42)*. From March to July, winged males and females emerge from mature colonies to mate. The males then die and the females leave to start a new colony. When the colony matures, it will contain about three thousand female workers. Mostly active in the evening, the ants feed on aphid honeydew, plant and fruit juice, and insects and other arthropods. They don't sting, but they can bite. If they start nesting in the walls of a house, it is a sign of decaying wood in the structure.

HABITAT
Dead wood of tree trunks, cut logs in deciduous forests, and sometimes in wooden buildings
RANGE
Eastern United States and southeastern Canada
SIZE
Workers 0.1 to 0.5 inch (3 to 13 mm); queens 0.5 to 0.7 inch (13 to 17 mm)
LIFE CYCLE
Holometabolous

FAIRYFLY / *Anaphes flavipes*

Fairyflies (family Mymaridae) are little known because they are among the smallest insects in the world. They are parasites of insect eggs and, as larvae, of the insects themselves. One fairyfly species, *Anaphes flavipes*, a native of Europe, was introduced to the United States in 1966 as a biological control of cereal-leaf beetle pest *Oulema melanopus*. When a female *A. flavipes* finds the eggs of a cereal-leaf beetle, she lays one egg in each host egg. She can lay about twenty eggs in two to three days. After a fairyfly egg hatches, the larva eats its way through the yolk of the host's egg and then pupates inside the shell. The adult chews its way out. Fairyflies have a very short life cycle; in good conditions, development from egg to adult takes about ten to eleven days. Within an hour after emerging from the host's egg, a female fairyfly is already looking for another host egg to attack.

HABITAT
Open fields or on fence rows near forests
RANGE
Northeastern United States, Ontario, and northern Europe
SIZE
0.03 inch (0.75 mm)
LIFE CYCLE
Holometabolous

GIANT MAYFLY / Hexagenia limbata

Hexagenia limbata is a common species of mayfly (family Ephemeridae) that is sometimes found in large numbers near lakes. Huge swarms made up of more than hundred mayflies per square yard (sq m) sometimes emerge in areas around the Great Lakes. The females lay as many as eight thousand eggs on the surface of the water. The eggs sink to the bottom and hatch after a few days or months, depending on the water temperature. The naiads have front legs adapted for digging, and they burrow in the sand or mud at the bottom of lakes or streams, feeding on small particles such as diatoms. They molt twenty to thirty times over a year or two, the frequency also depending on water temperature. Eventually, the naiads molt to winged mayflies called subimagos, which swim up to the surface of the water. There, the subimagos molt again and the adult mayflies emerge. Adult males and females fly to the shore, swarming there and finding mates. Just after mating, the females lay eggs and die. Fishermen use artificial mayflies as bait because mayflies are an important food source for fish.

HABITAT
Near rivers and lakes
RANGE
Widespread in eastern North America
SIZE
0.7 to 1.2 inches (18 to 30 mm), excluding tail filaments
LIFE CYCLE
Hemimetabolous

NORTHERN WALKINGSTICK / Diapheromera femorata

Sometimes called a stickbug, *Diapheromera femorata* (family Heteronemiidae) has a skinny, elongated, wingless, brown body that makes it look exactly like a twig—a camouflage that provides a defense against predators. Adults are found only on certain species of deciduous trees, such as oaks and hazelnut, where they feed on the leaves. Their eggs overwinter on the forest floor. The nymphs emerge in spring and feed on leaves of low-lying vegetation such as roses, blueberries, and strawberries. Later, the larger nymphs move onto the same trees as the adults and continue to feed.

HABITAT
On trees in deciduous forests
RANGE
Eastern United States west to New Mexico; Quebec to Manitoba
SIZE
Females 4 inches (95 mm); males 3 inches (75 mm)
LIFE CYCLE
Hemimetabolous

PRAYING MANTIS / *Mantis religiosa*

Also known as the European mantid, the praying mantis (family Mantidae) was accidentally carried from Europe to New York in 1899 and rapidly spread far afield. Its elongated green or brown body offers excellent camouflage among leaves and twigs. Like other mantids, *Mantis religiosa* has sharp spines on its powerful forelegs for grasping food. It preys on insect pests, including caterpillars, aphids, grasshoppers, and moths, and also on beneficial insects such as bees. As the mantid molts and grows, it sometimes attacks other mantids and other insects that outmatch it in size. The females often eat the males during or after mating; sometimes the male finishes mating even after she has eaten his head. The nymphs, too, are cannibalistic, especially when in crowded conditions. In these situations they may eat each other until there is only one left. Each fall the female lays fifty to two hundred eggs in a foamy mass attached to a branch or grasses. The foam hardens and protects the eggs through the winter. They hatch the following June.

HABITAT
On branches, leaves, and flowers in woodlands and open areas
RANGE
Eastern United States, central Canada, and Europe
SIZE
2 to 2.6 inches (50 to 65 mm)
LIFE CYCLE
Hemimetabolous

FALSE MANTID / *Climaciella brunnea*

The elusive insects known as mantispids or mantidflies (order Neuroptera) are of particular interest because they bear a strong resemblance to the praying mantis (order Mantodea)—even though they belong a to different order. However, real mantids do not have a pupal stage, while mantidflies go through complete metamorphosis, looking very different from the adult in their immature stage. One of the most common North American mantidflies is *Climaciella brunnea*, which, unlike other mantidflies, is active mainly during the day. Its brown and yellow coloration makes it look like a paper wasp, a useful mimicry as defense against predators. The adults prey on other insects from June to late October. The females lay eggs on vegetation; they hatch two to four weeks later. The larvae are also predators, but specialize on spiders and their eggs.

HABITAT
On low vegetation in dry deciduous forests
RANGE
Widespread in North and South America
SIZE
1 inch (25 mm)
LIFE CYCLE
Holometabolous

EASTERN DOBSONFLY / *Corydalus cornutus*

Eastern dobsonflies, along with alderflies, belong to the order Megaloptera. Large brownish green insects with long, translucent gray wings crossed by dark veins, their most impressive characteristic is the males' long mandibles. They use these curved jaws, which can be an inch (25 mm) long, to hold the females during mating. The females have a much shorter mandible, but they can grip tightly. Although the adults don't eat, the aquatic larvae prey on other aquatic insects. These larvae, called hellgrammites, are large and active, with long spiny hairs. They take three years to reach maturity. The larvae are sometimes used by fishermen for bait. When mature, they crawl out of the water to pupate under stones for the winter. In early summer, the adults emerge and stay close to water.

HABITAT
Near rivers, usually on trees
RANGE
Widespread in North America
east of Rocky Mountains
SIZE
Body 2 inches (50 mm);
wingspan 5 inches (125 mm)
LIFE CYCLE
Holometabolous

HANGINGFLY / *Bittacus stigmateus*

The members of the family Bittacidae are commonly known as hangingflies or hanging scorpionflies because they spend most of their time suspended from stems and leaves; their legs are so long and skinny

that the insects cannot stand up well on flat surfaces. Even mating is done while hanging. Often confused with craneflies *(page 130)*, these slender, yellow or light-brown insect predators are the only insects to catch their prey with their hindlegs. A poor aerialist, *Bittacus stigmateus* flies only when disturbed or when prey pulls it from its hanging spot. The female leaves the vegetation to lay eggs on damp ground in the summer. After the eggs hatch the following spring, the larvae scavenge on the forest floor.

HABITAT
On leaves or stems in shady woodlands
RANGE
Eastern United States
SIZE
Body 1 inch (25 mm), wingspan 2 to 2.2 inches
(51 to 57 mm)
LIFE CYCLE
Holometabolous

SPIDERS

ARROW-SHAPED MICRATHENA / *Micrathena sagittata*

Arrow-shaped micra-thenas are small, colorful orb weavers (family Araneidae). Their abdomen is yellow and triangular; on the females' abdomen are two long red spines that stick out in opposite directions from the abdominal tip. Arrow-shaped micra-thenas build vertical orb webs, leaving holes in the middle so they can move easily from one side of the web to the other. They feed on small insects that fall into their silken traps. They are most often seen in the woods in the fall, when the females lay eggs on leaves near the webs. The eggs are covered with silk and left to overwinter. Young spiders—looking similar to adults except for their longer abdomen—emerge in the spring.

HABITAT
Webs among vegetation along woodland edges and in shrubby meadows
RANGE
Eastern United States west to Nebraska
SIZE
Females 0.31 to 0.35 inch (8 to 9 mm); males 0.18 to 0.2 inch (4 to 5 mm)

EUROPEAN GARDEN SPIDER / *Araneus diadematus*

The European garden spider (family Araneidae), which now lives on both sides of the Atlantic, is orange-brown with dark orange legs and a distinct white cross on the abdomen. It has very small eyes and can detect only shadows and patterns of light and dark. Like most orb weavers, the female is much larger than the male. Every night the spider eats its old web to conserve the silk protein and spins a new one. In the fall, the female leaves her web, usually laying her three hundred to eight hundred eggs under peeling bark or other sheltered areas. She covers the eggs in silk and guards them until the first frost, when she dies. The bite of the European garden spider is harmless.

HABITAT
Webs among vegetation and trees
RANGE
West coast of North America; Europe
SIZE
Females 0.5 inch (12 mm), excluding legs; males 0.2 inch (6 mm), excluding legs

FOREST WOLF SPIDER / *Gladicosa gulosa*

The dark-brown forest wolf spiders (family Lycosidae) are distinguished by a yellowish stripe running along the middle of the cephalothorax. Like other wolf spiders, they are good hunters and have excellent vision. They hunt at night and hide during the day in leaf litter. They don't build webs, but instead prowl on the forest floor. To attract females, the males of some wolf-spider species have rough structures on the mouthparts that they can scrape to produce sounds to which only females respond. Male forest wolf spiders produce sound by tapping dry leaves on the ground with their palps and abdomen. The females wrap their eggs in a spherical silk sac that they carry attached to the back of their abdomen until the eggs hatch. The spiderlings will ride for a while on the mother until they are old enough to hunt for themselves.

HABITAT
In woodland leaf litter
RANGE
Eastern United States west to Utah and north to southern Manitoba
SIZE
Females 0.4 to 0.5 inch (10 to 13 mm); males 0.4 inch (10 mm)

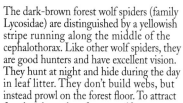

ORCHARD SPIDER / *Leucauge venusta*

Because most spiders in the family Tetragnathidae build orb webs, they are sometimes included in the family Araneidae with the other orb weavers. But to many arachnologists, they look different enough to rate their own family. The most striking characteristic of these long-legged orb weavers is their large chelicerae. The male's chelicerae are bigger than the female's and they interlock them during mating. *Leucauge venusta* constructs its orb web almost horizontally among shrubs or trees. When waiting for an insect to fly into its trap, the spider hangs from the web or nearby it on a stem with one leg in contact with it. This way, the spider can sense the arrival of prey by the vibrations it makes on the thread.

HABITAT
Webs among vegetation at woodland edges and in shrubby meadows
RANGE
Eastern United States west to Nebraska
SIZE
Females 0.2 to 0.3 inch (5 to 7 mm); males 0.2 inch (4 mm)

Taiga

Taiga is the biome made up of the coniferous or boreal forests spread across high-latitude areas of North America, northern Europe, and Asia. The vegetation that grows in this biome's sandy soil is less diverse than in the woodlands and forests farther south; it consists mainly of spruce, fir, pine, and larch, along with some deciduous trees such as birch, willow, and poplar. The taiga's vegetation also includes shrubs, low herbs, lichens, and mosses.

There is not much precipitation in the taiga and most of it occurs during the summer, when rainfall amounts to only about ten to twenty inches (250 to 500 mm). The rain and snow that falls doesn't drain away easily; instead, it collects in ponds and bogs.

The biome's limited plant diversity as well as the long, cold winters that hold sway over the land have discouraged many types of insects and spiders from adapting to this biome.

SHARED SPECIES

Many of the insects and spiders that populate the taiga are also found in woodlands and forests. The most common groups of insects are those in the orders Diptera (often featuring an aquatic larval stage), Lepidoptera, and Coleoptera. Among taiga spiders, there are representatives from a number of families, including Pisauridae (nursery web spiders), Thomisidae (crab spiders), and Salticidae (jumping spiders).

The species of insects and spiders that thrive in these northern conditions have had to make special adaptations to survive. For example, most insect species in the taiga have only one generation per year. They spend the long winter in a resting stage, such as in an egg or as a pupa, and come out in early spring when more food is available. Because the summer is so short, it is a time of extreme activity. And since there are fewer different types of plants for the plant-eating insects to feed on, many of them are not as specialized as their temperate forest counterparts. Instead, they are dietary generalists.

Biting midges, also called punkies or no-see-ums, are the smallest of all the biting flies. Some species suck blood from other insects; others attack humans and large animals. Most of the species that bite people belong to the genus Culicoides (family Ceratopogonidae).

COMMON ALPINE / Erebia epipsodea

Butterflies in the genus *Erebia* (family Nymphalidae) include small and medium-sized species commonly known as alpines. They are dark brown or blackish, often with lighter brown, orange, or reddish wing markings. Their wings are broad and well-developed, but they are weak fliers and spend most of their time close to the ground. The common alpine, *E. epipsodea*, is a strictly North American species. The adults are dark brown with a row of orange-winged black eyespots. The caterpillars are light green with brown and yellow stripes. Like other

species of *Erebia*, the common alpine has only one generation per year. The adults are active from May to October in the southern part of their range, until late August farther north. The females lay eggs on grasses and the caterpillars feed on the grasses, then overwinter. In early spring, the caterpillars feed again for a short period of time, then pupate to emerge in May as adults.

HABITAT
Forest clearings, mountain meadows, and alpine tundra
RANGE
Northwestern United States, western Canada, and eastern Alaska
SIZE
1.3 to 1.8 inches (34 to 45 mm)
LIFE CYCLE
Holometabolous

BLACK FLY / Simulium decorum

The family Simuliidae includes the black flies. Small and dark with short legs and wings, they have a stout humpbacked body. All species of the genus *Simulium* are blood feeders, but as with mosquitoes, only the females bite. The males feed on nectar or pollen of flowers. *Simulium decorum* is widespread in boreal forests. The first adults come out in mid-May, but the females of this generation do not need blood for the development of eggs, so they don't bite. Later generations, however, do need a blood meal for the eggs, and they are the ones that become annoying to humans in the summer. The females lay eggs in flowing water, often around natural dams. The larvae live in fast-flowing water and are equipped with a sucker at the end of the abdomen for attaching themselves to stones and branches. Their mouthparts are modified into wide fans that they use to catch small bits of organic debris in the water.

HABITAT
Near rivers in forests
RANGE
Widespread in North America
SIZE
0.08 to 0.16 inch (2 to 4 mm)
LIFE CYCLE
Holometabolous

CRANEFLY / *Tipula* spp.

Craneflies are large and elongated flies, with long, narrow wings, and very long, skinny legs that can break off easily, which is why they are often seen with only four or five legs. Slow fliers, they look a lot like large mosquitoes, but they don't bite. One species of *Tipula*, the European cranefly (*T. paludosa*), is today found in both Europe and North America. The adults are most active in the evenings or early mornings in late summer. They do not feed and do not live very long. The females lay eggs in moist soil, and the young larvae feed on decayed plant material. As the larvae get bigger, they start to feed on a variety of live plants, sometimes becoming serious threats to lawns and grains. The larvae overwinter in the soil and pupate in late May.

HABITAT
Moist woodlands and fields close to streams or lakes
RANGE
North America and Eurasia
SIZE
0.7 to 1 inch (17 to 25 mm)
LIFE CYCLE
Holometabolous

GREEN MIDGE / Chironomidae

The midges (family Chironomidae) are small and slender flies, with long legs and feathery antennae. They are sometimes mistaken for mosquitoes, but unlike mosquitoes, they don't bite. The larvae of some species are called bloodworms because they have hemoglobin in their blood, which gives them a bright red color. Midge larvae are aquatic and are often the dominant insects found in freshwater habitats, serving as an important food source for other insects, fish, and other aquatic animals. Sometimes the adults emerge simultaneously and form huge mating swarms. *Tanytarsus* species are commonly seen swarming in the evenings, producing a humming sound that can be heard from quite far away. The swarm is made up of males. When a female enters, she is caught by a male and the two fly free to mate below the swarm. The female lays eggs in a pond or marsh and the larvae feed on decomposing organic material at the bottom.

HABITAT
Woods and meadows near wetlands
RANGE
Widespread in North America and Eurasia
SIZE
0.2 to 0.4 inch (5 to 10 mm)
LIFE CYCLE
Holometabolous

HORSE FLY / *Tabanus* spp.

hundred) close to water or wet ground. The larvae live in wet soil and prey on other insects and invertebrates. The genus *Tabanus* contains most species of horse flies. They are stout-bodied flies, usually dark brown, gray, or black in color. The flies possess large eyes; those of the females are sometimes brilliant green. Strong fliers, they are unaffected by light winds, but they don't do much flying on cloudy days.

Female horse flies (family Tabanidae), like mosquitoes, feed on the blood of humans and animals. When they bite, they cut out a piece of skin with their sharp mouthparts and sponge up the blood that flows out—which is why their bite is more painful than that of a mosquito. Four to eight days after she has taken a blood meal, the female lays a large mass of eggs (up to as many as seven

HABITAT
Near ponds, swamps, and marshes
RANGE
Widespread in North America; genus *Tabanus* widespread in Eurasia
SIZE
0.3 to 1.1 inches (8 to 27 mm)
LIFE CYCLE
Holometabolous

NORTHERN CLOUDY-WING SKIPPER / *Thorybes pylades*

The skippers (family Hesperiidae) have a rapid and erratic flight pattern. They are distinguished from other butterflies by the small hook at the tip of the antennae (others have a club, but no hook). *Thorybes pylades* is a medium-sized, dark-brown species. The adults feed on the nectar of various flowers. The larvae feed on a variety of plants in the pea family. The females lay their eggs under leaves of the food plants. Only one egg is laid on each leaf. The caterpillar rolls or folds the leaf and lives inside this shelter for protection. The fully grown caterpillar will also overwinter in this shelter. In the northern part of North America, this species produces one generation a year, and the adults are active from mid-May until July. In the southern part of the range, there are two broods, adult activity extending from March to September.

HABITAT
On low vegetation in open forests
RANGE
Widespread in North America
SIZE
Wingspan 1.1 to 1.5 inches (28 to 38 mm)
LIFE CYCLE
Holometabolous

OLD WORLD SWALLOWTAIL / *Papilio machaon*

The butterfly *Papilio machaon* (family Papilionidae) is basically yellow with blue and brown or black markings. It can usually be recognized by the reddish spot on the upper side of the hindwings. A highly variable species, it is sometimes divided into numerous subspecies. Males are territorial and actively patrol their area, usually hilltops, keeping out other males. Females fly up from nearby valleys to mate.

HABITAT
Hilltops and open areas throughout taiga and temperate regions
RANGE
Widespread in North America and Eurasia
SIZE
Wingspan 2 to 3.7 inches (51 to 95 mm)
LIFE CYCLE
Holometabolous

SPRING AZURE / *Celastrina ladon*

The blues, from the family Lycaenidae, are small, delicate butterflies. As the common name of the group suggests, the upper surface of their wings is blue. Females are usually a darker blue than males. *Celastrina ladon*, one of the more widespread species in this family, is pale blue, and the females have a gray border on the forewings. But this butterfly varies a lot in color and size, depending on the region and the season. For example, it is more purplish blue in western North America and the second brood that appears in the summer is paler than the spring brood. The larvae feed on a variety of flowering trees and bushes such as cherry and blueberry. They eat the flowers and developing fruits, then pupate for the winter. The spring azure is one of the earliest butterflies to come out in the spring. The first adults are active in early April in the southern part of their range, but emerge later in April in northern Canada.

HABITAT
Moist forests and forest openings
RANGE
Widespread in North America
SIZE
Wingspan 0.7 to 1 inch (18 to 26 mm)
LIFE CYCLE
Holometabolous

SPRUCE BUDWORM / *Choristoneura fumiferana*

The spruce budworm moth (family Tortricidae) is probably the most important pest insect of fir and spruce forests. The adult is a small moth with the front wings mottled orange-brown and yellow, usually with a dark spot in the middle; the hindwings are gray. The larvae are pale to dark brown and about an inch (25 mm) long. It is the larvae that cause the damage, feeding on the buds and the needles of the tree. They attack mostly firs and spruces, but also larches, hemlocks, and pines. The female moth lays about 150 eggs on the underside of the needles late in the summer and the eggs hatch in about twelve days. Each caterpillar makes a silky case that protects it during the winter. The caterpillars emerge from their cases in the spring and feed until late June. They then pupate until the middle of July, when the adult moths emerge. The adults live for only two weeks. The spruce budworm has one generation a year.

HABITAT
Coniferous trees
RANGE
Widespread in North America
SIZE
Wingspan 0.8 to 1.2 inches (20 to 30 mm)
LIFE CYCLE
Holometabolous

BURYING BEETLE / *Nicrophorus defodiens*

Most burying beetles (family Silphidae) are large, red and black beetles with short elytra that feed on dead animals. The male and female *Nicrophorus defodiens* search at night for a small dead animal, such as a mouse or a bird, which they bury by digging a hole under the body. If the ground is too hard where the animal is found, the beetles will drag the body to a better place for burial. Interring the animal keeps it away from other scavengers. During the process of burial, the adult beetles chew off the fur or feathers and lay eggs on the body. When the eggs hatch, the parents stay with the larvae and feed them regurgitated food. The parents will remain with the nest until the larvae pupate.

HABITAT
Mixed forests
RANGE
Widespread in northern United States and Canada
SIZE
0.6 to 1.1 inches (14 to 28 mm)
LIFE CYCLE
Holometabolous

FLAT-HEADED TREE BORER / *Chrysobothris* spp.

The flat-headed tree borers (family Buprestidae) are usually metallic-looking, dark bronze, green, and purplish. The females lay eggs in cracks or openings in the bark of trees that are usually already weakened. When the eggs hatch, the larvae quickly bore through the bark and into the trees, making tunnels and feeding on the sapwood—also the bark if the tree is old. The head of the larvae is pulled back into the thorax—hence their common name. When fully grown, the larvae make a small chamber in which to pass the winter. They pupate the following spring, then the adults chew through the bark to emerge from the tree. The flat-headed tree borer is a pest of many species of trees and shrubs.

HABITAT
Deciduous and coniferous trees
RANGE
Widespread in North America
SIZE
0.2 to 0.6 inch (5 to 16 mm)
LIFE CYCLE
Holometabolous

GOLDEN BUPRESTID / *Cypriacis aurulenta*

The golden buprestid is a metallic green or blue beetle with some copper along the margins of the elytra. The larvae of this species are wood borers of conifer trees and can be very destructive. The adults feed on the foliage of Douglas fir, but also on the pollen and nectar of other plants. In late spring or early summer, females lay eggs on the bark of trees, preferably Douglas fir, but also pine, spruce, and some other conifers. The trees that are chosen for egg-laying are already injured and the eggs are laid in crevices or scars in the bark. When the eggs hatch, the larvae tunnel through the wood, enlarging the tunnels as they grow. In late summer, the larvae pupate inside a tunnel, becoming adults in the fall. The adults overwinter inside the tunnel and the following spring they chew their way out, leaving a permanent hole into the wood.

HABITAT
Adults on foliage of coniferous trees; larvae under bark
RANGE
Western North America
SIZE
0.5 to 0.8 inch (12 to 20 mm)
LIFE CYCLE
Holometabolous

NORTHEASTERN SAWYER BEETLE / *Monochamus notatus*

The sawyer beetles in the genus *Monochamus* (family Cerambycidae) are usually large, dark beetles with elongated bodies and very long antennae. Many of them are pests of forest trees. The name sawyer comes from the sawing sound that the larvae make as they chew their way through the wood of newly cut logs and sometimes living trees. *M. notatus* is a large brown species with black, gray, and white spots on its elytra. The male's antennae are twice as long as its body, while the female's antennae are half that size. After mating, the females chew small holes in the bark of pine, spruce, or fir trees, where they lay their eggs. The larvae pupate inside the wood. When the adults emerge from the pupae, they chew their way out, leaving behind a large hole.

HABITAT
On living trees or fallen logs in coniferous forests
RANGE
Widespread in North America
SIZE
0.6 to 1.4 inches (16 to 35 mm)
LIFE CYCLE
Holometabolous

RED TURPENTINE BEETLE / *Dendroctonus valens*

The Scolytidae are small cylindrical beetles, usually dark brown or black. They include the bark beetles and the ambrosia beetles. The bark beetles attack living trees, especially conifers, and feed on the inside surface of the bark. The adults make branching tunnels, called galleries, between the bark and the wood, where the eggs are laid. The larvae hatch and tunnel in the wood. This makes a distinct pattern in the wood that is different for each species of bark beetle. Some of the most important species belong to the genus *Dendroctonus*. The largest species in this group is the hairy red turpentine beetle. It feeds mainly under the bark of pine trees. The adults tunnel into the bark and lay eggs within twenty feet (6.1 m) of the ground. This often causes serious damage to the tree.

The ambrosia beetles bore into the wood of a dead or dying tree that has already been attacked by bark beetles and they feed on a fungus in the wood.

HABITAT
Larvae in bark of coniferous trees
RANGE
Widespread in North America
SIZE
0.2 to 0.4 inch (6 to 9 mm)
LIFE CYCLE
Holometabolous

BLUE HORNTAIL / *Sirex cyanus*

The horntails (family Siricidae) do not sting people. Unlike the related wasps, bees, and ants, horntails don't have a narrow wasp waist between the thorax and the abdomen. They get their common name from a hard spearlike projection at the end of the abdomen of both sexes. The larvae are wood borers. *Sirex cyanus* (also known as wood wasps) prefer to feed on already injured conifer trees. The female uses an ovipositor to drill holes about a half inch (1.5 cm) deep into the wood and lays a single egg in each hole. She then deposits spores of a special fungus into the hole. Scientists have not yet determined whether the larvae eat the fungus or just feed on the wood that is broken down as the fungus grows. The larvae tunnel inside the wood for one or two years, then pupate inside the tree. The adults emerge by chewing their way through the wood.

HABITAT
On hardwood and coniferous trees in mixed forests

RANGE
Widespread in North America

SIZE
0.8 inch (20 mm)

LIFE CYCLE
Holometabolous

GIANT ICHNEUMON / *Megarhyssa nortoni*

Members of the family Ichneumonidae are almost all parasitic wasps and many are beneficial in controlling insect pests. Those in the genus *Megarhyssa* are large, but what makes them so impressive is the female's extremely long ovipositor, which can measure up to about four inches (110 mm). The larvae parasitize the larvae of the wood-boring horntail (Hymenoptera: Siricidae). The widespread species *M. nortoni* lives in coniferous forests. The female lands on a tree and uses her antennae to detect vibrations made by the horntail larvae in the wood. She inserts her long ovipositor into the wood until she reaches the horntail's tunnel and then lays one egg per tunnel. The wasp larva gets inside the horntail larva through the mouth or the spiracle openings on the abdomen and starts eating the horntail from the inside. The horntail larva stays alive until the ichneumon larva is fully grown.

HABITAT
Adults on trees in coniferous forests; larvae parasitic

RANGE
Widespread in North America, New Zealand, and Australia

SIZE
Females 1.4 to 3 inches (35 to 75 mm), excluding ovipositor; males 1 to 1.5 inches (25 to 38 mm)

LIFE CYCLE
Holometabolous

RED-HEADED PINE SAWFLY / *Neodiprion lecontei*

Members of the family Diprionidae are commonly known as the conifer sawflies. The male is completely black, but the head and the first thoracic segment of the female are brownish red. The name "sawfly" comes from the shape of their ovipositor, which is stiff and covered with rows of sharp teeth. The female uses it to cut slits into the needles of pine trees, usually young trees that are less than ten feet (3 m) high. Then, she inserts up to thirty-five eggs per needle, ultimately laying from 100 to 140 eggs. After the eggs hatch, the larvae stay together in colonies and feed mostly on the old needles. When the old needles are consumed, they switch to new ones and will even feed on the bark of young twigs. A colony of red-headed pine sawfly larvae can strip an entire twig of its needles very rapidly. In eastern Canada and the United States, this species is considered one of the most serious pests of young pines.

HABITAT
Larvae live on pine trees; adults usually found nearby
RANGE
Eastern North America
SIZE
Females 0.2 to 0.4 inch (6 to 9 mm); males 0.2 to 0.24 inch (5 to 6 mm)
LIFE CYCLE
Holometabolous

SNOW FLEA / *Hypogastrura nivicola*

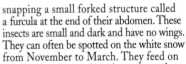

Snow fleas (family Hypogastruridae), unlike fleas that belong to the order Siphonaptera, are springtails from the order Collembola. The name "springtail" comes from their ability to launch themselves into the air by snapping a small forked structure called a furcula at the end of their abdomen. These insects are small and dark and have no wings. They can often be spotted on the white snow from November to March. They feed on algae, bacteria, and fungal spores. The eggs, which are laid in leaf litter, hatch later in the spring. The young develop throughout the summer to become adults in the fall.

HABITAT
Leaf litter on forest floor
RANGE
Northeastern United States, Ontario, and Europe
SIZE
0.08 inch (2 mm)
LIFE CYCLE
Ametabolous

SMALL WINTER STONEFLY / *Allocapnia pygmea*

Many species of *Allocapnia* (family Capniidae), especially the males, are wingless. Those belonging to *A. pygmea* are one of the most abundant groups of insects that are active during the winter. The adults emerge from streams and rivers in February and live for only a few days to a few weeks. During their short life, they disperse and feed on algae growing on tree bark. The

females need the algae for the development of their eggs. Once the eggs are developed, the females fly along the surface of small streams and dip their abdomen into the water to wash the eggs away. The eggs hatch about three weeks later and the larvae feed on algae and fungi in the water for a few weeks, then dig themselves into the bottom for a diapause that lasts for the summer. In the fall, the larvae start feeding again. The adults emerge in February.

HABITAT
Near streams
RANGE
Eastern North America
SIZE
0.3 to 0.4 inch (8 to 10 mm)
LIFE CYCLE
Hemimetabolous

ASH-WINGED LARGE CADDISFLY / *Phryganea cinerea*

The caddisflies of the family Phryganeidae can be recognized by their large size and mottled gray and brown wings. They live close to lakes, ponds, marshes, and slow-moving parts of rivers and streams, where the larvae have developed. *Phryganea cinerea* is brown with gray and brown patches on the forewings that form triangular markings when the wings are folded. The adults rest on trees during the day, where they are very hard to see, and are active just before and after

dark. They do not feed and do not live for long. The females lay their eggs on aquatic plants just below the surface of the water. When the larvae hatch, they build a portable case from bits of leaves to protect themselves. They feed on algae until they reach maturity, then close their case and pupate inside for two to three weeks. The adults chew their way out of the pupal case and come to the surface of the water before taking flight.

HABITAT
Adults found on trees or bushes near water, larvae are aquatic.
RANGE
Northern United States, Canada
SIZE
0.7 to 0.8 inch (18 to 20 mm)
LIFE CYCLE
Holometabolous

SPIDERS

BROWNISH-GRAY FISHING SPIDER / *Dolomedes tenebrosus*

Brownish-gray fishing spiders (family Pisauridae) are large with black markings all over the body. They live close to streams or ponds, where they feed on aquatic insects and sometimes small fish or tadpoles. They can walk easily on the surface of the water and can stay underwater for thirty minutes or more. Like other pisaurids, they look like wolf spiders (family Lycosidae), but they have a different eye pattern. They don't spin webs to catch insects; instead, they chase their prey. Those that hunt in the water are called fishing spiders.

HABITAT
Close to streams or ponds in forests
RANGE
Northeastern North America
SIZE
Females 0.6 to 1 inch (15 to 26 mm), with leg span of 3 inches (75 mm); males 0.3 to 0.5 inch (7 to12 mm)

THRICE-BANDED CRAB SPIDER / *Xysticus triguttatus*

Members of the family Thomisidae are known as crab spiders because of their similar shape, the way they hold their legs outstretched, and their ability to walk sideways or backward. They are small and usually dark colored, and their body is stout and flattened. The male *Xysticus triguttatus* is dark brown with yellow crossbands on the abdomen. The female is whitish with black crossbands. For defense, they rely on camouflage and their flat body allows them to hide in narrow crevices and under bark. They do not build webs to catch their prey, but instead sit and wait for a small insect to pass, grabbing it with their outstretched front legs, then holding it and sucking out its fluids. The female crab spider lays eggs in a silk sac attached to a plant and guards them until they hatch.

HABITAT
On forest floor, under rocks, or on bark
RANGE
Newfoundland to Alberta
SIZE
Females 0.2 to 0.24 inch (4 to 6 mm), excluding legs; males 0.11 to 0.2 inch (3 to 5 mm)

Grasslands & Meadows

Almost every continent has its native grasslands, large regions dominated by a nearly continuous cover of grasses. Hot, at least in summer, and drier than forest biomes—though not as dry as the desert—the natural grasslands include the Great Plains of North America, the steppes of Asia, the veldt in South Africa, the pampas in Argentina, and the Sahel, the vast tropical grassland that stretches across western and north-central Africa, south of the Sahara.

The most common insects in these regions are the jumpers: grasshoppers of various kinds and leafhoppers. But they have much company—flies gliding above the grass; butterflies hovering over the flowers; predatory wasps; and spiders searching for prey. A closer look will reveal colonies of aphids sucking on plant juice, bubbles on grass stems left by spittlebugs, and millions of ants marching to and fro.

A number of insects that live in these regions could not survive anywhere else, often because they are associated with one type of native prairie grass. Thus, as portions of the native grasslands disappear with the introduction of cereal crops or from burning and heavy grazing, some of the specialized insects, including the Dakota skipper (*Hesperia dacotae*) and the prairie mole cricket (*Neocurtilla major*) are threatened.

As the vegetation is changed, new species of insects and spiders that are not as specialized have entered the altered ecosystem. Meadows, parklands, fields, and other artificial grasslands have all attracted insects and spiders that have come from elsewhere quite recently.

Common insects, green lacewings (order Neuroptera, family Chrysopidae) possess four light-green, oval-shaped wings. Their prominent eyes are coppery or bright gold.

CAROLINA GRASSHOPPER / *Dissosteira carolina*

The Carolina grasshopper (family Acrididae) is one of the most common species of band-winged grasshoppers. The color of dry soil, these large grasshoppers are well camouflaged on the ground. When they fly, they expose their hind-wings, which are black with a broad, pale-yellow band around the edge. Carolina grasshoppers are widespread in areas of grassland that have been disturbed by humans; they can often be seen along dry roadsides in late summer. They eat many kinds of weeds, but they also feed on wheat, alfalfa, and beans. Excellent flyers, the males are sometimes seen flying straight up about three to six feet (1 to 2 m) into the air, where they hover for several seconds while making a soft sound with their wings. They then drop back to the ground close to where they started. They repeat this hovering flight four or five times—all to attract females. Even though they are not considered a major pest, a large population of Carolina grasshoppers can seriously damage crops.

HABITAT
Weedy grasslands
RANGE
Widespread in North America
SIZE
1.4 to 2 inches (35 to 50 mm)
LIFE CYCLE
Hemimetabolous

GLADIATOR KATYDID / *Orchelimum gladiator*

The gladiator katydid (family Tettigoniidae), also known as the American meadow katydid, lives in dense, grassy vegetation. The adults are green with brown markings on the back. They and the nymphs both feed on grass. The females lay eggs in the grass stems to overwinter. The nymphs emerge in spring and become adults by late summer. The males often form big groups in the summer and sing throughout the day to attract the non-singing females. Their song is made up of a few simple "ticks" alternating with a "buzz," and it lasts only a few seconds. But because they repeat it over and over without any break, it sounds like one long continuous song. The males in a group are usually about five feet (1.5 m) away from each other, but often one male will leave its singing post to fight with its closest rival. The fight is a real wrestling match, involving much kicking and biting—hence their common name.

HABITAT
Ground and low grasses
RANGE
Widespread in United States and southern Canada
SIZE
1.3 to 1.4 inches (34 to 36 mm)
LIFE CYCLE
Hemimetabolous

PRAIRIE MOLE CRICKET / *Neocurtilla major*

The prairie mole cricket (family Gryllotalpidae) is the largest North American cricket. Little is known about this uncommon species; it is restricted to the prairie vegetation of central United States and at one point was believed to have disappeared. Like other mole crickets, the males of *Neocurtilla major* sing in the spring to attract mates, the only time of the year that the males can be located. They conduct this courtship ritual from their horn-shaped burrows, which are designed to amplify the song. A male by himself will usually sing for no more than thirty minutes per evening, but when joined by others in a large group, the calling song may last for about an hour. The males never sing in the rain and rarely on cool or windy nights.

HABITAT
Underground burrows in prairie vegetation
RANGE
Illinois, Kansas, Missouri, and Oklahoma
SIZE
Up to 2 inches (50 mm)
LIFE CYCLE
Hemimetabolous

SCARLET PLANT BUG / *Lopidea* spp.

The family Miridae (plant bugs) is the largest family of true bugs. They are elongated or oval, with a short head and long antennae. Many species are brightly colored. Some are considered beneficial because they prey on soft-bodied insects such as aphids. But most are plant feeders, often causing serious damage to vegetation. The bugs use their long beak to suck the plant juices from leaves, stems, roots, and fruit. Species in the genus *Lopidea* are either black and white or red and black; they all have black legs. They live in open meadows and feed on a variety of plants. The females have a sharp ovipositor, which they use to cut into soft leaf stems and insert eggs. When the eggs hatch, the nymphs start to feed on the plant right away. If the brightly colored nymphs are disturbed, they drop to the ground and play dead. The adults sometimes play dead as well, although they also escape predators by taking flight.

HABITAT
On vegetation in dry meadows, mixed prairies, and other grassy areas
RANGE
Widespread in North America
SIZE
0.2 to 0.4 inch (6 to 9 mm)
LIFE CYCLE
Hemimetabolous

STILT BUG / *Jalysus* spp.

Stilt bugs (family Berytidae) are very slender and elongated insects. They look a bit like small craneflies *(page 130)* or thin spiders, but their wings are those of typical true bugs and their antennae are very distinctive; the first two segments are long, sometimes as long as the stilt bug's body, and the last segment forms a spindle-shaped club.

Stilt bugs live on vegetation in dry open areas. Most species are plant feeders, but a few prey on smaller insects. Stilt bugs in the genus *Jalysus* are pale brown and the last segment of their antennae is black. They have a long beak to suck the juices of a variety of grasses, alfalfa, and other plants. The adults overwinter and lay eggs on plants in the spring; the nymphs feed on these plants and develop quickly into adults. Their shape works in their favor: Even though they are common, most people (and predators) never notice them.

HABITAT
Tall grasses, weedy meadows, and crop fields
RANGE
Widespread in United States and southern Canada
SIZE
0.31 to 0.36 inch (8 to 9 mm)
LIFE CYCLE
Hemimetabolous

APHID / Aphididae

Pear-shaped and often wingless, aphids sport long antennae and a pair of narrow tubes, called cornicles, which project from the end of the abdomen and produce a defensive fluid. They vary in color from green, yellow, and red to brown or black. For most of the year, wingless females produce nymphs without mating, then switch in late summer to produce fully winged males and females. Aphids, including those of the genus *Microsiphum*, use their long beak to suck sap from leaves and roots, damaging grasses, cereals, and other plants. Undigested sap is mixed with sugar and waste materials and excreted as honeydew, a liquid vital to the relationships aphids have with other insects, such as ants *(page 147)*.

HABITAT
On leaves or roots of grasses and other plants
RANGE
Widespread and common in North America and Europe
SIZE
0.08 to 0.16 inch (2 to 4 mm)
LIFE CYCLE
Hemimetabolous

MEADOW SPITTLEBUG / *Philaenus spumarius*

The white frothy masses that look like spit on the stems of grasses are made by the immature stages of the meadow spittlebug

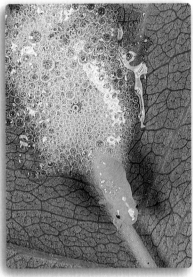

(family Cercopidae). Each mass of spittle contains one or more spittlebugs, positioned head down on the grass stem and feeding on plant juices. The nymphs mix the plant juice with secretions from glands in the gut, then with air as the liquid exits their anus, producing bubbles that protect the insect from wind, rain, and predators. The adults do not produce spittle. They are small brown or gray hopping insects that look like tiny frogs, and so are called froghoppers. The females lay eggs in the stems or sheaths of grasses and other plants. The feeding of the nymph can cause the plant to grow poorly, which is why it is considered a pest of cereal crops.

HABITAT
Nymphs and adults on vegetation in meadows and prairies
RANGE
Widespread in United States and southern Canada
SIZE
0.35 to 0.39 inch (9 to 10 mm)
LIFE CYCLE
Hemimetabolous

SCARLET AND GREEN LEAFHOPPER / *Graphocephala coccinea*

Leafhoppers (family Cicadellidae) are similar to their relatives the froghoppers, but are usually more abundant and more colorful. Leafhoppers use their small beak to suck the juices from grasses, flowers, and low shrubs. Like aphids, many leafhoppers produce honeydew while they feed, attracting ants that feed on the honeydew. A common species of leafhopper, *Graphocephala coccinea*, has orange or red stripes alternating with green or blue stripes on the forewings. The eggs are laid on

plants in early spring, and the pale green nymphs start feeding as soon as they emerge. The saliva injected into the plant when the leafhoppers feed blocks the passage of sap through the plant, causing the leaves to eventually fall off and the entire plant to become wrinkled and stunted.

HABITAT
Meadows and prairies
RANGE
Common in eastern United States and southern Canada
SIZE
0.31 to 0.35 inch (8 to 9 mm)
LIFE CYCLE
Hemimetabolous

AMERICAN HOVER FLY / *Eupeodes americanus*

The flies in the family Syrphidae are iridescent blue, green, yellow, orange, or black. Many are excellent mimics of bees and wasps. They have very large eyes, clear shiny wings, and vary from stout-bodied and hairy to elongated and brightly colored. The adults feed on flower nectar; their common name comes from their ability to hover motionless in the air above flowers. Some syrphid larvae live in decaying vegetation, others in highly polluted water, and a few feed on plants. But the great majority, including *Eupeodes americanus*, feed on aphids *(page 143)* and so are considered beneficial. The female lays eggs on an aphid-infested plant and when the eggs hatch, the larvae attack the aphids. The larvae leave the plant to pupate in the soil and overwinter.

HABITAT
Prairies and open meadows
RANGE
Widespread in North America
SIZE
0.3 to 0.4 inch (7 to 11 mm)
LIFE CYCLE
Holometabolous

BIG-HEADED FLY / *Pipunculus* spp.

Members of the family Pipunculidae have a huge head attached to a small, thin body; their head is almost completely covered by their enormous eyes. They are small to medium in size, with clear wings that are

longer than the body. Like their relatives the hover flies *(above)*, they are good fliers and are often seen hovering over meadows looking for leafhoppers *(page 144)*, which they parasitize. The female picks up a leafhopper with her legs, sticks her sharp pointed ovipositor into it, and lays one egg inside before dropping the leafhopper back onto the ground. The hatched pipunculid larva eats its host from the inside out. Eventually the leafhopper dies and the larva crawls out to pupate in the soil. Many male pipunculids are territorial, defending their small area of land from other males while they wait for females.

HABITAT
Larvae internal parasites of leafhoppers; adults in grasslands and open meadows
RANGE
Many species widespread in grassland regions of North America and Eurasia
SIZE
0.1 to 0.3 inch (3 to 7 mm)
LIFE CYCLE
Holometabolous

DAKOTA SKIPPER / Hesperia dacotae

Hesperia dacotae (family Hesperiidae) is a small butterfly that has the usual characteristics of skippers: a short, stout body; hooked antennae; and a rapid, erratic flight. The males are pale orange on the upper side and yellow underneath. Females vary from dark brown to pale orange. Once found from southern Manitoba through the midwestern United States, the Dakota skipper is now limited to a few small areas of native prairie because of agricultural development. It has only one generation a year. The females lay eggs on grasses and broad-leaf plants such as vetches. The eggs hatch in seven to twenty days and each caterpillar constructs a silken tube where it hides during the day. It leaves the tube at night to feed on a variety of grasses, showing a preference for bluestem. The half-grown caterpillar overwinters in this tube and starts feeding again in the following spring. Pupation occurs in late spring and the adults emerge in June.

HABITAT
Native tallgrass prairie
RANGE
Scattered sites in southern Manitoba, Iowa, Minnesota, and South Dakota
SIZE
1 to 1.3 inches (25 to 32 mm)
LIFE CYCLE
Holometabolous

WESTERN WHITE / Pontia occidentalis

The butterfly family Pieridae includes the sulphurs, the orange-tips, and the whites. The whites are almost completely white or pale yellowish, often with small dark patterns. *Pontia occidentalis* has a checkered appearance on the upper side of the wings and the underside of the hindwing has some green along the veins. This species lives in open habitats in western Canada, including prairies, mountain valleys, and badlands. It is also found in open grassy areas farther north in the Yukon. The caterpillar has green and gray stripes and feeds on a variety of plants, including wild mustard and stinkweed. It overwinters as a pupa and the adult emerges in spring or early summer. In the southern part of its range, this species produces two broods between April and October; in the north, a single brood between June and July.

HABITAT
Open areas, including prairies and other grasslands
RANGE
Western North America
SIZE
Wingspan 1.3 to 1.9 inches (33 to 48 mm)
LIFE CYCLE
Holometabolous

BLUEGRASS BILLBUG / *Sphenophorus parvulus*

The bluegrass billbug (family Curculionidae) is a weevil that feeds on many species of grasses, including bluegrass, fescue, and ryegrass. In some areas it is considered a pest of bluegrass and cereal crops. The adults are gray, black, or brown, with many deep punctures on the thorax and long grooves on the elytra. They feed by inserting their long snout into the grass stem. The females lay eggs one at a time into the feeding punctures between the leaf sheaths. The small white larvae hatch in about two weeks and start to feed inside the grass stem. The larvae leave piles of white frass—a mix of feces and dead grass—on the stem (which is often more noticeable then the larvae itself). As each larva grows, it moves down the stem, below the soil level until it reaches the roots and starts feeding there. This is the stage that causes the most damage to the grass. The larvae pupate in the soil in late summer and the adults emerge in early fall and overwinter.

HABITAT
In and on grass stems in open prairies and other grassy areas
RANGE
Widespread in North America
SIZE
0.28 to 0.31 inch (7 to 8 mm)
LIFE CYCLE
Holometabolous

LARGE YELLOW ANT / *Acanthomyops interjectus*

Ants (family Formicidae) are a very important part of the grassland fauna. About sixty species of ants typically are found in the prairies. Some are predators, others scavengers, and some live in symbiosis with aphids. Workers of *Acanthomyops interjectus*, for example, protect aphids from predators. In return, the aphids provide the ants with honeydew, a partially digested sap that is mixed with other substances and released from their anus. Some *A. interjectus* even collect the eggs of aphids and store them for the winter in a special chamber in the sandy mound where they nest. When the eggs hatch, the ants carry the young aphids out of the nest and place them on plant roots.

HABITAT
In sandy soil of grassland areas
RANGE
Southern and eastern United States
SIZE
0.08 to 0.16 inch (2 to 4 mm)
LIFE CYCLE
Holometabolous

SPIDERS

BANDED ARGIOPE / *Argiope trifasciata*

The banded argiope (family Araneidae) has an oval abdomen that is pointed at the back end. The spiders are usually silvery white or yellowish with thin silver and yellow transverse lines and larger spotted black lines across its body. The females are about four times the size of the males. They construct large webs in grasses and on herbaceous plants or shrubs. They rest in the middle of the web all day long and often all night, waiting for small insects to fly into the trap. Their webs are sometimes low enough to catch jumping insects such as grasshoppers and crickets. After feeding on the insects, the spider pulls the body free of the web and throws it away. The females produce a large silk egg sac, which they attach to nearby vegetation. The eggs overwinter in this sac and hatch in spring, with the spiderlings dispersing to look for sites to construct their own webs. They grow throughout the summer and reach maturity in late August and September.

HABITAT
Webs in grasslands and other open, dry areas
RANGE
Worldwide
SIZE
Females 0.6 to 1 inch (15 to 25 mm); males 0.16 to 0.2 inch (4 to 5 mm)

GREEN LYNX SPIDER / *Peucetia viridans*

Lynx spiders (family Oxyopidae) have yellowish legs distinguished by a row of long black spines. They don't construct webs; usually, they hunt during the day by chasing their prey, running with agility and jumping from one stem to another. Some, however, are less active; they tend to wait for prey on flowers or on dry stems, standing on their hindlegs and raising their front legs, a posture that makes them look a little like praying mantises. The green lynx spider is a common species in this family, found in the southern United States and Mexico. Most of those from the southeastern states are bright green, but in the southwestern states they are yellow or brown. The female spins a large egg sac, which she attaches to vegetation. As she rests on the egg sac, she extends lines of silk from it to nearby vegetation, forming a nursery web for the spiderlings when they hatch. Here they live and hunt until they are ready to disperse and live by themselves.

HABITAT
On flowers or ground in fields of tall grass
RANGE
Southern United States and Mexico
SIZE
Females 0.55 to 0.63 inch (14 to 16 mm); males 0.47 to 0.55 inch (12 to 14 mm)

Arid Lands

Dry forest, savanna, and shrubland together make up what are sometimes referred to as arid lands. Although each of these life zones possesses certain unique features, they share a similar climate—a long dry season with little or no rain, broken once a year by a period of rainfall. Because of this climatic similarity, they share many of the same insects and spiders.

The striped chafer, also known as the ten-lined beetle, is a scarabaeid beetle of arid regions in North America. On warm nights, the beetle can be seen flying toward light. When handled, it sometimes makes a squeaking sound.

VEGETATION IN A DRY LAND

The southwestern United States, Patagonia, southern and central Africa, and northern Australia all have arid areas that manage to support a surprisingly diverse assortment of vegetation—mostly tropical grasses, with small thorny shrubs and a few scattered trees that can survive several months with little water. Also evident in these regions are patches of bare soil and sand dunes. Savanna, which is more of a transition between dry forest and grassland, has a greater abundance of species than shrubland.

Most of the insects that have adapted to these arid lands are plant-eaters, such as grasshoppers, termites, and ants, although parasitic wasps, scavenging beetles, and predatory spiders are also abundant. Particularly prevalent are the locusts, species of grasshoppers that are periodically transformed by crowding and food scarcity into devastating hordes that cut great swathes through the countryside, devouring any green vegetation in their path.

Because there is a comparative paucity of vegetation in this biome to provide shelter from the blazing hot sun, sudden rain, wind, and the sharp eyes of winged predators, many insects and spiders in the arid lands have developed the ability to dig into the soil. A number of spiders, for instance, live in burrows, attuned to the vibrations of passing prey. Some insects don't dig their own burrows, but instead use the nests of mammals or other insects for shelter. Many bury their prey and lay eggs on it so the larvae can develop underground. Dung beetles take a different approach: They bury feces in the ground to conserve the moisture content for their larvae.

MIGRATORY LOCUST / *Schistocerca gregaria*

Commonly known as short-horned grasshoppers, locusts (family Acrididae) are distinguished from other grasshoppers by their ability to change their behavior when food becomes scarce. Normally they are solitary, but if they become crowded and their food sources diminish, they gather in huge swarms, migrating long distances to find a better place to feed and to breed.

Schistocerca gregaria can travel especially great distances and increase its population very rapidly, so it is considered the most damaging species in the family. Also known as desert locusts, *S. gregaria* can form swarms containing from 100 to 200 million locusts in a square mile (2.6 sq km). Each locust will eat its own weight in live plants in a day—not just the leaves, but also the fruits, flowers, and other parts. A swarm can devour all plants in an area within hours of landing.

HABITAT
Arid shrublands and semi-deserts
RANGE
North Africa and southwest Asia
SIZE
Wingspan 4 inches (100 mm)
LIFE CYCLE
Hemimetabolous

JERUSALEM CRICKET / *Stenopelmatus fuscus*

The Jerusalem cricket (family Gryllacrididae) is a slow-moving, hump-backed, shiny red-brown cricket. It has a large, round head with widely separated eyes and very long antennae. In Mexico its supposed resemblance to a small person has led it to be called *niña de la tierra*, meaning "child of the earth." The crickets are also known as sand crickets or potato bugs. They live under rocks on hillsides and are active both day and night. Sometimes they leave tracks in the soil or sand as they move about slowly, dragging their abdomen along the ground. Their diet includes other insects, plant roots, decaying vegetation, and potatoes. The females are sometimes cannibalistic, eating the males after mating. The females dig a burrow in the soil using their large head. The burrow is typically

about six to ten inches (15 to 25 cm) deep, with a tunnel at the bottom that ends at a chamber where eggs are laid.

HABITAT
Under rocks on hillsides and valley slopes
RANGE
Widespread in United States and Mexico
SIZE
1.2 to 2 inches (30 to 50 mm)
LIFE CYCLE
Hemimetabolous

LEICHARDT'S GRASSHOPPER / *Petasida ephippigera*

In Australian aboriginal legends, Namarrgon, the lightning god, causes the rains each year. Just before the rains start, *Petasida ephippigera* (family Pyrgomorphidae) come out in abundance—hence their local aboriginal name, Namarrgon's children. A dark-blue and bright-orange species of grasshopper, *P. ephippigera* feeds on a shrub species that contains aromatic chemical compounds, which give it a bad taste. Its colors are a warning that this grasshopper will make an unpleasant meal. *P. ephippigera* was described more than seventy years ago, then more or less forgotten until the 1970s. It is unclear whether this lack of attention was due to a sudden decline in the grasshopper population or because nobody looked for them.

HABITAT
Shrubby areas
RANGE
Northern Australia
SIZE
1.7 to 2 inches (44 to 50 mm)
LIFE CYCLE
Hemimetabolous

PAINTED GRASSHOPPER / *Dactylotum bicolor*

As the common name suggests, the painted grasshopper (family Acrididae) is patterned in bright colors: red, black, yellow, and white. The colors, like those of Leichardt's grasshopper *(above)* warn of its foul taste. The females use the tip of their abdomen to dig a hole in soft soil, where they lay up to twelve masses of eggs, each containing about a hundred eggs. The eggs overwinter until late spring, when the nymphs emerge and start to feed on low-growing plants. The nymphs become adults by the end of July.

HABITAT
Desert grasslands, dry open hillsides, and sparsely covered rocky soil
RANGE
Montana, North Dakota south to New Mexico, and Texas
SIZE
Females 1.1 to 1.4 inches (29 to 35 mm); males 0.8 to 0.9 inch (20 to 24 mm)
LIFE CYCLE
Hemimetabolous

KISSING BUG / *Triatoma infestans*

The family Reduviidae, also known as assassin bugs, is a large group of predatory hemipterans that feed mostly on other insects, although a few, such as those in the genus *Triatoma*, feed on blood. Like most other assassin bugs, *T. infestans* have such an elongated head that they appear to possess a neck. Dangerous insect pests, they feed on the blood of mammals, often entering houses and biting sleeping humans. They attack any exposed parts of the body and often bite near the mouth—hence their common name. Kissing bugs transmit Chagas' disease, a sometimes fatal illness caused by a microscopic parasite called a trypanosome. After the bug has fed on blood, it leaves droppings close to the bite. Scratching the bite will transfer the feces—and the trypanosome organisms they contain—into the wound. In parts of South America, more than half of the population may be infected. Efforts to control the disease have focused on the insect carriers.

HABITAT
Nests of small mammals and cracks in walls of houses
RANGE
United States; Central and South America
SIZE
0.7 to 0.8 inch (19 to 20 mm)
LIFE CYCLE
Hemimetabolous

BEE FLY / *Anthrax analis*

Bee flies (family Bombyliidae) are large, stout-bodied, hairy members of the order Diptera. Their common name derives from their resemblance to small bumblebees. Equipped with a long, slender proboscis for sucking nectar from flowers, they, like bumblebees, are important pollinators of many different types of wildflowers. They are often seen hovering over or resting on a flower or alighting on the ground with their wings outstretched. The females of many *Anthrax* species pick up and store sand grains in a special chamber at the end of their abdomen; they use the sand later to cover their eggs. The larvae of most bee fly species, including *A. analis*, are parasites of the immature stages of other insects, including butterflies, beetles, and wasps. Some prey on grasshopper eggs.

HABITAT
Sunny spots in arid and desertlike areas
RANGE
Widespread in North America
SIZE
0.4 to 0.8 inch (10 to 20 mm)
LIFE CYCLE
Holometabolous

GIANT ROBBER FLY / *Proctacanthus rodecki*

The robber flies (family Asilidae) are fairly large and common flies. They have long spiny legs, a beardlike patch of face hairs, and eyes so large that they project above the top of the head. Some are stout-bodied, very hairy, and mimic bumblebees; others are elongated with a tapered abdomen. Most species in the family occur in semi-arid and arid regions, where

they live in dry and sandy areas, moving around during the hottest part of the day. Both adults and larvae are predaceous, known for their aggressive attacks on other insects. *Proctacanthus rodecki* waits on a perch for a bee or other large insect to fly by, then rushes out to grab it in flight. The fly spears the prey with its sharp beak, injecting a venom to paralyze and liquefy tissues, which are then sucked up. The larvae of the giant robber fly live in the soil and feed on other insect larvae.

HABITAT
Sandy areas and open fields
RANGE
Kansas, Colorado, and New Mexico
SIZE
0.9 to 1.2 inches (24 to 30 mm)
LIFE CYCLE
Holometabolous

MANROOT BORER / *Melittia gloriosa*

Most moths and butterflies have scales on the wings, which gives them their distinctive wing colors and patterns. But the wings of the clearwing moths (family Sesiidae) are mostly devoid of scales and so are partly transparent like those of a fly or a wasp. Many Sesiidae are brightly colored, and in some species only the males have clear spots on the wings. They are all active during the day. The caterpillars bore into the roots or stems of a variety of plants and trees; some species are considered serious pests. The manroot borer is very popular among collectors. The female has gray-to-brown front wings and feathery hindwings that are orange with some purple; the male has transparent wings. They fly quickly and are hard to approach. The caterpillars bore into the roots of wild plants from the cucumber family, including manroot.

HABITAT
Dry open areas
RANGE
Western United States
SIZE
1.6 to 2.4 inches (40 to 60 mm)
LIFE CYCLE
Holometabolous

YUCCA MOTH / *Tegeticula yuccasella*

In a classic case of coevolution *(page 33)*, the yucca moth (family Incurvariidae) and the yucca plant have evolved a close, symbiotic relationship. The female moth visits the yucca plant at night and with the long mouthparts that curl below her head, she forms a ball of pollen that she carries to a second yucca plant of the same species, thereby pollinating it. She then lays one or two eggs in the plant's ovary, where the cactus seeds develop. The caterpillars eat some of the seeds, but leave enough to produce new yucca plants.

HABITAT
Arid areas where yucca cactus plants grow
RANGE
Southern United States
SIZE
0.7 to 1 inch (19 to 25 mm)
LIFE CYCLE
Holometabolous

GIANT TIGER BEETLE / *Mantichora* spp.

Tiger beetles (family Cicindelidae) are a common group of predaceous beetles usually associated with dry sandy areas. Among the most voracious of insect species, they are usually less than an inch (25 mm) long and brightly colored, with some blue, green, or purple; most are strong, fast fliers. One group of African tiger beetles does not fit this description—those belonging to the genus *Mantichora*, which includes the largest species of tiger beetles in the world. These beetles are black and have a wide abdomen and enormous jaws that can inflict a painful bite. They have no hindwings and so cannot fly, but they can run very rapidly when trying to escape or chase down insect prey.

HABITAT
Open ground in dry, scrubby areas
RANGE
Southern Africa
SIZE
Up to about 2.8 inches (70 mm)
LIFE CYCLE
Holometabolous

MARBLE DIVING BEETLE / *Thermonectus marmoratus*

Members of the family Dytiscidae, commonly known as predaceous diving beetles, are oval-shaped, shiny black, brown, or dark green, with back legs that are flattened and fringed. They move their back legs simulta-

neously when they swim, rather than alternately like most other aquatic beetles. They carry a bubble of air under their elytra for breathing, which allows them to stay underwater for long periods of time. The adults and larvae (also called water tigers) prey on a variety of aquatic animals, including other insects, worms, and even small fish. The marble diving beetle has gold markings on the elytra. During dry periods when water levels drop, these beetles survive by burrowing into the mud at the bottom of pond beds. At night the adults sometimes leave the water in large swarms. They are attracted to light.

HABITAT
Ponds in arid regions
RANGE
Western Texas, Arizona, California, and Mexico
SIZE
0.4 to 0.6 inch (10 to 15 mm)
LIFE CYCLE
Holometabolous

SACRED SCARAB / *Scarabeus sacer*

The sacred scarab (family Scarabaeidae) is a dung beetle that feeds on cattle dung, helping to break it down and fertilize the soil. When the female is ready to lay eggs, she rolls a ball of dung into a shallow burrow she has dug, lays an egg in the dung, and then buries them together. To the ancient Egyptians, the sacred scarab was a symbol of immortality and fertil-

ity. They saw the beetle's habit of rolling a ball of dung as a metaphor for the gods rolling the sun across the sky and the emergence of the larvae from the buried ball of dung as signifying new life reborn after death. They used the scarab beetle design in jewelry and amulets and carved it in burial chambers. It is believed that the Egyptian mummy in its tomb may have been designed as a parallel of the sacred scarab pupa lying in its ball of dung.

HABITAT
On open ground in arid regions
RANGE
Northern Africa
SIZE
0.8 to 1 inch (20 to 25 mm)
LIFE CYCLE
Holometabolous

TUMBLEBUG / *Canthon* spp.

Many insects are found on dung, but most feed on the other insects or the microorganisms occurring there. Tumblebugs (family Scarabaeidae) are a type of scarab that eat the dung itself. They are considered beneficial because they fertilize the soil and speed up the decomposition of dung, thus removing breeding sites for pest species such as flies. The name tumblebug comes from the insects' habit of forming dung into a small ball and rolling it away to bury it. Most species of tumblebugs are in the genus *Canthon*. Male and female cooperate to chew off a piece of dung, which they pack into a ball. The couple rolls the ball with their hindlegs, one pushing and one pulling. One large egg is laid in the ball and buried. The larva develops inside the ball, feeding on the dung. In some species, the parents stay in the burrow with the larva.

HABITAT
Desert grasslands and dry open areas
RANGE
Widespread in United States; Central and South America
SIZE
0.4 to 0.8 inch (10 to 20 mm)
LIFE CYCLE
Holometabolous

 ## GREAT GOLDEN DIGGER WASP / *Sphex ichneumoneus*

The great golden digger wasp (family Sphecidae) is a species of solitary wasp that nests in the ground. It is medium-sized, reddish brown and black, with yellow hairs on the thorax and the head. It has a short, narrow waist, called a pedicel, linking its thorax and its abdomen. The adults feed on nectar, the larvae on a variety of orthopterans, such as true crickets, camel crickets, and long-horned grasshoppers. The female builds a vertical burrow in the soil with many side tunnels. She catches insects by paralyzing them with her sting and stores them live in the tunnels. Then, she lays one egg on top of each insect. When the egg hatches, the larva feeds on the paralyzed prey. The golden digger wasp produces one generation a year. The adults are active from July to August.

HABITAT
Bare sandy soil in open areas
RANGE
United States and southern Canada
SIZE
0.6 to 0.9 inch (15 to 23 mm)
LIFE CYCLE
Holometabolous

RED IMPORTED FIRE ANT / *Solenopsis invicta*

Solenopsis invicta (family Formicidae) was introduced from South America into Alabama in the 1930s and since then has spread throughout the southeastern United States. Fire ants reproduce very rapidly: The queen mates only once and lays one hundred to two hundred eggs per hour for up to six years. She nests in piles of sand up to three feet (1 m) in height with a huge population of workers. These ants are very aggressive and have a painful sting. If disturbed, they will swarm out of their nest in seconds, crawling onto the intruder and hanging by their mandibles to sting repeatedly. They feed primarily on other insects, but will eat any plant or animal matter. Small mammals and birds are often killed by these ants. An attack by fire ants is a very painful experience for humans.

HABITAT
Dry sandy soil in open areas
RANGE
South and Central America; southern United States
SIZE
Workers 0.1 to 0.2 inch (3 to 6 mm)
LIFE CYCLE
Holometabolous

TARANTULA HAWK / *Pepsis* spp.

Members of the family Pompilidae are commonly known as spider wasps. They are solitary wasps that provision their nests with spiders. The tarantula hawk is a genus of large spider wasp, easily recognized by its metallic, bluish-black body and orange wings. The adults feed on nectar, but the female also preys on tarantulas—one of the few creatures to do so. When she is ready to lay eggs, she searches out a tarantula's burrow, disturbing the area until the spider rushes out. She immediately stings the spider between the legs, injecting a paralyzing venom. Quickly, she digs a burrow and drags the tarantula inside—sometimes she will use the spider's burrow instead. Then she lays an egg on the abdomen of her captive and closes the burrow with sand. When the egg hatches, the wasp larva feeds on the tarantula, which eventually dies.

HABITAT
Desert shrublands, dry hillsides, and rolling arid plains
RANGE
Southwestern United States; Central and South America
SIZE
0.5 to 0.8 inch (12 to 20 mm)
LIFE CYCLE
Holometabolous

COMPASS TERMITE / *Amitermes meridionalis*

Some termite species build very simple nests that consist of galleries excavated in wood. Others create somewhat more elaborate nests in the soil, a log, or the trunk of a living tree. But the most spectacular termite nests are those constructed in the form of mounds. These mounds are made of soil cemented by the termites' saliva. Termite mounds are of different sizes and shapes, ranging from low domes to high columns. Those made by *Amitermes meridionalis* of northern Australia are wedge-shaped mounds a few inches wide that can be more than ten feet (3 m) high and seven feet (2 m) long. All of the mounds in an area are positioned to face the same direction, their broad sides oriented east and west. This minimizes the amount of surface exposed to direct sunlight, helping to keep the nest cool. The directional nature of their design also explains the common name of these termites.

HABITAT
Mounds constructed in open arid areas
RANGE
Northern Australia
SIZE
Workers 0.2 to 0.4 inch (5 to 10 mm)
LIFE CYCLE
Hemimetabolous

STRIPED DESERT COCKROACH / *Desmozosteria cincta*

Cockroaches (family Blattidae) are easily recognized by their oval, flattened body, their large pronotum that conceals the head, their long antennae, and their long, spiny legs. Some species have well-developed wings and can fly very well; others have reduced wings or no wings at all and use their long legs to run on the ground. Cockroaches are often considered as creepy and disgusting insects, but in fact some of the world's cockroaches are remarkably beautiful. Some species live in houses and other buildings and can become serious pests, but most species are associated with a particular outdoor habitat and could not survive anywhere else. The striped desert cockroach lives among twigs and branches at the base of eucalyptus trees in central Australia. It is a colorful reddish brown with yellow stripes. Like many other species of cockroach, the desert cockroach is nocturnal and so it is rarely seen.

HABITAT
Vegetation on ground in arid areas
RANGE
Central Australia
SIZE
0.6 to 1 inch (15 to 25 mm)
LIFE CYCLE
Hemimetabolous

WESTERN FLOWER THRIPS / *Frankliniella occidentalis*

The family Thripidae (common thrips) includes many damaging species of thrips, fond of cultivated plants. One of them is *Frankliniella occidentalis*, a native North American thrips that was introduced to Europe and Australia in the 1980s. A tiny species, usually yellow or dark brown, *F. occidentalis* feeds on a wide range of plants, including weeds, field crops, and trees, sometimes transmitting a plant virus as it eats. It causes serious damage to the fruits of many trees; as it feeds, it creates scars on the surface of the fruit that expand as the fruit grows. It usually feeds in protected places on the plant, such as inside the stem and under the leaves, thus reducing its exposure to insecticides. Because it has developed resistance to many insecticides, scientists are trying to develop biological controls, such as the use of predators and parasites.

HABITAT
On plants in arid regions
RANGE
Widespread in North America, Europe, and Australia
SIZE
0.06 inch (1.5 mm)
LIFE CYCLE
Hemimetabolous

OWLFLY / Ascalaphidae

The owlflies (family Ascalaphidae) are very similar to dragonflies in appearance and they, too, are strong, rapid flyers. Still, owlflies can always be distinguished by their long, clubbed antennae and their dull coloring. Some are nocturnal and thus not commonly seen, but both adults and larvae of the diurnal species can be observed preying on other insects. The females lay their eggs on twigs. When the eggs hatch about a week later, the larvae drop to the ground, covering themselves with debris. There they wait with their mandibles spread open until a small insect comes close enough to be snapped up and injected with a paralyzing poison.

HABITAT
Larvae on open ground; adults often on sunny plants or rocks
RANGE
South and southwest United States; Central and South America
SIZE
1.4 to 1.6 inches (35 to 40 mm)
LIFE CYCLE
Holometabolous

BURROWING WOLF SPIDER / *Geolycosa turricola*

Although wolf spiders (family Lycosidae) do not hunt in packs like wolves, when conditions are just right they sometimes occur in large numbers in a single habitat. These spiders spend most of their time inside their burrow, waiting for insects to come near. They dig the burrow in the sand straight down to a depth of about six to twelve inches (15 to 30 cm), lining it with silk to prevent the sand from collapsing. They often plug the burrow with sand to keep out predatory wasps. The burrow appears as a hole about the diameter of a large pencil. (Dig down beside a burrow and you might find a spider inside.) Like the nursery web spiders (family Pisauridae), the females of *Geolycosa* carry the egg sac until the eggs hatch. Then, the spiderlings move onto their mother's back, where they remain until they are ready to live on their own.

HABITAT
Open sand dunes in arid areas
RANGE
Widespread in North America and northern Mexico
SIZE
Females 0.7 to 0.9 inch (18 to 22 mm); males 0.6 to 0.9 inch (14 to 22 mm)

CALIFORNIAN TRAPDOOR SPIDER / *Bothriocyrtum californicum*

Like many other spiders, trapdoor spiders (family Ctenizidae) live in a burrow in the ground, but they are unique in one respect: They also make a door at the entrance. Some species fashion their door out of silk, others make it out of a combination of soil, debris, and silk to hold everything together. The door is usually hidden from predators by a covering of moss, twigs, and leaves. But if a predator does see the door and tries to open it, the spider will grab the door with its legs and chelicerae to hold it closed. One of the species in this group, *Bothriocyrtum californicum*, has spines on its chelicerae for digging burrows, which are deep enough for the spider to easily move around. It sits and waits just inside the trapdoor for passing prey—a small insect, a millipede, or another spider. When *B. californicum* senses prey by the vibrations it makes, the spider darts out to grab it, then pulls it back into the burrow to kill and devour it.

HABITAT
Hard soil on sunny hillsides and slopes
RANGE
Southern California
SIZE
Females 1.1 to 1.3 inches (28 to 33 mm); males 0.8 to 1 inch (18 to 26 mm)

GREEN LYSSOMANES / *Lyssomanes virides*

The Salticidae, commonly known as jumping spiders, is the largest family of spiders in the world. Found worldwide, these small, sun-loving spiders are most common in warm regions. They have very good vision, which makes them excellent hunters. Two of their eight eyes are much larger than the others, giving them an unexpected intelligent look. They can spot their prey from a distance and sneak up on it. They construct silken retreats in crevices, under stones, or on the leaves of plants, where the females lay their eggs. The females of the species *Lyssomanes virides* show some parental care by enclosing their eggs in a silken cocoon and guarding them until the spiderlings emerge.

HABITAT
Low bushes in dry sandy areas
RANGE
North Carolina to Florida and west to Texas
SIZE
Females 0.2 to 0.3 inch (7 to 9 mm); males 0.2 to 0.3 inch (5 to 7 mm)

DESERT VIOLIN SPIDER / *Loxosceles deserta*

Members of the small family Loxoscelidae are commonly called violin spiders because some species have a violin-shaped marking on the cephalothorax. They are usually dull yellowish or brown spiders with long legs and only six eyes. Species can be found in North America, Africa, Europe, and Australia, where some have been introduced. The violin spiders are known for their venomous bite that can cause illness. A bite from these spiders can take several weeks to heal. *Loxosceles deserta* is the least venomous of the violin spiders. This species is pale yellow, brownish gray, or sand-colored; its violin-shaped mark is less obvious and sometimes absent. Like most other violin spiders, this species hides in cracks and crevices of logs and rocks where it spins an irregular web to catch small prey.

HABITAT
Under stones or logs in arid areas
RANGE
Arizona, Nevada, Utah, and California
SIZE
0.2 to 0.3 inch (6 to 8 mm)

Tundra

In the high northern and southern latitudes near the poles, the air is so cold and dry that trees cannot survive. Instead low-growing plants, including shrubs, sedges, lichens, and mosses, cling to rocky ground and shallow soil to create the basis of a harsh biome called arctic tundra. A similar biome, alpine tundra, occurs high up in the mountains at lower latitudes.

In these regions, the temperature may drop to minus sixty degrees Fahrenheit (-50°C) or even lower during the winter. But despite the cold, many insects and spiders manage to thrive, in part because their size, shape, and colors are designed to absorb heat from the sun and preserve the warmth inside their body.

Most tundra species are diminutive and hide in warm, small habitats on the ground. Those that are bigger, such as bumblebees, caterpillars, and some butterflies, are often covered with dark hairs to keep them warm. Many flying insects stay close to the ground where it is warmer and there is less wind. Because food is scarce here and the summers are short, some insects have a long life cycle, which allows them to feed voraciously for a few weeks in the summer, then become dormant for the winter.

ARCTIC GRASSHOPPER / *Bohemanella frigida*

Grasshoppers (family Acrididae) are usually considered to be primarily a tropical or subtropical group, but some species have adapted to temperate regions and a few others flourish in the arctic. Those that live in the subarctic or the arctic produce no more than one generation a year, and often their life cycle lasts two years or more. The species that have one generation a year overwinter in the egg stage; those that take two years to complete their life cycle spend the first winter in the egg stage and the second winter as a nymph. *Bohemanella frigida* is an arctic species of short-horned grasshopper that has one generation a year. The females lay their eggs in the soil in the fall, where they remain for the winter. The eggs hatch the following summer, usually in June or July, and the nymphs feed very quickly on the leaves of low-lying vegetation, maturing to adult grasshoppers about four weeks later.

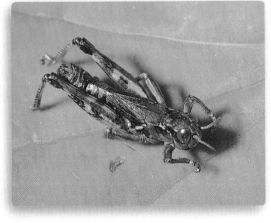

HABITAT
Low vegetation in tundra
RANGE
Alaska, Yukon, Northwest Territories, and northern Asia
SIZE
0.7 to 1 inch (18 to 27 mm)
LIFE CYCLE
Hemimetabolous

ARCTIC BLACK FLY / *Gymnopais holopticus*

The biting species of black flies (family Simuliidae) are very abundant in the north during the summer. But about a quarter of the species of black flies that reside on the tundra, including *Gymnopais holopticus*, do not require blood for the development of their eggs. Instead, the females accumulate enough protein while still larvae and can later produce eggs without a blood meal first. In fact, the mouthparts of *G. holopticus* are too small to pierce the skin of larger animals. The larvae are aquatic, but unlike most black-fly species, they do not have the head fans to catch organic particles in the water. Instead, they scrape algae and other organic matter off rocks with their mandibles. Both sexes fly reasonably well, like their southern counterparts.

HABITAT
Larvae (shown below) in mountain streams; adults in flight near streams
RANGE
Alaska and Yukon
SIZE
0.08 to 0.16 inch (2 to 4 mm)
LIFE CYCLE
Holometabolous

ARCTIC TACHINID FLY / Tachinidae

The family Tachinidae is a very large, highly diverse group of flies that live almost everywhere, including the arctic. They vary in color, size, and shape, with some species being quite hairy and resembling bees or wasps, others looking more like house flies. All are considered beneficial because they parasitize other insects, many of which are pests. Most parasitize only a single host or a small number of species, but a few attack a variety of hosts. One of the most common arctic species is *Chetogena gelida*, a parasite of the lymantriid moths of the genus *Gynaephora*, which includes the arctic woolybear moth *(page 164)*. The female fly lays eggs on a *Gynaephora* caterpillar and the fly larva penetrates the caterpillar's body, feeding internally and eventually killing the host. When the larva is fully grown, it leaves the host's body and pupates in the ground.

HABITAT
Dry tundra
RANGE
Alaska, Yukon, and Northwest Territories
SIZE
0.3 to 0.5 inch (7 to 13 mm)
LIFE CYCLE
Holometabolous

ARCTIC WOOLLYBEAR / *Gynaephora groenlandica*

Gynaephora groenlandica (family Lymantriidae) lives farther north than almost any other species of Lepidoptera. Found at the limit of vegetation in the high arctic, it has the longest life cycle of any butterfly or moth, lasting from seven to fourteen years. The caterpillars overwinter every year and come out every spring for a few weeks to feed as much as they can before going back into diapause. The larvae feed mostly on arctic willows. Adults are active during the long arctic summer days. The females have wings but never fly, a common condition among arctic Lepidoptera. The males are good aerialists and, unlike many arctic Lepidoptera, they fly high above the ground.

HABITAT
Dry rocky tundra
RANGE
Arctic Canada and Greenland
SIZE
1.4 to 1.6 inches (35 to 40 mm)
LIFE CYCLE
Holometabolous

 CRANBERRY BLUE / *Vacciniina optilete*

The wings of male cranberry blues (family Lycaenidae) have deep purplish-blue upper sides. The females are less conspicuous, with wide brown margins and a small part of the wing bases purplish. In both sexes, the underside of the wings is pale gray with two rows of large dark spots. Also called Yukon blue, the cranberry blue has an orange spot near the lower corner of each wing that differentiates it from other similar species. The adults are active in July. Weak fliers, they are usually seen close to the ground among low-lying vegetation. The caterpillars feed mostly on the leaves of blueberry and cranberry plants; thus, they are common in bogs and wet tundra, where these plants are most abundant. There is one generation per year that overwinters as caterpillars.

HABITAT
Wet tundra and northern peat bogs
RANGE
Hudson Bay to Alaska; Manitoba to northern British Columbia; and Eurasia
SIZE
0.7 to 0.9 inch (18 to 24 mm)
LIFE CYCLE
Holometabolous

GREENLAND SULPHUR / *Colias hecla*

The sulphurs are yellow or orange butterflies, often with black wing margins, belonging to the family Pieridae, which also contains the whites and orange-tip butterflies. Some of them are among the most northern butterflies in the world. Members of the genus *Colias* that live in the arctic have much darker wing undersides than those of species farther south. When they are

resting and their wings are raised, the dark surfaces absorb the sunlight. Adult Greenland sulphurs, also called hecla sulphurs, live as far north as Ellesmere Island. Strong fliers, they are active from late June to early August, when they are seen (like many other arctic species) flying low over the tundra vegetation. The caterpillars are green with lateral stripes. They feed mostly on alpine milk vetch, but also eat a variety of related plants, such as lupines. It is believed they take two years to complete their life cycle, overwintering as caterpillars or pupae.

HABITAT
Arctic shrub tundra
RANGE
Arctic North America south to northern Manitoba and British Columbia, Greenland, and Eurasia
SIZE
1.3 to 1.8 inches (33 to 45 mm)
LIFE CYCLE
Holometabolous

PHOEBUS PARNASSIAN / *Parnassius phoebus*

The butterfly family Papilionidae includes the swallowtails and the parnassians. The parnassians are usually white or gray with dark markings, sometimes with small reddish spots on the hindwings. Many live in mountains, including *Parnassius phoebus,* which lives in the high mountain ranges of the Yukon and other far-northern regions. The males have white forewings with a band of

pale gray on the outer margins, as well as red spots on both forewings and hindwings. The females are a creamier white and have more dark markings; they have red spots on only the hindwings. The caterpillars feed only on certain species of stonecrop, especially roseroot. The adults are active from early June until late August and are usually found near the larval food plants, where eggs are laid. This species is very similar to the Rocky Mountain parnassian, a butterfly that can be found farther south in high alpine meadows.

HABITAT
Wet tundra and alpine meadows
RANGE
Western Yukon and northern Asia
SIZE
1.8 to 2.3 inches (45 to 58 mm)
LIFE CYCLE
Holometabolous

POLAR BUMBLEBEE / *Bombus* spp.

The bumblebees (family Apidae) are one insect group that is well represented in the far north. Because of their large size, their hairy bodies, and their tendency to be darker-colored in the north, bumblebees are well adapted to stay warm in the cool arctic summer. Several species of *Bombus* occur in the arctic; three among them, including *B. polaris*, get as far north as the high arctic. All are social insects. They fly very close to the ground where it is usually warmer.

Most species of *Bombus* in the temperate zones nest in abandoned rodent nests, but because a rodent's nest in the arctic is too cold and often wet, *B. polaris* construct their nests in warm, dry sedge meadows, positioning the entrance to face the sun. The nest starts with a fertilized queen that has overwintered. Once the non-breeding workers emerge, they take care of the nest and the larvae. Males and queens are produced at the end of the summer and only the queens will survive the winter to start a new colony the following spring.

HABITAT
Arctic and alpine tundra
RANGE
Arctic Canada, Alaska, Greenland, and parts of arctic Eurasia
SIZE
0.6 inch (15 mm)
LIFE CYCLE
Holometabolous

ROCK CRAWLER / *Grylloblatta* spp.

The rock crawlers (family Grylloblattidae) look like pale, slender, wingless cockroaches. They have long antennae and their eyes are small or absent. There are only twenty known species of rock crawlers in the world and thirteen of these, all in the genus *Grylloblatta*, live in western North America. Mostly nocturnal, they are found on bare rocks at the edge of glaciers and snow beds or in ice caves, usually high in the mountains—hence their other common name, ice insects. Because of their isolation, they were not discovered until 1914. The first to be described, *G. campodeiformis* lives in the Canadian Rockies. Like other rock crawlers, it feeds on dead insects and other decaying organic debris found on snow, ice, and rocks. They can handle only a small range of temperatures and will die quickly if they become too warm or cold. (They can get overheated just being held in your hand.)

HABITAT
Edges of snow and ice in rocky, mountainous areas
RANGE
Rockies and other mountains in western North America
SIZE
0.6 to 1 inch (15 to 30 mm)
LIFE CYCLE
Hemimetabolous

SPIDERS

DWARF SPIDER / *Erigone* spp.

Members of the subfamily Erigoninae (family Linyphiidae) are very small spiders and are commonly referred to as dwarf spiders. They are a dominant spider group in colder regions, with thirty-four species living in the tundra and a dozen more that live as far north as the high arctic. The best known species belong to the genus *Erigone*. Dark brown or black spiders with a smooth and shiny exoskeleton, they have spines on their sides, their pedipalps, and their chelicerae. They construct tiny webs among the vegetation. When they leave their webs to run on the ground, they can be found under leaves, moss, and organic debris. Some species prey particularly on mites (order Acari) and springtails (order Collembola), but also eat other insects.

HABITAT
Arctic species found on ground in tundra
RANGE
Arctic species widespread in arctic Canada and Eurasia
SIZE
0.1 inch (3 mm)

GROUND SPIDER / Gnaphosidae

The Gnaphosidae is a large family of ground spiders with more than two thousand species worldwide. Many are dull colored, covered with very short, velvety, gray, brown, and black hairs. A few are more colorful. Seven species of *Gnaphosa* live in the arctic. Small to medium-sized, they are oval-shaped and appear somewhat flattened. Their carapace is light orange to dark brown, with some dark margins and also many erect dark hairs. Like other ground spiders, the species of *Gnaphosa* hunt at night. During the day, they are found under stones or logs in silken retreats. The females spin an egg sac that is characteristically flattened and can contain up to 250 eggs. They spend most of their time guarding the egg sacs in their retreats. The males are more active, wandering around to hunt.

HABITAT
Arctic species found on ground in tundra or around small willows
RANGE
Widespread in North America, including arctic Canada, and in arctic Eurasia
SIZE
0.1 to 0.5 inch (3 to 12 mm)

Desert

Because the desert biome receives very little rainfall, the vegetation there usually has roots that reach down deep to find water. Such desert plants include a variety of short grasses, shrubs, sagebrush, cactus, and other succulent plants. Most deserts experience very hot days, cold nights, and, since there are so few plants to serve as obstacles, strong surface-level winds. Despite these challenging conditions, many types of insects and spiders occur here, including flies, cockroaches, termites, ants, beetles, mantids, and tarantulas.

Many desert-dwelling insects and spiders find shelter in the sand or under rocks by day and disperse, feed, and mate at night. Others, however, can tolerate great heat and spend the day outside. Some velvet ants and darkling beetles *(page 171)*, for example, can survive temperatures of more than 122 degrees Fahrenheit (50°C). Since water is rare, many species get their moisture from their food and must eat a lot to obtain what liquid they need. Others, such as the darkling beetles, have special ways of accumulating drinking water on their bodies.

GIANT MESQUITE BUG / *Thasus acutangulus*

Members of the family Coreidae (leaf-footed bugs) are medium to large bugs with a small head compared to their elongated body. They have well-developed scent glands and when handled, they release a strong odor. The giant mesquite bug is the largest species of Coreidae in North America, also one of the largest species of the order Hemiptera. Its hindlegs have enlarged femora with sharp spines, which they use to defend their territory against other males. Most species are plant feeders. The bright orange, yellow, and black nymphs form large feeding aggregations on mesquite trees.

When disturbed by predators, they spray jets of fluid into the air from their anus while their scent glands release a foul-smelling secretion. All of this creates a nasty cloud that scares off most intruders.

HABITAT
On mesquite bushes in desert areas
RANGE
Arizona and New Mexico
SIZE
1.4 to 1.6 inches (35 to 40 mm)
LIFE CYCLE
Hemimetabolous

DELHI SANDS FLOWER-LOVING FLY / *Raphiomidas terminatus abdominalis*

The flies in the genus *Raphiomidas* (family Apioceridae) are restricted to small areas of desert regions in southwestern United States and northern Mexico. Some species are very abundant during certain times of the year, while other species are quite rare. One of these rare species, *Raphiomidas terminatus*, is the first fly ever to have been placed on the United States Endangered Species List. There may be only five hundred individuals still alive. A large, robust fly, it is covered with short golden hairs that gradually fade to gray a few days after emergence. The female lays her eggs deep in the sand by extending her telescopic abdomen to about twice its normal length. The larvae live in the soil and are believed to be predators. The adults feed on flowers of the desert plant *Eriogonum fasciculatum* by inserting their pro-

boscis into the flowers while hovering like hummingbirds; they usually spend only a few seconds at each flower.

HABITAT
On flowers in open desert areas
RANGE
Small area of southeastern California; possibly northern Mexico
SIZE
1 inch (25 mm)
LIFE CYCLE
Holometabolous

CALIFORNIA CANKERWORM MOTH / *Paleacrita longiciliata*

The larvae of the geometrid moths are the familiar inchworms, also called measuring worms. The caterpillars have only two or three pairs of unsegmented legs (prolegs) at

their posterior end and none in the middle, causing them to walk in a distinctive looping way. The adults are small and slender-bodied, and have broad, delicate wings frequently marked with fine wavy lines. The males and females often differ in color and in a few species the females have only small undeveloped wings or are completely wingless. *Paleacrita longiciliata* is one of the species in which the female cannot fly; its wings are tiny stubs less than 0.04 inch (1 mm) long. The male's wings are normal-sized and dull brown or gray. The adults are active from November to May. Eggs are laid on a variety of species of desert shrubs in the rose family and the hatched caterpillars feed on the foliage.

HABITAT
Deserts and open scrub areas
RANGE
California
SIZE
1 to 1.4 inches (25 to 35 mm)
LIFE CYCLE
Holometabolous

WRIGHT'S METALMARK / *Calephelis wrighti*

Metalmarks (family Riodinidae) are small, dark-colored butterflies. The name metalmark comes from the shiny metallic markings that many species have on the upper side of the front wings. They all are strong fliers and many of them have the habit of landing upside down under a leaf with their wings flat open. *Calephelis wrighti* is a species of metalmark that is dull reddish brown, with small white iridescent spots and silver metallic markings. The caterpillar is purplish gray and covered with long hairs. The eggs are laid on the outer stems of sweetbush and the caterpillars feed on the plant.

HABITAT
Near water courses and by sweetbush in arid deserts
RANGE
Southwestern United States; Central and South America
SIZE
0.7 to 1 inch (19 to 25 mm)
LIFE CYCLE
Holometabolous

DESERT BLISTER BEETLE / *Cysteodemus wislizeni*

Blister beetles get their common name from a defensive chemical called cantharidin that causes blisters when it contacts the skin or other soft parts of large animals. Most species of blister beetles are elongated and cylindrical, but those in the genus *Cysteodemus* (family Meloidae) are broadly oval and convex. *C. wislizeni* is dark metallic blue or purple and shaped a little like a large spider. It has short spines on the sides of the thorax and the elytra are covered with large, deep punctures. When these beetles are threatened and release their defensive fluids, they tip their abdomen into the air as though they were doing a headstand. The adults are usually seen walking on the open sand, but they can also be found feeding on flowers. The larvae, like that of other blister beetles, prey on grasshopper eggs and feed on bee eggs and the food that bees store in their cells.

HABITAT
Open ground and flowers in desert areas
RANGE
Arizona and New Mexico
SIZE
0.4 to 0.6 inch (10 to 15 mm)
LIFE CYCLE
Holometabolous

DESERT DARKLING BEETLE / *Onymacris meridionalis*

Of all the beetle families, the Tenebrionidae (darkling beetles) are the best represented in the desert. Their common name comes from their nocturnal habits rather than their colors, although most species are black. Most feed on plant material. They usually have a compact body to minimize their surface area and they often have thick elytra that are fused in the back to reduce water evaporation. Some tene-brionid species in the genus *Onymacris* that live on sand dunes in the Namib Desert of southern Africa have long, spiny legs and long, curved claws that give them a good grip on the sand when they run. To make the most of the available moisture, they allow dew to collect on their body at night, then tilt their head down so that it runs toward their mouth for drinking.

HABITAT
Sand dunes and along dry river courses
RANGE
Southern Africa
SIZE
0.5 to 0.6 inch (12 to 15 mm)
LIFE CYCLE
Holometabolous

THISTLEDOWN VELVET ANT / *Dasymutilla gloriosa*

Most species of Mutillidae are velvet ants that live in arid areas. Both wingless females and winged males are densely covered with hair—hence their common name. The females have a curved stinger that is sometimes as long as their abdomen and they can deliver a very painful sting. *Dasymutilla gloriosa* is black and covered with long white hairs. It has an extremely high resistance to heat and can survive temperatures up to 130 degrees Fahrenheit (55°C). Even so, at times the males fly into vegetation or shade and the females climb on vegetation or into a burrow to cool off. The females spend a lot of time running along the ground searching for nests of sand wasps, where they lay their eggs. The parasitic larvae thrive by feeding on the larvae of the sand wasps.

HABITAT
Females on open sand in desert areas; males on sand and vegetation
RANGE
Southwestern United States and Mexico
SIZE
0.5 to 0.6 inch (13 to 16 mm)
LIFE CYCLE
Holometabolous

DESERT BURROWING COCKROACH / *Arenivaga investigata*

The desert burrowing cockroaches (family Polyphagidae) are active throughout the year, but they avoid water loss and extreme heat by spending almost their entire life buried about eight to twenty-four inches (20 to 60 cm) deep in the sand, where the temperature is lower and the humidity is higher. There, they feed on decaying leaves and also on the roots of desert shrubs, which are their main source of water. During spring, summer, and fall nights, they crawl up close to the surface, still staying about an inch (2.5 cm) deep in the sand; sometimes they come out and walk for a short distance before burrowing again. When digging just beneath ground level, they leave tiny tracks on the surface like tiny moles. Before they come out of the sand, they test the air by extending their antennae, which are equipped with sense organs that detect the level of humidity and the air temperature. During the winter, they stay deep in the sand both day and night.

HABITAT
Deep in desert sand
RANGE
California
SIZE
0.6 to 0.8 inch (15 to 20 mm)
LIFE CYCLE
Hemimetabolous

ANTLIONS / *Brachynemurus* spp.

Antlions (family Myrmeleontidae) live in arid regions around the world; some are particularly common in the desert. With their long, narrow body and four long, slender wings, the adults look much like damselflies, except that they have a smaller head and long, clubbed antennae. They are also much weaker fliers. The better-known larvae are large and hairy, with a small head and long, spiny mandibles. Sometimes called doodlebugs, the larvae are predators; they dig a cone-shaped pit in the sand and bury themselves at the bottom, where they wait for small insects to tumble in. The walls of the pit are so steep that the insects cannot escape; when they fall to the bottom, the antlions snap their mandibles shut over the prey. Antlions pupate in the sand in a cocoon made of silk and sand.

HABITAT
Larvae in open sand in deserts; adults in flight in open areas
RANGE
Genus *Brachynemurus* found in arid regions of North America, Africa, and Australia
SIZE
Body 1.8 inches (45 mm); wingspan 2.6 inches (65 mm)
LIFE CYCLE
Holometabolous

SPIDERS

DESERT TARANTULA / *Aphonopelma chalcodes*

Aphonopelma chalcodes (family Theraphosidae) is a large gray to dark-brown tarantula found in North America. The males are usually darker and slimmer than the females and stop molting when they reach maturity. The females continue to molt, in total about thirty to forty times, for the rest of their life, which can be up to twenty years. They lay many eggs—about 450 to 500 per egg sac. After the young hatch, they stay in the egg sac for more than a month for protection. Once they leave, they remain in the burrow for a short period before leaving to find their own burrow. A tarantula's bite is about as painful as a bee sting.

HABITAT
Open soil in desert regions
RANGE
Arizona, New Mexico, and southern California
SIZE
Females 2 to 2.8 inches (50 to 70 mm), leg span 4 inches (100 mm); males 2 to 2.6 inches (50-65 mm)

GIANT CRAB SPIDER / *Carparachne alba*

Members of the family Heteropodidae are commonly known as huntsman spiders, but the larger species are also called giant crab spiders. They are mainly tropical in distribution and live in habitats ranging from tropical rain forests to deserts. *Carparachne alba*, also known as dancing dune spiders, look very similar to the crab spiders in the family Thomisidae *(page 59)*, but they are larger. They hunt on the open sand of the Namib Desert; sometimes they will take on the larger web-footed dune gecko, a small lizard also native to that harsh region. The spiders sometimes point their legs forward so they can slip their somewhat flattened carapace under stones and into small cracks. Their legs are modified to dig rapidly in the sand.

HABITAT
Desert soil
RANGE
Namib Desert of southwest Africa
SIZE
0.8 to 1 inch (20 to 25 mm)

RESOURCE GUIDE

This handy reference guide contains information to help you develop a deeper understanding of insects and spiders. A selection of useful addresses and websites is listed on the page opposite, followed by an explanation of insect and spider taxonomy (pages 176 to 178) and a list of some of the world's endangered species (page 179). Finally, a glossary of terms can be found on pages 180 to 183.

International Directory

URLs Only

http://www.si.edu/
resource/faq/nmnh/
buginfo/start.htm
Fun bug facts from the
Smithsonian Institution

http://www.ento.vt.
edu/Courses/Under
graduate/IHS/Insects
onWWW/
Links to dozens of
insect-related sites

http://www.fws.gov/
r9endspp/endspp.html
U.S. Fish and Wildlife
Service Endangered
Species home page:
lists; news releases;
links; maps; programs;
FAQs; contacts

http://www.insecton
line.com/
Insectarium of Victoria;
Australian insect,
spider, invertebrates;
information; links

http://viceroy.eeb.
uconn.edu/ALAS/
ALAS.html
Project ALAS; tropical
studies; collections; information; publications

http://www.ufsia.ac.
be/Arachnology/
Arachnology.html
Directory of arachnologi-
cal information on the
web; links; publications;
discussion groups

http://www.bishop.
hawaii.org/bishop/
ento/codens-r-us.html
Insect and spider collec-
tions of the world;
information; links

http://www.naba.org.
North American Butterfly
Association (NABA)

http://gnv.ifas.ufl.edu/
~tjw/recbk.htm
University of Florida book
of insect records; champi-
ons; achievements

http://members.aol.
com/YESbugs/bugsclub.
html
Young Entomologist's
Society Inc.

ADDRESSES

**The Amateur
Entomologist's Society
(AES)**
P.O. Box 8774
London, UK
SW7 5ZG
aes@theaes.org
http://www.theaes.org/
welcome2.htm

**Canadian Museum
of Nature**
P.O. Box 3443
Station D, Ottawa
Ontario, Canada
K1P 6P4
http://www.nature.ca/
english/nhblinks.htm#
invert

**Connecticut Valley
Biological Supply Co.**
82 Valley Road
P.O. Box 326
Southampton
MA 01073
Tel: (413) 527-4030

**National Museum
of Natural History,
Smithsonian
Institution**
10th Street and
Constitution Avenue NW
Washington
DC 20560-0105
Tel: (202) 357-2078
webmaster@www.nmnh.s
i.edu.
http://www.nmnh.si.edu/
departments/entom.html

**The Natural
History Museum**
Cromwell Road
London, UK
SW7 5BD
Tel: +44 (0)20 7942 5000
insects@nhm.ac.uk
http://www.nhm.ac.uk/
entomology/

**Royal Entomological
Society of London**
41 Queen's Gate
London, UK
SW7 5HU
Tel: + 44 (0)71-584 8361

Xerces Society
(conservation society)
4828 SE Hawthorne Blvd.
Portland
OR 97215
Tel: (503) 232-6639

Wings for the Earth
(non-profit; supports
worldwide tropical
insect-rearing projects)
6341 Longcroft Dr.
Oakland
CA 94611
Tel: (510) 531-8959
Fax: (510) 531-6659

**World Conservation
Monitoring Centre**
219 Huntingdon Road
Cambridge, UK
CB3 0DL
Tel: +44 1223 277314;
Fax: +44 1223 277136.
info@wcmc.org.uk
http://www.wcmc.org.uk/

***Special note about
U.S. Department of
Agriculture's coopera-
tive extension service**
For information on insect
pests and pest manage-
ment, contact your local
university's cooperative
extension unit.

Species to Kingdom

Insects are classified using a system that dates back to the mid-eighteenth century. At that time, Carolus Linnaeus, known as "the father of taxonomy," introduced a structure of classification that used biological characteristics to reveal relationships in broader and broader groupings, from genera to order to class to kingdom. Later biologists added other ranks to express additional relationships based on various interpretations of evolution, so today a minimum of seven categories are generally recognized (box opposite, left). Linnaeus also was the first to consistently use a binomial system for naming species, employing one Latin word for genus and another for species— e.g. *Papilion machaon*, the Latin name for the swallowtail butterfly. A third word indicating subspecies is sometimes added, often referring to the

MAJOR ORDERS (pages 72 to 81)	SELECTED FAMILIES	KNOWN SPECIES
Odonata "Jaw-toothed flies"	Aeshnidae (Darners) Gomphidae (Gomphid dragonflies) Calopterygidae (Broad-winged damselflies)	5,500
Orthoptera "Straight wings"	Acrididae (Short-horned grasshoppers) Gryllidae (True crickets) Gryllotalpidae (Mole crickets)	20,500
Hemiptera "Half wings"	Corixidae (Water boatmen) Cimicidae (Bed bugs) Lygaeidae (Seed bugs)	40,000
Homoptera "Similar wings"	Cicadidae (Cicadas) Membracidae (Treehoppers) Aphididae (Aphids)	45,000
Diptera "Two wings"	Culicidae (Mosquitos) Simuliidae (Black flies) Chironomidae (Midges)	120,000
Coleoptera "Hard wings"	Lucanidae (Stag beetles) Cicindelidae (Tiger beetles) Carabidae (Ground beetles)	400,000
Lepidoptera "Scaly wings"	Danaidae (Milkweed butterflies) Saturniidae (Giant silkworm moths) Sesiidae (Clear-winged moths)	150,000
Hymenoptera "Membrane wings"	Tiphiidae (Tiphiid wasps) Formicidae (Ants) Apidae (Bees)	130,000

geographic location of distinct populations—e.g. *Papilio machaon aliaska*. Latin names may change as more is learned, but they do so less often than common names, which often vary from place to place. In the charts here, the English meaning of the names for insect orders indicates the importance taxonomists give to wings: The suffix "ptera" derives from the Greek word for wing, *pteron*.

Included in the charts here is the approximate number of known species by order. Only an estimated 5 to 20 percent of species have been formally classified and debate continues on how to organize them. In the system applied here, the swallowtail butterfly falls under Hexapoda ("six legs"), a class that includes insects and three non-insect orders. Other systems place insects in a class of their own, called Insecta.

There are at least twenty-five insect orders—again depending on the system used. In the system followed in

this book, Hemiptera *(page 74)* is a separate order from Homoptera *(page 74)* and Mallophaga (chewing lice) and Anoplura (sucking lice) are grouped together under Phthiraptera *(page 70)*. Regardless of the system used, the swallowtail butterfly is always placed in the order Lepidoptera.

SELECTED MINOR ORDERS *(page 82)*	KNOWN SPECIES
Ephemeroptera "Living for one day"	2,100
Phasmatodea "Like a ghost"	2,500
Grylloblattodea "Crickets that avoid light"	10
Dermaptera "Leathery wings"	1,800
Isoptera "Equal wings"	2,300
Blattodea "Avoiding light"	3,700
Mantodea "Like a prophet"	1,800
Plecoptera "Wickerwork wings"	2,000
Embiidina "Web spinners"	150
Thysanoptera "Fringed wings"	5,000
Anoplura "Like a ghost"	250
Phthiraptera "Lice without wings"	3,000
Neuroptera "Nerve wings"	5,000
Megaloptera "Ample wings"	180
Trichoptera "Hairy wings"	10,000
Mecoptera "Long wings"	400

OLD WORLD SWALLOWTAIL

Kingdom: Animalia
Phylum: Arthropoda
Class: Hexapoda
Order: Lepidoptera
Family: Papilionidae
Genus: *Papilio*
Species: *Papilio machaon*

Spider Traits

The spider order Aranea is the most prominent subdivision of the class Arachnida—creatures possessing four pairs of walking legs. This main order is divided into three suborders: Araneomorphae, Mygalomorphae, and Mesothelae. Araneomorphae, or "true spiders," make up the vast majority of known spider species. The most prominent trait separating Araneomorphae from the other two suborders is the orientation of the jawlike chelicerae. The jaws of the Mygalomorphae and Mesothelae suborders strike forward and down when attacking, while those

> **FOREST WOLF SPIDER**
>
> **Kingdom:** Animalia
> **Phylum:** Arthropoda
> **Class:** Arachnida
> **Order:** Aranea
> **Suborder:** Araneomorphae
> **Family:** Lycosidae
> **Genus:** *Gladicosa*
> **Species:** *Gladicosa gulosa*

of the Araneomorphae open from side to side, giving the jaws of these true spiders a greater span. The Mesolathae have the additional distinction of a segmented abdomen—like that of insects.

ORDER: ARANEAE

SUBORDER	SELECTED FAMILIES (of 90)	KNOWN SPECIES
Araneomorphae (true spiders)	Araneidae (orb weavers), Salticidae (jumping spiders), Lycosidae (wolf spiders), Pisauridae (nursery-web or fishing spiders), Linyphiidae (sheet-web weavers), Agelenidae (funnel-web spiders), Theridiidae (cobweb weavers), Thomisidae (crab spiders), Sicariidae (violin spiders), Scytodidae (spitting spiders), Dictynidae (dictynid spiders), Oxyopidae (lynx spiders), Ctenidae (wandering spiders), Clubionidae (sac spiders)	32,000

SUBORDER	SELECTED FAMILIES (of 15)	KNOWN SPECIES
Mygalomorphae (primitive spiders)	Theraphosidae (tarantulas), Dipluridae (funnel-web tarantulas), Ctenizidae (trapdoor spiders), Antrodiaetidae (folding trapdoor spiders)	3,000

SUBORDER	FAMILY (1)	KNOWN SPECIES
Mesothelae (segmented spiders)	Liphistiidae (segmented spiders)	40

Situation Critical

Below is a selection of the World Conservation Monitoring Center's list of threatened insect species. These insects are critically endangered (facing extremely high risk of extinction in the wild in the immediate future). While no arachnid species are listed as critical, the U.S. Kauai Cave wolf spider (*Adelocosa anops*) is endangered (facing very high risk of extinction in the near future.)

CRITICALLY ENDANGERED INSECT SPECIES (by order)		DISTRIBUTION
ODONATA	*Argiocnemis solitaria*	Mauritius
	Austrocordulia leonardi	Australia
	Boninagrion ezoin	Japan
	Boninthemis insularis	Japan
	Brachythemis liberiensis	Guinea-Bissau
	Burmagomphus sivalikensis	India
	Chlorogomphus brunneus keramensis	Japan
	Frey's damselfly (*Coenagrion hylas freyi*)	Austria, Germany, Switzerland
	Indolestes boninensis	Japan
	Libellula angelina	Japan
	Mecistogaster pronoti	Brazil
	Palpopleura albifrons	Gabon
	Pele damselfly (*Megalagrion amaurodytum peles*)	United States
	Platycnemis mauriciana	Mauritius
	Rhinocypha ogasawarensis	Japan
	Seychellibasis alluaudi alluaudi	Seychelles
	Trithemis nigra	Sao Tome, Principe
ORTHOPTERA	*Hemisaga elongata*	Australia
	Ixalodectes flectocercus	Australia
	Middlekauf's shieldback katydid (*Idiostatus middlekaufi*)	United States
	Nanodectes bulbicercus	Australia
	Pachysaga strobila	Australia
	Santa Monica shieldback katydid (*Neduba longipennis*)	United States
	Schayera baiulus	Australia
	Torreya pygmy grasshopper (*Tettigidea empedonepia*)	United States
COLEOPTERA	American burying beetle (*Nicrophorus americanus*)	United States (extinct in Canada)
	Colophon berrisfordi, C. cassoni, C. montisatris, C. primosi	South Africa
	Cromwell chafer (*Prodontria lewisi*)	New Zealand
	Delta green ground beetle (*Elaphrus viridis*)	United States
	Frigate Island giant tenebrionid beetle (*Polposipus herculeanus*)	Seychelles
	Hydrotarsus compunctus	Spain
	Meladema imbricata	Spain
LEPIDOPTERA	*Chrysoritis cotrelli*	South Africa
	David's tiger (*Parantica davidi*)	Philippines
	Lepidochrysops lotana	South Africa
	Natterer's longwing (*Heliconius nattereri*)	Brazil
	Piedmont anomalous blue (*Polyommatus humedasae*)	Italy
	Prairie sphinx moth (*Euproserpinus wiesti*)	United States
	Sri Lankan rose (*Atrophaneura jophon*)	Sri Lanka
HYMENOPTERA	*Adetomyrma venatrix*	Madagascar
	Australian ant (*Nothomyrmecia macrops*)	Australia
	Sri Lankan relict ant (*Aneuretus simoni*)	Sri Lanka

Glossary

Ametabolous:
Development with no metamorphosis; eggs hatch into larvae resembling small adults with undeveloped gonads. Larval size increases with each molt.

Apterygote: "Wingless insects," literally. Insects that have never developed wings during their evolutionary history.

Arachnology: A branch of zoology that deals with the study of spiders, scorpions, mites, and ticks.

Bees' honey: Nectar that has been chemically modified in the queen's crop, then regurgitated.

Biological altruism: Behavior seemingly costly to the individual, but beneficial to its group.

Bioluminescence: Organism-produced cold light.

Bridal gift (nuptial gift): A gift, typically food, offered by the male of a usually sexually dimorphic insect species to secure the female's willingness to mate.

Castes: Morphologically and behaviorally distinct groups within a single species of social insect (e.g. workers, drones).

Cerci (sing. **cercus**): Paired appendages that spring from the tip of the abdomen in many arthropods. They probably have a sensory purpose.

Chelicera (plur. chelicerae): The fangs of arachnids; the pair of anterior head appendages of subphylum chelicerata.

Chitin: Tough, thick, horny material made up of polysaccharides that forms the main component of the exoskeleton or cuticle.

Chromosome: A linear assemblage of DNA making up a portion of an organism's genes.

Chrysalis: The pupa of a butterfly.

Class: A taxonomic division between the phylum and order (e.g. class Insecta).

Cocoon: Protective covering of a resting or developmental arthropod stage, made partially or completely of silk. In moths, the cocoon is made by the larva before it pupates.

Coevolution: The evolutionary interactions between two species, e.g. plants and pollinators, hosts and parasites.

Coleopterans: insects in the order Coleoptera: beetles.

Compound eye: An insect eye that is divided into smaller eyes, or ommatidia, each with its own lens.

Cornicles: Pair of small tubular outgrowths on the hind end of the aphid abdomen that release defensive secretions, especially alarm pheromones.

Cuticle: An inert material of chitin and protein that makes up the exoskeleton and is secreted by the epidermis. It comprises several differentiated layers.

Diapause: A period of suspended development in the life of many insects, in which an insect is highly resistant to unfavorable external conditions.

Diploid: With two sets of chromosomes.

Dipterans: Insects in the order Diptera: flies.

Diurnal: Active during the day.

Drone: Male bees, especially honeybees and bumblebees, born of unfertilized eggs; one of the caste groups of social insects.

Egg sac: A silk bag or blanketlike covering spun by some spiders around their eggs.

Elytra (sing. **elytrum**): The tough, horny forewings of a beetle or earwig that protect the hindwings.

Entomology: A branch of zoology that deals with the study of insects.

Epidermis: A layer of cells that secretes the cuticle.

Eusocial: Insects that exhibit cooperation in division of labor and reproduction, with an overlap of generations.

Exoskeleton: An insect's hardened outer cuticle, or protective shell, to which muscles are attached internally.

Family: A taxonomic subdivision of an order, suborder, or superfamily; it contains a group of related subfamilies, tribes, and genera. In the animal family, names always end in "idae" (e.g. family Salticidae).

Frenulum: The single bristle or group of bristles found on the leading edge of the hindwing of moths and some butterflies, enabling the fore- and hindwings to operate together in flight.

Furcula: A forked spring at the tip of springtails' abdomens; allows them to jump.

Ganglia (sing. **ganglion**): Small nerve centers, made up of pairs of bodies linked by nerve cords.

Genus (plur. **genera**): A taxonomic division between family and species; a grouping of one or more species believed to be of a single evolutionary origin.

Genome: The entire genetic information of an organism encoded in its cells.

Halteres: Pair of modified, club-shaped hindwings in Diptera, acting as balancers.

Haploid: With one set of chromosomes.

Hemelytra: Forewings of Hemiptera, with thickened basal section and membranous apex.

Hemimetabolous: Incomplete metamorphosis with no pupal stage. Egg hatches into a larva (or nymph) that resembles adult in looks and lifestyle. Wing buds enlarge with each molt.

Hemipterans: Insects in the order Hemiptera: true bugs.

Hemolymph: Fluid in some invertebrate bodies, akin to blood and lymph, that transports nutrients, hormones, and wastes.

Holometabolous: Complete metamorphosis; egg develops through larval and pupal stages, which are distinct from adult.

Homopterans: Insects in the order Homoptera: aphids, cicadas, and hoppers.

Honeydew: The sugary liquid emitted from the anus of Homoptera, especially aphids.

Hormone: A chemical messenger that regulates some body activity at a distance from the endocrine organ that produced it.

Hymenopterans: Insects in the order Hymenoptera: bees, ants, and wasps.

Instar: The stage in an insect's life history between any two molts. The adult (imago) is the final instar.

Larva: An immature insect after emerging from the egg. Larvae look and act markedly different from the adults. Term often restricted for holometabolous groups.

Lepidopterans: Insects in the order Lepidoptera: moths and butterflies.

Malpighian tubules: Thin, blind-ended tubules originating from the gut; involved in regulation of salt, water, and nitrogenous waste excretion.

Maggot: A legless larval insect, frequently a fly.

Mandibles: The front jaws of an insect; they vary in shape and usage, depending on the species.

Maxillae: The secondary pair of jaws of an insect.

Metamorphosis: The change in body form between end of immature development and onset of adult phase.

Molting: Developing a new cuticle, then shedding the old one.

Naiad: The immature, gill-bearing form of an aquatic hemimetabolous insect.

Nocturnal: Active during the night.

Nymph: The immature, growing form of a terrestrial hemimetabolous insect.

Ocelli (sing. **ocellus**): Simple eyes of adult and nymphal insects, and some holometabolous larvae.

Odonatans: Insects in the order Odonata: dragonflies and damselflies.

Ommatidium (plur. **ommatidia**): A single element of the compound eye.

Orthopterans: Insects in the order Orthoptera: grasshoppers, katydids, and crickets.

Overwinter: To spend an extended period of time in suspended developmental and physiological animation, awaiting the passage of harsh environmental conditions.

Ovipositor: A tubular or valved structure at the posterior end of the abdomen of many female insects, used for laying eggs.

Palp: Fingerlike, usually segmented appendage of the secondary pair of jaws (maxillae) and lower lip (labium).

Parasite: An organism that lives at the expense of another, but does not usually kill it.

Parasitoid: A parasite, usually of the same taxonomic class, that lives at the expense of another and eventually kills it.

Parthenogenesis: Development from an unfertilized egg; common in social insects and aphids.

Pheromone: A hormone that when released in small amounts causes a specific behavioral or physiological reaction within individuals of the same species. Pheromones play a role in courtship, communicating alarm, and trail-marking.

Phylum: A major division of all living things, containing various orders, suborders, classes, etc. (e.g. phylum Arthropoda).

Pollinator: An organism that transfers pollen from male to female flower parts.

Proboscis: Elongated mouthparts.

Pronotum: Thick plates of cuticle on the dorsal surface of the first thoracic segment. Sometimes it covers the entire thorax.

Pterygote: "Wing bearers," literally. Winged insects that eventually replaced wingless apterygotes.

Pupa (plur. pupae): Non-feeding and usually inactive post-larval form of holometabolous insects. Also called a chrysalis in butterflies.

Pupal stage: The third stage in the life history of a holometabolous insect.

Raptorial forelegs: Spiny limbs, found on praying mantids and other predatory insects, used to help grasp and impale prey.

Royal jelly: Fortified bees' milk secreted by glands in the worker's head. Used to feed larvae during the first few days after hatching.

Sensillum: A sense organ; it can be simple and isolated or part of a more complex organ.

Seta (plur. setae): A hairlike sensillum.

Sexual dimorphism: The occurrence of two distinct forms, sizes, colors, etc., for the male and female of the same species.

Social: Insects living together in organized colonies, with varying degrees of interaction. See also *Eusocial*.

Species: Group of individuals that can interbreed and produce fertile offspring; members of the same species share similar appearance, behavior, and common evolutionary history.

Spermatheca: The female insect's sperm receptacle.

Spinneret: A spider's silk-producing organ, located near the tip of the abdomen.

Spiracles: Sphincterlike openings of the Arthropod tracheal system found on the thorax and abdomen, through which diffusion of gases and water occurs.

Stridulation: The production of sound by rubbing two ridged or rough body parts together. Notable in grasshoppers and other orthopterans.

Taxonomy: The scientific classification and naming system used for animals and plants.

Terminalia: The terminal abdominal segments involved in the formation of insect genitalia.

Venation: Pattern of veins on insect wings; varies among species and is used as identification tool, especially for butterflies.

Workers: In social insects, a member of the sterile caste born from fertilized eggs; performs the work of the colony and assists the reproductive insects.

Index

Text references are in plain type; illustrations in *italic*; photographs in **bold**; insect and spider biographies in **bold** with asterisk (*).

The common names of insects and spiders are listed under major groups.

A

Acanthomyops interjectus, 147*
Acrididae, 176
Acripela reticulata, 73
Acrocinus longimanus, 20, 98*
Acrosternum hilare, 74
Actias luna, 40, 114*
adaptation, 32-33
addresses, 175
Aeshnidae, 176
Africanized bees, 81, *81*
Agaonidae, 100*
Agelena republicana, 57
Agelenidae, 178
Alaptus magnanimus, 9
Alaus oculatus, 118*
alcoholism, studies of, using fruit flies, 51
alderflies (Megaloptera), 83, 177
Allocapnia pygmea, 138*
altruism, biological, 43, 180
Amaurobius ferox, 65
Amaurobius similis, 65
ametabolous life cycle, *24,* 25, 180
Amitermes meridionalis, 45, 158*
Anaphes flavipes, 122*
Anastrepha fraterculus, 93*
anatomy
  insects, 10-23, *12*
  spiders, *54,* 54-56
Anax junius, 109*
Anelosimus eximius, 57
Anopheles freeborni, 93*
Anoplura, 177
ant farms, 180
antennae, 22-23, 22-23, *22-23*
  chemoreceptors on, 40, *40*
  Johnston's organ, 22, 23
Antheraea polyphemus, 22-23, 26
Anthonomus grandis (boll weevil), 41, 48, 77
Anthrax analis, 152*
Anthrobia mammouthia, 55
antlions, 35, 83, 172*
Antrodiaetidae, 178
ants
  antennae, 23, *23*
  caste system, 42, 80
  communication, 43
  family Formicidae, 176
  mass battles, 80
  metamorphosis, 25
  order Hymenoptera, 70, 71, 80-81, 176, 179, 182
  pheromones, 41
  strength, 10
  stridulating, 39
ant(s)
  Amazon, 42
  army, 42, 100*
  black carpenter, 122*
  Formica yessensis, 45
  honey pot, 43
  large yellow, 147*
  leafcutter, 39, 101*
  Pseudomyrmex ferruginea, 33, *33*
  red, *81*
  red imported fire, 157*
  thistledown velvet, 171*
aphid, rosy apple, *74*
Aphididae, 143*, 176
aphids
  cornicles, 180
  family Aphididae, 143*, 176
  honeydew, 181
  order Homoptera, 70, 71, 74-75, 176, 181
  parthenogenesis, 27, 182
  pheromone glands, 39
Aphonopelma chalcodes, 84, 173*
Apidae, 176
Apis mellifera. See honeybees
apterygotes, 10, 180
Arachnida, 8, 54
arachnology, 180
Araneae, 178
Araneidae, 178
araneomorph spiders, *55, 58,* 178
Araneomorphae, 178
Araneus diadematus (garden spider), 56, 63, 126*
Arenivaga investigata, 172*
Argia violacea, 72
Argiope argentata, 58, 107*
Argiope aurantia, 84
Argiope trifasciata, 148*
Argyroneta aquatica, 59, 62-63
arid lands insects, 149, *149,* 150-159*
arid lands spiders, 149, 160-161*
Arthropoda, 8
Ascalaphidae, 159*

Atrax robustus, 85, 107*
Atta cephalotes, 39, 101*
Attacus atlas, 94*
Automeris io, 17

B

ballooning in spiders, 62-63, 65
bees
  antennae, 23
  bumblebee nests, 45
  caste system, 42
  color vision, 21
  family Apidae, 176
  flight, 16
  metamorphosis, 25
  nests, 45
  order Hymenoptera, 70, 71, 80-81, 176, 182
bee(s)
  golden northern bumblebee, *80*
  killer (Africanized), 81, *81*
  orchid, 101*
  polar bumblebee, 166*
  stingless, 41, 102*
  See also honeybees
bees' honey, 180
beetles
  antennae, *22*
  order Coleoptera, 71, 76-77, 176, 179, 180
  stridulating, 39
  subsocial organization, 42
beetle(s)
  African goliath, 96*
  Australian stag, 97*
  black oak acorn weevil, *76,* 116*
  bluegrass billbug weevil, 147*
  boll weevil, 41, 48, 77
  bombardier, 35
  bruchid, 32
  burying, 133*
  carrion, 77
  cereal-leaf, 122
  click, *22,* 118*
  Colorado potato, 25, 47-48
  convergent lady, 116*
  darkling, 77, 171*
  dermestid, 30
  desert blister, 170*
  desert darkling, 171*
  diving, *18,* 19, 155*
  dung, 48, 77
  elder borer, 117*
  elm bark, 77
  European caterpillar hunter, 117*

European stag, *76*, 118*
eyed click, 118*
fire-colored, *23*
flat-headed tree borer, 134*
flower, 29
giant metallic wood-boring, 97*
giant tiger, 154*
golden buprestid, 134*
ground, 176
harlequin, 20, 98*
hercules, 98*
hister, 30
horned fungus, 119*
horned passalus, 39
June, 77, 119*
ladybird, 14-15, 49, 77
longhorn, 32
marble diving, 155*
Melanophila spp., 19
metallic leaf chafer, 99*
northeastern sawyer, 135*
red milkweed, 120*
red turpentine, 135*
rove, 30
sacred scarab, 155*
six-spotted tiger, *9*, 77, 121*
stag, *76*, 77, 97*, 118*, 176
striped chafer, 149
ten-lined, 149
tiger, *9*, *13*, 35, 44, 76, *76*, *77*, 121*, 154*, 176
tortoise, 76, 99*
tumblebug, 156*
weevils, 41, 48, *76*, 77, 116*, 147*
whirligig, 19, 77
wrinkled bark, *22*
benefits of insects, 46, 46-47, 47, 50-51
Bibio spp., 28-29
bioluminescence, 38, 180
  mimicry of, 37
biomes, 86-87, *86-87*
  arid lands insects and spiders, 149, 149, 150-161*
  desert insects and spiders, 168, 168-173*
  grassland and meadow insects and spiders, 140, 140, 141-148*
  rain forest insects and spiders, 88, 88, 89-107*
  taiga insects and spiders, 128, *128*, 129-139*
  tundra insects and spiders, 162, 162-167*
  woodland and forest insects and spiders, 108, 108, 109-127*
Bittacus stigmateus, 125*
Blattodea, 82, 177

identification chart, 70, 71
Blissus leucopterus, 47
Bolitotherus cornutus, 119*
Bombus fervidus, *80*
Bombus polaris, 166*
Bombyx mori, 25
book lungs, *54*, 55
Borrelia burgdorferi, 69
Bothriocyrtum californicum, 160*
Brachinus spp., 35
Brachynemurus spp. (antlions), 35, 83, 172*
brain
  insects, *12*, 13
  spiders, *54*
bridal gift, 180
bug(s)
  ambush, 84
  backswimmers, 74
  bed, 176
  chinch, 47
  fulgorid lantern, 37, 38
  giant mesquite, 168*
  giant water, 24, 32, 111*
  green stink, *74*
  kissing, 152*
  oak lace, 32
  scarlet plant, 142*
  seed, 176
  shield, 35
  stilt, 143*
  toad, 90*
  water boatmen, 74, 176
  water strider, 19, 74
bugs, true
  metamorphosis, 25
  order Hemiptera, 71, 74, 176, 181
  stridulating, 39
burrows, spider, 62
butterflies
  color vision, 21
  flight, 16
  metamorphosis, 25, 78-79
  order Lepidoptera, 70, 78-79, 176, 179, 182
  pheromones, 39-40
  proboscis, *13*
  subsocial organization, 42
butterfly(ies)
  citrus swallowtail, 36
  common alpine, 129*
  cranberry blue, 164*
  Dakota skipper, 140, 146*
  dark-winged arctic, 17
  European cabbage white, 78
  gossamer-winged, 32
  gray pansy, 46
  great spangled fritillary, 78, 114*
  greenland sulphur, 165*

hackberry, 59
hairstreak, 37
milkweed, 176
monarch, 14, 33, 34, 34, 36-37, 78
morpho, 95*
mourning cloak, 115*
northern cloudy-wing skipper, 131*
Old World swallowtail, *9*, *78*, 132*, 177
painted lady, 115*
phoebus parnassian, 165*
Priam's birdwing, 95*
queen, 40, 41
Queen Alexandra birdwing, 95
South American morpho, 17, 17
spring azure, 132*
sulphur, 79
swallowtails, *9*, 27, 36, *78*, 132*, 177
viceroy, 36-37
western white, 146*
Wright's metalmark, 170*
Yukon blue, 164
zebra, 96*

C

caddisflies
  metamorphosis, 25, *26*
  order Trichoptera, 71, 83, 177
  shelter, 44
caddisfly, ash-winged large, 138*
Calephelis wrighti, 170*
Calopterygidae, 176
Calopteryx sp., 29
  See also damselflies
Calosoma sycophanta, 117*
camouflage
  in insects, 36, 36-37, 37
  in spiders, 59
Campylenchia latipes, 75
cannibalism in spiders, 65
Canthon spp., 156*
Carabidae, 176
Carparachne alba, 173*
caste systems, 42-43, 80, 180
catching insects and spiders, 68-69
Catocala amatrix, 37
Celestrina ladon, 132*
centipedes, 8
cerci, 180
Cetonia polyphema, 29
Chaeradodis rhombicollis, 105*
Chaoborus genus, 23
chelicerae, *54*, *58*, 180
chemoreceptors, 40, 40
Chetogena gelida, 163*
chiggers, 31

Chilopoda, 8
Chironomidae, 130*, 176
chitin, 11, 180
Choristoneura fumiferana, 133*
chromosomes, 180
chrysalis, 79, 180
Chrysobothris spp., 134*
Chrysops callidus, 112*
cicadas
    family Cicadidae, 91*, 176
    molting, 27
    order Homoptera, 70, 71,
        74-75, 176, 181
    stridulating, 39, 74-75, 91
cicada(s)
    Periodical, 75, *75*, 112*
    Tacua speciosa, 91
Cicadidae, 91*, 176
Cicindela sexguttata, 9, 77, 121*
Cicindelidae, 176
Cimicidae, 176
circulatory system, *12*
class, 8, 180
classification. *See* taxonomy
classifications, social, 42-43
Climaciella brunnea, 124*
Clubionidae, 178
cockroach
    desert burrowing, 172*
    Madagascar hissing, 104*
    striped desert, 158*
cockroaches
    antennae, 23
    dispersal of, 33
    metamorphosis, 25
    order Blattodea, 70, 71,
        82, 177
    as pests, 48
cocoons, 25, 79, 180
coevolution, 33, *33*, 180
Coleoptera, 76-77, 176, 180
    endangered insects, 179
    identification chart, 71
Colias hecla, 165*
Collembola, 82
    identification chart, 70
communication, 38-41, 43
Companotus pennsylvanicus,
    122*
control methods, 49
Corixidae (water boatmen),
    74, 176
cornicles, 180
Corydalus cornutus, 125*
Corythuca arcuata, 32
courtship
    bridal gift, 180
    in insects, 17, 28, 28-29,
        29, 38
    in spiders, 57, *64*, 64-65,
        65, 65
crickets

antennae, 23
metamorphosis, 25, 73
order Orthoptera, 70, 71, 73,
    176, 179, 182
stridulating, 39, 73
cricket(s)
    European mole, 110*
    Jerusalem, 150*
    mole, 19, 39, 44, 176
    northern mole, *73*
    prairie mole, 44, 140, 142*
    stone, 37
    tree, 24
    true, 176
crop, *12*
Ctenidae, 178
Ctenizidae, 178
Culicidae, 93, 176
Curculio rectus, 76, 116*
cuticle, 11, 13, 180
cuticular lens, *21*
Cypriacis aurulenta, 134*
Cysteodemus wislizeni, 170*

D

Dactylotum bicolor, 151*
daddy longlegs, 54
damselflies
    eyes, 21
    mating, 29, *29*, 72
    order Odonata, 71, 72-73,
        176, 179, 182
    sperm displacement, 29
damselfly(ies)
    broad-winged, 176
    helicopter, 89*
    narrow-winged, 21
    violet-tail, *72*
Danaidae, 176
Danaus gilippus (queen
    butterfly), 40, 41
Danaus plexippus (monarch
    butterfly), 14, 33, 34, 34,
    36-37, 78
Dasymutilla gloriosa, 171*
defensive tactics, 35
    toxic sprays, 35, 77
    See also camouflage; mimicry;
        pheromones
Deinopis longipes, 106*
Deinopis spinosa, 55
Dendroctonus valens, 135*
Dermaptera, 82, 103*, 176
    identification chart, 71
Dermatobia hominis, 92*
desert insects, 168, 168-172*
desert spiders, 168, 173*
Desmocerus palliatus, 117*
Desmonota variolosa, 99*
Desmozosteria cincta, 158*
diapause, 27, 180
Diapheromera femorata, 123*

Dichonia aprilina, 36
Dictynidae, 178
digestion, 12-13
diploid, 181
Diplopoda, 8
Dipluridae, 178
Diptera, 75, 176, 181
    identification chart, 70
disease carriers, 47, 47-49,
    48, 49
Dissosteira carolina, 141*
diurnal, 181
dobsonfly, eastern, 125*
Dolomedes tenebrosus, 139*
dragonflies
    antennae, *22*, 23
    communication through
        color, 38
    eggs, 24
    eyes, 20, 72
    family Gomphidae, 176
    flight, 16
    mating, 29, 72
    metamorphosis, 25, *26*
    order Odonata, 71, 72, 176,
        179, 182
    rectal pumps, 12
    speed, *16*
    sperm displacement, 29
dragonfly(ies)
    darners, 176
    green darner, 109*
    white-tailed skimmer,
        72, 109*
drones, 26, 42, 181
Drosophila melanogaster
    (fruit fly)
    adaptation in, 33
    and genetic research, 46, 50,
        50-51, *51*
Dynastes hercules, 98*
Dysaphis plantaginea, 74

E

earwigs
    order Dermaptera, 71, 82,
        103*, 176
    subsocial organization, 42
earwig(s)
    rain-forest, 103*
Eciton hamatum (army ant),
    42, 100*
egg laying, 24-27, *25*
egg sacs, *62*, 181
elimination, 12-13
elytra, 14-15, 181
Embiidina, 83, 177
Empis spp., 28
endangered insects, 179
entomology, 181
entomology, forensic, 30-31
Ephemeroptera, 82, 176

identification chart, 71
Ephydra buresi, 9
epidermis, 181
epigynum, *54*, 55, 57
equipment for catching insects
    and spiders, 68
Erebia epipsodea, 129*
Erigone spp., 167*
Euchroma gigantea, 97*
Euglossa spp., 101*
Eupeodes americanus, 145*
Eurycnema goliath, 102*
eusocial insects, 42-43, 181
evolution, 10
Exoprosopa spp., 75
exoskeleton, 11, 181
eyes (insects), 10-11, 20, 20-21,
    21, *21*
    compound eye, *21*, 180
    ocelli, 10, 20, 182
    ommatidia, 20, *21*, 182
    vision, 20-21, 73
eyes (spiders), 55

F

Fabre, Jean-Henri, 10
fairyfly, 122*
families, 181
    of insects, 176, 177
    of spiders, 178
feeding, 32, 32-35, 33
fireflies
    and bioluminescence,
        37-38
    lampyrid, and
        bioluminencence
        mimicry, 37
firefly(ies)
    pyralis, 38, 120*
    Southeast Asian, 38
fleas
    antennae, 23
    as disease carriers, 48, 48
    dispersal of, 33
    legs, 18
    metamorphosis, 25
    wings, lack of, 17
flea(s)
    rat, 48, 49
    snow, 137*
flies
    antennae, *23*
    bioluminescence, 38
    as disease carriers, 48, 48
    flight, 16-17
    foot pads, 18
    maggots, 182
    maggots and forensic
        entomology, 31
    metamorphosis, 25
    order Diptera, 70, 75, 176,
       181

proboscis, *13*
flight, *15, 16*
    See also wings
fly(ies)
    American hover, 145*
    arctic black, 163*
    arctic tachinid, 163*
    bee, 152*
    big-headed, 145*
    black, 86, 129*, 176
    blow, 20, 30, 31
    bluebottle, 75
    brine, 9
    callidus deer, 112*
    craneflies, 75, 130*
    dance, 28
    Delhi sands flower-loving,
       169*
    fruit *(Drosophila
       melanogaster)*, 33, 46,
       50, 50-51, 51
    giant robber, 153*
    Hessian, 47
    horse, *16*, 131*
    house, 19, *19*, 21, *23*
    human botfly, 92*
    March, 28-29
    parasitic, 39
    progressive bee, 75
    robber, 35, 36, 75
    screw-worm, 49
    shore, 9
    South American fruit, 93*
    syrphid, 36
    tsetse, 48
    See also mosquitos
forensic entomology, 30-31
forest and woodland insects,
    108, 108, 109-125*
forest and woodland spiders,
    108, 126-127*
Formica spp., *81*
Formica yessensis, 45
Formicidae, 176
Frankliniella occidentalis, 159*
frass, 79
frenulum, 181
Frisch, Karl von, 41
Fulgora laternaria (fulgorid
    lantern bug), 37, 38
Fulgoridae, 91
furcula, 181

G

ganglia, *12*, 13, 181
Gelastocridae, 90*
genome, 181
genus, 181
Geolycosa turricola, 160*
Gladicosa gulosa, 127*
glossary, 180-183
Gnaphosidae, 167*

Goliathus goliatus, 96*
Gomphidae, 176
Graphocephala coccinea, 144*
Graphosidae, 167*
Graphosoma italicum, 35
grasshoppers
    flight, 16
    labium, *13*
    legs, 18
    maxillae, *13*
    metamorphosis, *26*, 73
    order Orthoptera, 70, 71, 73,
       176, 179, 182
    stridulating, 39, 73
grasshopper(s)
    arctic, 162*
    Carolina, 141*
    Leichardt's, 151*
    long-horned, 73
    mountain, 73
    painted, 151*
    pyrgomorph, 89*
    short-horned, 28, 73, 176
grassland and meadow insects,
    140, 140, 141-147*
grassland and meadow spiders,
    140, 148*
Gromphadorina portentosa, 104*
Gryllidae, 176
Grylloblatta spp., 166*
Grylloblattodea, 82, 177
    identification chart, 70
Gryllotalpa gryllotalpa, 110*
Gryllotalpa hexadactyla, 73
Gryllotalpa spp. (mole crickets),
    19, 39, 44, 176
Gryllotalpidae, 176
Gymnopais holopticus, 163*
Gynaephora groenlandica, 164*

H

habitats of individual insects,
    89-105, 109-125, 129-138,
    141-147, 150-159, 162-166,
    168-172
habitats of individual spiders,
    106-107, 126-127, 139, 148,
    160-161, 167, 173
halteres, 16-17, 181
hangingflies, 41
hangingfly, 125*
haploid, 181
Harpobittacus sp.
    See scorpionflies
harvestmen (daddy longlegs), 54
Helaeopmyia petrolia, 9
Heliconius charitonius, 96*
hemelytra, 181
hemimetabolous life cycle,
    24, 25, 181
Hemiptera, 74, 176, 181
    identification chart, 71

hemolymph, 181
Hesperia dacotae, 140, 146*
Heteronotus glandiguler, 92*
Hexagenia limbata, 123*
Hexapoda, 8
highest-altitude land animal, 63
Hippodamia convergens, 116*
holometabolous life cycle, 24, 25-26, 181
Homoptera, 74-75, 176, 181
   honeydew, 181
   identification chart, 70, 71
honeybees
   bees' honey, 180
   caste system, 26-27, 42-43, 180
   dance, 41, 41, 43
   hive, 45
   legs, 19
   pheromones, 41
   royal jelly, 26, 183
   sex differentiation, 26-27
   speed, 16
honeydew, 181
hoppers, 74-75
   See also treehoppers
hormones, 182
hornet, bald-faced, 45
horntail, blue, 136*
Hyalophora cecropia, 40-41, 79, 113*
Hymenoptera, 80-81, 176, 182
   endangered insects, 179
   identification chart, 70, 71
Hypogastrura nivicola, 137*

I-J

identification chart, 70-71
imago, 182
infrared-wavelength detecting legs, 19
insecticides, 49
instar stage, 27, 182
Internet URLs, 175
Isoptera, 82, 177
   identification chart, 70, 71
Ixodes dammini, 69
Ixodes pacificus, 69
Ixodes ricinus, 69
Jalysus spp., 143*
Johnston's organ, 22, 23

K

katydids
   legs, 19
   order Orthoptera, 70, 71, 73, 176, 179, 182
   sound perception, 19
   stridulating, 39
katydid(s)
   broad-winged, 110*
   gladiator, 141*

rain-forest, 90*
killer bees, 81, 81

L

labium, 13
labrum, 13
lacewings, 25, 83
   green, 140
ladybugs, 33
   See also beetle(s)
lanternfly, 91
larvae, 25-26, 182
Laternaria phosporea, 91*
Latrodectus hasselti, 65
Latrodectus mactans, 85
leaf insect, 103*
leaf insects
   order Phasmatodea, 70, 71, 82, 177
leafhopper, scarlet and green, 144*
leafhoppers, 58-59
legs, 18, 18-19, 19, 19
   raptorial forelegs, 183
Lepidoptera, 78-79, 176, 182
   endangered insects, 179
   identification chart, 70
Leptinotarsa decemlineata, 25, 47-48
Lethocerus americanus (giant water bug), 24, 32, 111*
Leucauge venusta, 127*
lice
   as disease carriers, 48
   dispersal of, 33
   wings, lack of, 14
life cycles, 24, 24-27, 26
   See also metamorphosis
life cycles of individual insects, 89-105, 109-125, 129-138, 141-147, 150-159, 162-166, 168-172
life span of spiders, 57
Limenitis archippus, 36-37
Linnaeus, Carolus, 9, 176
Linyphiidae, 178
Liphistiidae, 178
locusts
   eyes, 20
   gliding, 16
locust(s)
   migratory, 14, 150*
   red-legged, 9, 73
Lopidea spp., 142*
loudest insect, 91
Loxosceles deserta, 161*
Loxosceles reclusa, 85
Loxosceles spp., 85
Lucanidae, 176
Lucanus cervus, 76, 118*
Lycosidae, 178
Lygaeidae, 176

Lymantria dispar, 113*
Lyme disease, 69
Lyssomanes virides, 161*

M

Macrotermes natalensis, 44
maggots, 31, 182
Magicicada septendecim, 75, 75, 112*
Malpighian tubules, 12, 13, 182
mandibles, 13, 182
Mantichora spp., 154*
mantid
   European (*Mantis religiosa*), 124*
   false, 124*
   praying mantis (*Chaeradodis rhombicollis*), 105*
   praying mantis (*Mantis religiosa*), 124*
mantids
   flight, 16
   metamorphosis, 25
   order Mantodea, 71, 83, 177
   praying mantids, camouflage of, 36
   praying mantids, mating of, 13
   praying mantids, raptorial forelegs of, 19, 19, 183
Mantis religiosa, 124*
Mantodea, 83, 177
   identification chart, 71
maps
   biomes, 86-87
   spread of Africanized bee, 81
Mastophora spp. (bolas spiders), 56, 59
mating
   in insects, 28, 28-29, 29
   in spiders, 57, 64, 64-65, 65
maxillae, 13, 182
Mayetiola destructor, 47
mayflies
   antennae, 23
   metamorphosis, 25
   order Ephemeroptera, 71, 82, 176
mayfly, giant, 123*
meadow and grassland insects, 140, 140, 141-147*
meadow and grassland spiders, 140, 148*
mealybugs, 32
Mecoptera, 83, 177
   identification chart, 71
Megaloprepus coerulatus, 89*
Megaloptera, 83, 177
Megarhyssa lumator, 34
Megarhyssa nortoni, 136*
Melanophila spp., 19
Melanoplus femurrubrum, 9, 73

Melanopus frigidus, 162*
Melittia gloriosa, 153*
Membracidae, 92, 176
Mesothelae, 178
metamorphosis, 24, 24-27, 26, 78-79, 79, 182
Micrathena sagittata, 126*
Microcentrum rhombifolium, 110*
midges
  family Chironomidae, 130*, 176
  flight, 16
  food, 32
  metamorphosis and food intake, 26
  order Diptera, 70, 75, 176, 181
midge(s)
  biting, 128
  chironomid, 17, 23, 28-29
  glacier, 9
  green, 130*
millipedes, 8
mimicry
  in insects, 36-37, 37
  in spiders, 55, 56
Misumena vatia, 59
mites, 54
  gamasid, 30
molting, 182
  in insects, 11, 27, 27
  in spiders, 56, 57
Monochamus notatus, 135*
Morgan, Thomas Hunt, 50-51, 51
Morpho amathonte, 17, 17
Morpho rhetenor, 95*
mosquito, malaria-carrying, 93*
mosquitos
  antenna of male, 23
  as disease carriers, 48, 48-49, 93*
  family Culicidae, 176
  order Diptera, 70, 75, 176, 181
  proboscis, 13
  speed, 16
moths
  camouflage, 36-37
  metamorphosis, 25, 78-79
  mimicry, 36
  order Lepidoptera, 70, 78-79, 176, 179, 182
  pheromones, 39-40, 40
  proboscis, 13
moth(s)
  arctic woollybear, 164*
  atlas, 94*
  bagworm, 36
  California cankerworm, 169*
  cecropia, 40-41, 79, 113*

Chinese silk, 25
clear-winged, 176
Cynthia, 47
giant owlet, 94*
giant silkworm, 26, 28, 176
gypsy, 113*
Io, 17
leaf roller, 44
luna, 40, 114*
manroot borer, 153*
merveille du jour, 36
polyphemus, 22-23, 26
pyralid, 39-40
silk, 22
silver-Y, 14
sphinx, 16
spruce budworm, 133*
sweetheart underwing, 37
tineid, 30
yucca, 154*
mouthparts, 13
mygalomorph spiders, 54-55, 58
Mygalomorphae, 178
Myrmecocystus spp., 43

N

naiads, 182
Nasutitermes corniger, 104*
navigation using polarized light, 21
Neocurtilla major, 44, 140, 142*
Neodiprion lecontei, 137*
Nephila clavipes, 65
nests, 44, 44-45, 45
nets, 68
Neuroptera, 83, 140, 177
  identification chart, 71
Nicrophorus defodiens, 133*
nocturnal insects, 20, 88, 182
nocturnal spiders, 182
  use of silk by trapdoor spiders, 62
number of species
  insects, 8, 176, 177
  spiders, 54, 178
nuptial gift, 180
Nymphalis antiopa, 115*
nymphs, 25, 182

O

observing insects and spiders, 68-69
ocelli, 10, 20, 182
Odonata, 72, 176, 182
  endangered insects, 179
  identification chart, 71
Odontotaenius disjunctus, 39
Oestridae, 92
Oligotomidae, 105*
ommatidia, 20, 21, 182
Onymacris meridionalis, 171*
Orchelimum gladiator, 141*

orders (insects), 70-83, 176, 177
Ornithoptera alexandrae, 95
Ornithoptera priamus, 95*
Orthoptera, 73, 176, 182
  endangered insects, 179
  identification chart, 70, 71
Oulema melanopus, 122
overwinter, 182
ovipositor, 24, 182
owlflies, 159*
Oxyopidae, 178

P

Paleacrita longiciliata, 169*
palp, 55
Panorpa spp. *See* scorpionflies
Papilio machaon, 9, 78, 132*, 177
Papilio thoas, 36
parasites, 34, 182
parasitoids, 182
Parnassius phoebus, 165*
parthenogenesis, 27, 182
pedipalps, 54, 55
Pelecinus polyturator, 121*
Pepsis spp., 157*
pests, 47, 47-49, 48, 49
Petasida ephippigera, 151*
Peucetia viridans, 148*
Phalacrognathus muelleri, 97*
Phasmatodea, 82, 177
  identification chart, 70, 71
pheromones, 182
  in insects, 28, 39-41, 40
  in spiders, 59
Philaenus spumarius, 144*
Photinus pyralis, 38, 120*
Phricta spp., 90*
Phryganea cinerea, 138*
Phthiraptera, 177
  identification chart, 70
Phyllium siccifolium, 103*
Phyllophaga spp., 77, 119*
phylum, 8, 183
Pieris rapae, 78
Pipunculus spp., 145*
Pisauridae, 55, 59, 178
Pisaurina mira, 55
planthopper, peanut-headed, 91*
Plasmodium, 48, 93
Plathemis lydia, 72, 109*
Plecoptera, 83, 177
  identification chart, 71
Plusia gamma, 14
Plusiotis chrysargyrea, 99*
poison gland, 54
  venom, 85
pollination by insects, 46, 46, 78, 81
pollinators, 183
Pontia occidentalis, 146*
Precis atlites, 46

predatory behavior in spiders, *58,* 58-59, 58-59
   See also webs
proboscis, *13,* 183
Proctacanthus rodecki, 153*
pronotum, 92, 183
proventriculus, 12, *12*
Pseudomyrmex ferruginea, 33, 33
Psocoptera, 71
Pteroptyx sp., 38
pterygotes, 10, 183
pupae, 25, 27, 183
pupal stage, *26,* 183
Pyrgomorphidae, 89*

R

rain forest insects, 88, 88, 89-105*
rain forest spiders, 88, 106-107*
range of individual insects, 89-105, 109-125, 129-138, 141-147, 150-159, 162-166, 168-172
range of individual spiders, 106-107, 126-127, 139, 148, 160-161, 167, 173
Raphiomidos terminatus abdominalis, 169*
raptorial forelegs, 183
rectal pumps, 12
red light and insects, 73
repletes, 43
reproduction
   in insects, 28, 28-29, 29
   in spiders, 57, *64,* 64-65, *65*
rock crawlers, 82, 166*
   See also Grylloblattodea
royal jelly, 26, 183

S

salivary glands, *12*
Salticidae, 178
Samia cynthia, 47
Saturniidae, 176
sawfly(ies)
   cimbicid, *22*
   red-headed pine, 137*
scales, cottony cushion, 49
Scarabeus sacer, 155*
scavenging by insects, 34-35, 46
Schistocerca gregaria, 150*
Scolytus spp., 77
scorpionflies
   mating, 28
   nuptial feeding, 108
   order Mecoptera, 71, 83, 177
Scytodidae, 178
seducin, 40
sensillum, 183
sensory organs
   antennae, 22-23, 22-23,

22-23
   Johnston's organ, 22, 23
   sensilla, 22, 22-23, 23
Sesiidae, 176
setae, 183
sexual dimorphism, 183
   in spiders, 65
shelters, 44, 44-45, 45
Sicariidae, 178
silk, spider, 60-63, 60-63
   See also webs
silk glands, *54*
silk moths, 22
silverfish, 10, 25
Simuliidae, 176
Simulium decorum, 86, 129*
Siphonaptera, 70
Sirex cyanus, 136*
size, 9
   of ancestral insects, 11, 11
   largest insects, 10
   smallest insect, 9-10
size of individual insects, 89-105, 109-125, 129-138, 141-147, 150-159, 162-166, 168-172
size of individual spiders, 106-107, 126-127, 139, 148, 160-161, 167, 173
smallest insect, 9-10
social insects, 42-43, 183
Solenopsis invicta, 157*
sounds, producing, 38-39
   See also stridulating
sp.and spp., 86
species, 183
   number of insect species, 8, 176, 177
   number of spider species, 54, 178
speed of insects, *16*
sperm displacement, 29, 51
sperm webs, *62*
spermatheca, 29, 183
spermophors, *54,* 57
Speyeria cybele, 78, 114*
Sphex ichneumoneus, 156*
spiders, *84-85*
   ballooning, 62-63, 65
   bites, 85
   cannibalism, 65
   cohabitation, 57
   courtship, 57, *64,* 64-65, *65*
   families, 178
   sexual dimorphism, 65, *65*
   suborders, 178
   See also webs
spider(s)
   argiope, 58, *84,* 107*, 148*
   arrow-shaped micrathena, 126*
   Australian redback, 65

banded argiope, 148*
black widow, 85
black-and-yellow argiope, *84*
bolas, 56, 59
brown recluse, 85
brownish-gray fishing, 139*
burrowing wolf, 160*
Californian trapdoor, 160*
cobweb weaver, 61, 178
crab, 59, 65, 139*, 173*, 178
desert tarantula, *84,* 173*
desert violin, 161*
dictynid, 178
dwarf, 167*
fishing, 59, 139*, 178
folding trapdoor, 178
forest wolf, 127*, 178
funnel-web tarantula, 178
funnel-web weaver, 60-61, 178
garden, 56, 63, 126*
giant crab, 173*
goldenrod crab, 59
golden-silk, 65
goliath bird-eating tarantula, 106*
green lynx, 148*
green lyssomanes, 161*
ground, 167*
hammock-web, 85
huntsman, 57
jumping, 58, 58-59, 62, 65, 178
lynx, 178
midget, 55
nursery-web, 55, 57, 65, 178
ogre-faced, (*Deinopis longipes*), 106*
ogre-faced, (*Deinopis spinosa*), 55
orb-weaver, *60-61,* 61-62, 64, *64,* 178
orchard, 127*
pirate, 59
purse web, 55
recluse, 85
sac, 178
segmented, 178
sheet-web weaver, 60, 178
silver argiope, 58, 107*
spitting, 178
Sydney funnel-web, 85, 107*
tarantulas, *84,* 106*, 173*, 178
thrice-banded crab, 139*
trapdoor, 54-55, *62,* 160*, 178
violin, 178
wandering, *64,* 178
water, 59, 62-63
wolf, 57, 58-59, 62, 64-65, 85, 127*, 160*, 178
See also Agelena republicana;
   Anelosimus eximius;

Anthrobia mammouthia; harvestmen (daddy longlegs); tarantulas
Spilochalcis mariae, 47
spinnerets, *54*, 55, 60, 183
spiracles, 183
  insects, 12
  spiders, *54*, 56
spittlebug, meadow, 144*
springtails
  bioluminescence, 38
  furcula, 181
  metamorphosis, 25
  order Collembola, 70, 82
Stenopelmatus fuscus, 150*
stick insect, goliath, 102*
stick insects
  order Phasmatodea, 70, 71, 82, 177
stickbug, 123
Stictocephala spp., 111*
stoneflies
  order Plecoptera, 71, 83, 177
stonefly, small winter, 138*
stridulating, 38-39, 183
  cicadas, 39, 74-75, 92
  crickets, 39, 73
  grasshoppers, 39, 73
  stridulation amplification in mole cricket, 44
subsocial insects, 42
symbiosis, mutualistic, 33, 33

T

Tabanus spp. (horse flies), *16*, 131*
Tacua speciosa, 91
taiga insects, 128, *128*, 129-138*
taiga spiders, 128, 139*
tarantulas
  bites, 85
  family Theraphosidae, 178
  life span, 57
  mygalomorph, 55
  predatory behavior, 59
  use of silk, 62
  See also spider(s)
taxonomy, 8-9, 86, 183
  of insects, 176-177
  of spiders, 178
Tegeticula yuccasella, 154*
terminalia, 183
termites
  eusocial organization, 42, 42-43, 43
  nests, 44, 44
  order Isoptera, 70, 71, 82, 177
  queen, 42-43
termite(s)
  compass, 45, 158*
  fungus-farming, 44

nasute, 104*
Tetraopes tetraophthalmus, 120*
Thasus acutangulus, 168*
Theraphosa blondi, 106*
Theraphosidae, 178
Theridiidae, 178
Thermonectus marmoratus, 155*
Thomisidae, 178
thorn bugs, 92
Thorybes pylades, 131*
thrips
  order Thysanoptera, 70, 77, 83
thrips, western flower, 159*
Thysania agripina, 94*
Thysanoptera, 83, 177
  identification chart, 70
ticks, 54, 69, 69
Tiphiidae, 176
Tipula spp., *75*, 130*
Titanus giganteus, 88
trachea, *54*, 55
tracheal tubes, 12
trap doors, 62
treehoppers
  family Membracidae, 92, 176
  mimicry, 36
  order Homoptera, 70, 71, 74-75, 176, 181
treehopper(s)
  buffalo, 111*
  Heteronotus glandiguler, 92*
  thorn-mimic, *75*
Triatoma infestans, 152*
Trichoptera, 83, 177
  identification chart, 71
Trigona nigerrima, 102*
Trigona spp., 41
tundra insects, 162, 162-166*
tundra spiders, 162, 167*

U-V

usefulness of insects, 46, 46-47, 47, 50-51
Vacciniina optilete, 164*
Vanessa cardui, 115*
venation, 183
venom, 85
Vespula maculata, 45
Vespula spp., *81*
vision
  in insects, 20-21, 73
  in spiders, 55
  See also eyes (insects); eyes (spiders)
vivariums, 69

W

Walckenaeria acuminata, 55
walkingstick, northern, 123*
walkingsticks, 36
wasps

antennae, 22-23
caste system, 42
and forensic entomology, 30
metamorphosis, 25
nests, 45
order Hymenoptera, 70, 71, 80-81, 176, 179, 182
wasp(s)
  American pelecinid, 121*
  chalcid, 47
  fairyfly, 9
  fig, 100*
  giant ichneumon, 136*
  great golden digger, 156*
  ichneumon, 24, 81
  ichneumon (*Megarhyssa lumator*), 34
  Polistes, 45
  spider, 157
  tarantula hawk, 157*
  tiphiid, 176
  vespoid, 81
  wood, 136
  See also yellow jackets
waste elimination, 12-13
Web sites, 175
webs
  communal webs, 57
  drumming on, to attract mates, *65*
  funnel webs, 60-61
  observing, 84
  orb web, 52-53, *60-61*
  sheet webs, 60
webspinners, 83, 105*
wingless insects, 10, 14, 17
wings, 14-17
  elytra, 14-15, 181
  evolution, 14, 15
  flight, *15*
  flight speeds, *16*
  halteres, 16-17, 181
  scales, 17, 17, 78
  structure, 15-16
woodland and forest insects, 108, 108, 109-125*
woodland and forest spiders, 108, 126-127*
workers, 183

X-Y

Xenopsylla cheopis (rat flea), 48, 49
Xysticus triguttatus, 139*
yellow jackets, *81*

ST. REMY MEDIA

President: Pierre Léveillé
Vice-President, Finance: Natalie Watanabe
Managing Editor: Carolyn Jackson
Managing Art Director: Diane Denoncourt
Production Manager: Michelle Turbide
Director, Business Development: Christopher Jackson
Senior Editor: Elizabeth Lewis
Art Director: Michel Giguère
Assistant Editor: Stacey Berman
Writers: Stephanie Boucher, Alan Morantz,
    Jade Savage, Dan Schneider
Illustrators: Gyslain Caron, Patrick Jougla
Photo Researcher: Linda Castle
Indexer: Linda Cardella Cournoyer
Senior Editor, Production: Brian Parsons
Systems Director: Edward Renaud
Technical Support: Jean Sirois, Roberto Schulz
Scanner Operator: Martin Francoeur

The following persons also assisted in the preparation of this book:
Lorraine Doré, Dominique Gagné, Pierre Home-Douglas,
Pascale Hueber, Rob Labelle, Solange Laberge, Rob Lutes,
Ned Meredith, Esmé Terry.

ACKNOWLEDGMENTS
The editors wish to thank the following:
Stephanie Boucher; Dory Cameron, Canadian Museum of
Nature; Don Hilton, Bishop's University; George Constable;
Dr. David F. Greene, Concordia University; April Gower,
Entomological Society of America; Chia-Chi Hsiung, Curator,
Lyman Entomological Museum and Research Laboratory,
McGill University; Cendrine Huemer, Nature Canada; Steve
Manning, Discovery Channel; Richard Merritt, Michigan State
University; Melanie Rousseau, Concordia University; Luke
Russell, Concordia University; Lorraine Savoie, Montreal
Insectarium; Anne Schwab; Rachelle Wallage; Terry Wheeler,
McGill University; Ernest Williams, Hamilton College.

PICTURE CREDITS

Nancy Rotenberg/Animals Animals-4 (upper left), 6-7;
Mary Evans Picture Library-10 (upper), 41 (upper), 49;
Carol Hughes/Bruce Coleman Inc.-10 (lower); Robert
Noonan/Photo Researchers, Inc.-11; Stephen Dalton/Photo
Researchers, Inc.-14-15; L. West/Photo Researchers, Inc.-17
(upper); Dr. E.R. Degginger-17 (lower), 25 (lower), 34 (upper),
47, 96 (lower), 107 (upper), 126 (upper), 127 (lower), 140, 152
(lower); Gary R. Zahm/Bruce Coleman Inc.-19; George D.
Dodge/Bruce Coleman Inc.-20; Dwight R. Kuhn/Bruce
Coleman Inc.-21, 143 (lower); Rod Planck/Photo Researchers,
Inc.-22-23, 115 (lower); James Bell/Photo Researchers, Inc.-
23; J.C. Carton/ Bruce Coleman Inc.-25 (upper), 29 (upper),
45, 56 (upper); O.S.F./Animals Animals-26-27, 166 (lower);
Rene Limoges-27, 76, 142 (upper), 147 (upper), 171 (lower); Kenneth M. Highfill/Photo Researchers, Inc.-
28; Bill Beatty/Animals Animals-29 (lower); Yva Momatiuk
& John Eastcott/Photo Researchers, Inc.-31; John Mitchell/
Photo Researchers, Inc.-32, 106 (lower), 123 (lower); Gregory
G. Dimijian/Photo Researchers, Inc.-33, 89 (upper); Kenneth
H. Thomas/Photo Researchers, Inc.-4 (lower), 120 (lower), 139
(upper), 166 (upper); Thomas Eisner & Daniel Aneshansley/
Cornell University-35; Farrell Grehan/Photo Researchers, Inc.-
36; Stephen J. Krasemann/Photo Researchers, Inc.-37 (upper);
Michael P. Fogden/Bruce Coleman Inc.-37 (lower); Fletcher &
Baylis/Photo Researchers, Inc.-38; Gilbert S. Grant/Photo
Researchers, Inc.-39, 124 (lower), 154 (lower), 156 (upper);
Robert Lubeck/Animals Animals-40; Root, A., O.S.F./Animals
Animals-42-43; Bud Lehnhausen/Photo Researchers, Inc.-
42; Raymond A. Mendez/Animals Animals-43 (lower), 159
(lower), 164 (upper); K. Gunnar/Bruce Coleman Inc.-4 (upper
right), 44; John Shaw/Bruce Coleman Inc.-46; Robert J.
Ellison/Photo Researchers, Inc.-4 (lower left), 48 (a); TC
Nature/Animals Animals-48 (b); Sinclair Stammers/Science
Photo Library/Photo Researchers, Inc.-48 (c); George
Bernard/Animals Animals-48 (d); Oliver Meckes/Photo
Researchers, Inc.-50; Culver Pictures-51 (upper); Professors
P. Motta & T. Naguro/Science Photo Library/Photo
Researchers, Inc.-51 (lower); M. Abbey/Photo Researchers,
Inc.-5 (upper left), 52-53; K.G. Vock/OKAPIA/Photo
Researchers, Inc.-55; James H. Robinson/Photo
Researchers,Inc.-56 (lower), 61, 131 (upper), 136 (lower);
John Serras/Photo Researchers, Inc.-57; Larry West/Bruce
Coleman Inc.-58-59, 90 (upper), 160 (upper); Patti
Murray/Animals Animals-59, 87, 94 (upper), 132 (lower);
Bill Bachman/Photo Researchers, Inc.-60-61; H.L. Fox,
O.S.F./Animals Animals-62-63; Simon D. Pollard/Photo
Researchers, Inc.-63 (lower); Foelix "Biologie der Spinnen"
2. Aufl. 1992. Georg Thieme Verlag Stuttgart, New York-65
(upper); M.H. Sharp/Photo Researchers, Inc.-65; Byron
Jorjorian/Bruce Coleman Inc.-5 (lower left), 66-67; Robert
Chartier 68, 145 (lower), 158 (lower), 162, 169 (lower); Dr.
Morley Read/Science Photo Library/Photo Researchers,
Inc.-69; Kim Taylor/Bruce Coleman Inc.-79, 130 (lower);
Jacques De Tonnacour-88, 91 (both), 94 (lower), 95 (lower),
96 (upper), 97 (both), 98 (both), 99 (lower), 101 (lower), 103
(both), 105 (upper), 109 (lower), 111 (upper), 113 (both), 114
(lower), 115 (upper), 117 (both), 118 (upper), 120 (lower),
121 (both), 124 (upper), 125 (upper), 130 (upper), 134
(upper), 135 (upper), 136 (upper), 149, 150 (upper), 154
(lower), 155 (lower), 171 (upper); Arthur Gloor/Animals
Animals-89 (lower); David Rentz-90 (lower), 151(upper);
Kjell B. Sandved/Photo Researchers, Inc.-92 (upper), 100
(lower); Edward S. Ross-92 (lower), 93 (lower), 105 (lower),
106 (upper), 123 (upper), 125 (lower), 129 (both), 135
(lower), 138 (lower), 153 (both), 157 (lower), 163(both),
165 (lower), 173 (lower); Jack Clark/Animals Animals-93
(upper); E.R. Degginger/Bruce Coleman Inc.-95 (lower);
Michael Fogden/Oxford Scientific Films-99 (upper); Rudolf
Freund/Photo Researchers, Inc.-100 (upper); William
Ervin/Science Photo Library/Photo Researchers, Inc.-101
(upper); Morris, S., O.S.F./ Animals Animals-102 (upper);
Piotr Naskrecki, University of Connecticut, Storrs, USA-102
(lower); Michael Fogden/Animals Animals-104 (upper); E.R.
Degginger/Photo Researchers, Inc.-104 (lower), 114 (upper),
141 (upper); Tom McHugh/Photo Researchers, Inc.-107
(lower); Densey Clyne/Mantis Wildlife Films/Oxford
Scientific Films-108; Michael Lustbader/Photo Researchers,
Inc.-109 (lower); Robert J. Erwin/Photo Researchers, Inc.-
110 (upper), 146 (lower); Jorge Sierra/Oxford Scientific
Films-110 (lower); Christian Autotte-111 (lower), 112
(lower), 137 (lower), 142 (lower), 145 (upper); Jim Zipp/
Photo Researchers, Inc.-112 (upper); Ray Simons/Photo
Researchers, Inc.-116 (upper); Ray Coleman/Photo
Researchers, Inc.-116 (lower); J.H. Robinson/Animals
Animals-118 (lower), 148 (lower); Jeff Lepore/Photo
Researchers, Inc.-119 (lower); David T. Roberts/Nature's
Images Inc./Photo Researchers, Inc.-119 (lower), 122
(upper), 147 (lower), 151 (lower), 155 (upper), 157 (upper);
USDA, APHIS, PPQ,.Niles Plant Protection Center-122
(lower); Toni Angermayer/Photo Researchers, Inc.-126
(lower); Joe McDonald/Animals Animals-127 (upper); Ken
Brate/Photo Researchers, Inc.-131 (lower), 143 (upper);
Michael Giannechini/Photo Researchers, Inc.-132 (upper),
164 (lower); John Bova/Photo Researchers, Inc.-133 (upper);
Steve Trumbo/University of Connecticut-133 (lower); C.L.
Bellamy, Head Coleoptera Dept., Transvaal Museum,
Pretoria, South Africa-134 (lower); Frederick A. Coyle-137
(upper), 139 (lower), 167 (both); Bill P. Stark-138 (upper);
Harry Rogers/Photo Researchers, Inc.-141 (lower); Holt
Studios/Nigel Cattlin/Photo Researchers, Inc.-144 (upper),
159 (upper); Robert P. Carr/Bruce Coleman Inc.-144 (lower),
148 (upper); Paul A. Opler-146 (upper), 165 (upper); Mark
Smith/Photo Researchers, Inc.-150 (lower); Jany
Sauvanet/Photo Researchers, Inc.-152 (upper); Valerie
Giles/Photo Researchers, Inc.-156 (lower); Jean-Paul
Ferraro/Auscape-158 (upper); Dr. Paul A. Zahl/Photo
Researchers, Inc.-160 (lower); Larry West-161 (upper); Rick
Vetter-161 (lower); George Bryce/Animals Animals-168;
Gregory R. Ballmer-169 (upper), 170 (upper), 172 (upper);
Kjell B. Sandved/Bruce Coleman Inc.-170 (lower); Francois
Gohier/Photo Researchers, Inc.-173 (upper).